Schooling Ideology and the Curriculum

Schooling, Ideology and the Curriculum

*Edited
and Introduced by
Len Barton, Roland Meighan
and Stephen Walker.*

 The Falmer Press.

First published 1980

ISBN limp 0 905273 12 5
     cased 0 905273 13 3

Illustration by Peter Clason
Jacket design by Leonard Williams

Printed and bound by Taylor and Francis (Printers) Ltd
Basingstoke
for
The Falmer Press
(*A member of the Taylor & Francis Group*)
Falmer House
Barcombe, Lewes
Sussex BN8 5DL
England

Contents

Preface

The papers which appear in this collection originate from presentations made by the authors at the Sociology of Education Conference held in January, 1980 at Westhill College, Birmingham.

Introduction

Len Barton, *Westhill College*
Roland Meighan, *(Birmingham University)*
Stephen Walker, *Newman College*

Although the different contributions to this book range over a wide spectrum of substantive issues, they share a common interest. This is a concern to explore the ways in which notions of the relations between theory and practice, between belief and action, can be used to develop three kinds of sensitivity in the sociology of education. A sensitivity towards how school systems are created, maintained and made to function. A sensitivity towards developing a more refined, critical and constructive awareness of the reliability and validity of descriptions, analyses and explanations offered in this field of study. And finally, a sensitivity towards the ways in which changes take place within the education system and how the insights and realisations generated in the discipline might be used to control such occurrences.

However, although there is a commonality of *focus*, this should not be taken to mean that the contributors are united in their attitudes to how the issues under consideration can be conceptualised or investigated. Much of the material in the book reflects a tension arising from different convictions about the nature of the perspective which will make the most useful contribution to the development of the sensitivities outlined. It is a tension both complex and creative. Complex because the notions of the dialectical relationship between theory and practice penetrate the discourse at various levels; at the level of how this relationship is manifested in schools, at the level of how analysis is to be conducted and, crucially, at the level of how the theory and practice of analysis can be related to the theory and practice of life in educational settings. Creative because it exposes contradictions between and within theories and practices at different levels and thus provides a basis for making a more developed sensitivity.

It can be argued that the development of critical insights in any intellectual endeavour depends upon the cross-fertilisation of ideas and evaluations and whilst the authors of the papers in this collection differ in some of their interpretations, an important aspect of their work is that frequently their particular stances are being developed through the process of a dialogue. To this extent, this collection

I

should be regarded as a contribution to a debate which is likely to continue for some time. This debate has a specific direction which distinguishes it from other avenues of thought which have been developed in the sociology of education. In the past, investigations of the theories on which education systems are predicated have often been conducted as if they were dealing with something quite separate from that which is being analysed by those studying the practices of individuals inside the system, and vice versa. A major contention, of the movement in which we can locate the discussions in this book, is that the sociology of education needs to be quite consciously concerned with the ways in which theories and practices inter-penetrate and with the extent and consequences of this inter-penetration or, more concisely, with ideology in education. Of course, as a concept, the notion 'ideology is not easy to define. Its usage in sociology ranges from those instances where it is employed to refer to the series of images that men use which are an expression of their consciousness of their world, to those other instances where it is used to refer to whole collections of beliefs used by various interest groups to legitimate and maintain their status positions within a hierarchical social order.[1] The movement in the sociology of education to which we refer is mostly concerned with the latter usage. It makes, as a priority, an exploration of how the structure of the education system and the nature of the everyday practices in schools are directly or indirectly related to the ways in which dominant groups in society attempt to secure acceptance and conformity to their beliefs, attitudes and interests. To this extent this approach quite deliberately and adamantly seeks to move away from a position in which questions about the relationship between theory and practice in both educational analysis and actuality are treated as a-political towards one from which the relation-ship between the distribution of power in society and educational processes is a major focus of inquiry.[2]

A legitimate question to pose is why a concern with the impact of ideologies in education, including questions of politics and power, should assume such an important place in current debate in the sociology of education? We believe this has arisen for several reasons. The first, and arguably the most fundamental reason, relates to what we would describe as a sense of despondency which seems to have been felt by many engaged in sociological examinations of education and schooling. For the most part, this mood sprang from a belief that reformist policy prescriptions and action, aimed at developing a more liberal educational system by making use of insights gained from sociological analysis, had largely failed. This sense of failure is discussed by Reynolds and Sullivan in their paper in this book, and they assert:

> Educational policies have simply failed to attain their goals. Greatly increased levels of educational expenditure have clearly not been associated with any noticeable reduction in inequalities between the members of social classes in their benefit from their system in their obtained qualifications. The proportion of students from working class homes within the higher education sector, for example, has remained at around 25–27 per cent in spite of the large overall expansion in the total numbers obtaining higher education ...

If increases in the overall quality of resources have not brought social justice for disadvantaged groups, neither have they brought the higher levels of economic growth to those societies where such expansionist educational policies have been followed.

What gives this apparent lack of effectiveness a depressing quality is that the supposed increases in our awareness of how educational institutions work, which had been laboriously produced through analysis undertaken in the 1950s and 1960s, did not seem particularly helpful in attempts made to bring such processes into the more direct control of participants or policy-makers. Thus, the necessity to identify the nature and source of seemingly intractable elements of constraint at work, both upon and within education, became pressing and inevitably involved attempting to expose the ideological bed-rock upon which schooling is based and the connections this structural support might have with wider socio-political frameworks.

However, the mood of despondency can also be seen as a reflection of a reaction to events experienced more directly by those working in the sociology of education – cut-backs in the provision for higher education leading to closures, amalgamations of institutions and falling student-rolls. The last few years have been characterised by anxiety, low-morale and fear as individuals working in higher education wondered if, during a period of educational contraction and economic recession, their personal involvement in the system would come under threat. The highly explicit intervention by the State into the lived-experience of sociologists of education or their colleagues confirmed the relevance of making as a priority the exploration of how educational institutions are controlled and the nature of the ideologies which enable and legitimate such control. Furthermore, this intervention was not restricted to the direct experience of individuals in higher education engaged in educational research or training but was also being perceived as a crucial aspect of the object of their works, the world of schools and teachers, and thus gave further support to the general feeling of anxiety and the consequent need for the rapid development of a form of analysis which could deal with questions of power and control. In short, the apparent powerlessness of individuals, at all levels of education, to defend themselves against forces who wished to implement policies with which they did not necessarily agree, sharpened the need felt to identify the nature and authority base of such forces and to isolate the mechanisms used to achieve and sustain the position of dominance from which they operated.

It can be argued that a second and different feature which contributed to the emergence of a greater emphasis being placed upon ideological questions in the study of education was what has been described as a 'paradigm crisis' in both sociology and the sociology of education. As the availability of a plurality of perspectives in sociology increased in the late 1960s and 1970s (an increase which was accompanied by vociferous claims being made by some exponents of different perspectives as to the indispensable contribution the approach they espoused could make to the advancement of social scientific endeavour), many practitioners were compelled to make careful consideration of the relationship between their own research and teaching practices and the theoretical and political groundings on which these practices were based. It is interesting to note that some of these perspectives, themselves, were depressing in that they were predicated upon a deterministic view of social affairs which depicted the individual as powerless in the face of wider social forces. This, plus the proliferation of publications in which questions of *approach* were discussed and the complexity of the ideas and interpretations which were articulated during this period, added to the sense of frustration and bewilderment discussed above. More significantly, and perhaps paradoxically, conflict over where one's theoretical allegiance should be placed and, hence, the kind of practices which could be engaged in without contradicting the basic tenets of the particular theoretical position adopted, created the circumstances in which self-reflection was both necessary and consequential. Such self-reflection is both beneficial, in that it has led to sociologists of education making their own ideological position more explicit, and debilitating, in that it undermines the sense of sureness practitioners have for justifying these positions and their particular practices. This vulnerability has recently been exacerbated by an ideological attack mounted from sources external to the discipline. For example, in her paper in this collection, Janet Strivens explains that much of the work she describes in the paper has been developed, in part, as a reaction to this attack, a crucial dimension of which, she suggests, is illustrated in

> ... a recent trend in teacher education to reassess the role of theory in vocational training. The essential challenge is to the traditional status of the social sciences, questions being raised about the relevance of theoretical studies in the social sciences on courses where time is strictly limited and the first priority should be the acquisition of practical skills.

It is important to locate the kinds of troubles facing sociologists of education during recent years within a wider context of turbulence or what has been described as 'capitalism in crisis'.[3] Affairs like rampant inflation, high unemployment, low productivity and falling profits on the one hand, and experiments in political and economic management in the developing world on the other, have combined to produce a situation in which the organisation of economic life, the social relations related to this organisation and the appropriateness of the ideology which sustains and legitimates capitalist production become a public issue. The events which grew out of this crisis, in terms of reaction to it, involved increased intervention by dominant groups or their agents in social affairs. In education, the crushing experience of contraction, school closures, efforts to relate the curriculum in school more closely to the 'needs' of industry, attempts at increased state monitoring of educational performance and efficiency (which brought with them a consequent up-heaval in the encounters and relations of numerous groups of people), was a stark testimony that politics and education were inextricably linked. Thus, in an atmosphere of private despondency and public crisis, it is not surprising that many sociologists should begin to express increasing interest in an analytical approach which, in making what seemed to be the sources of these troubles the focal point of investigation, offered a means which, even if it did not represent the path to salvation, nevertheless appeared to be most useful in building some understanding of the situation.

However, what distinguishes the movement in the sociology of education we are describing is not just that it involves a concern with ideology and education *per se* but also the ways in which this concern have been translated into analysis. Although the relationship between patterns of education and wider ideological systems and practices has been made an area of analysis for some sociologists in the past,[4] the particular movement under consideration is characterised by a quite explicit interest in how power groups sustain and legitimise dominant ideologies and the impact these procedures have upon the form and content of educational life. This interest has been pursued along a variety of different lines. Bowles and Gintis, for example, in their influential book *Schooling in Capitalist America*,[5] maintain that we can advance our attempts to reveal the ideological basis of schooling and our understanding of the routine practices we find in schools by focussing our attention on ways in which social relations fostered in educational institutions are related to social relations in the economic and political order and the belief system which sustains these orders. Thus, they argue,

> The education system . . . reproduces and legitimates a pre-existing pattern in the process of training and stratifying the work force. How does this occur? The heart of the process is to be found not in the content of the educational encounter – or the process of information transfer – but in the form: the social relations of the educational encounter. These correspond closely to the social relations of dominance, subordination, and motivation in the economic sphere. Through the educational encounter, individuals are induced to accept the degree of powerlessness with which they will be faced as mature workers.[6]

Other writers have approached the issue differently. Rather than assuming a correspondence between the social relations of schooling and work, the ideological impact on education has been viewed by some in terms of how the ways in which knowledge and the curriculum is structured and defined in school serves to repro-duce the cultural conditions of the prevailing economic and political order whilst others have made a concentration upon how the social system creates the necessary conditions for the emergence and development of cultural forms which stand in close, or distant, relation to the process of education and which condition the ideological expectations of those pupil and teachers immersed in such forms.

A diversity of approach, then, represents the present climate of debate about ideology and education. Whilst we would not claim that the analyses and descrip-tions presented in the papers collected in this volume are going to provide final answers or definitive statements on this issue, we do feel that they offer insights into how we can conceptualise the problem and, more importantly, make significant contributions to extending what we described as a sensitivity towards the possibil-ities of change. It would be arrogant to assume that we could successfully summarise the many different arguments contained in the various papers in this book. Never-theless, we would like to isolate some elements from the papers which seem to us to be the main issues which emerge from the collection *as a whole* and, in so-doing, to communicate some idea of why we have arranged the papers in the order in which they appear.

As we indicated at the beginning of this introduction, a major consideration addressed in this book is how sociologists of education might, by using concepts of ideology and politics, proceed in building an understanding of how institutionalised forms of education are to be related to other aspects of the social system in which these forms emerge and are maintained. An important point at issue here is the question of the acceptability of a particular theoretical position developed by Bowles and Gintis in which, as noted earlier, they suggest that one way of conceptualising this relationship is by exploring the ways in which the social relations of schooling might be perceived as being remarkably similar to the social relations of work – the correspondence theory. The first five papers in this volume all contain discussion relevant to a critical re-appraisal of the correspondence principle as it was first expressed or of how it has been applied to later work. The correspondence principle, as Gintis and Bowles themselves acknowledge, is open to the criticism that it represents the relation between education and the economy as a mostly harmonious one. In his paper, Apple, developing this criticism, argues that approaches using the theory will be limited unless we can establish not only that schools might be seen as reproducing the social relations of the prevailing socio-economic order and its dominant ideologies, but also *how* such reproduction is accomplished and whether or not this is *all* that schools do. He suggests that we have to recognise that teachers and pupils in school not only *take* forms of curriculum and organised knowledge which may well be predicated upon dominant ideologies as a basis for their activities, but that they also *work back* on these for their own ends. In being able to develop relatively autonomous ideologies within school – ideologies which are constructed as teachers and pupils react to their day-to-day, concrete lived-experiences and draw upon the contradictions of their own lives – individuals in schools are able to develop meanings and practices which stand in opposition to dominant versions and provide a basis for struggle against such formulations. To this extent schools *produce* ideologies as well as having them imposed upon them.

MacDonald's paper illustrates the kind of analysis which takes as its object the *content* of education and examines quite specifically how the processes of legitimation and reproduction occur – in this case the legitimation and reproduction of class and gender relations in schools. It can be argued that the essay represents an attempt to supplement the insights to be gained from the application of the correspondence theory by exploring how the ideologies of the dominant groups in capitalist society (or, as she calls them, the 'ruling class') penetrate and are reproduced in the structure and content of the school culture as realised in the curriculum. We do not think MacDonald's work is in direct opposition to the principles of the correspondence theory (although this is not to say her stance does not imply certain reservations about its present adequacy) but rather that, like Apple, she is interested in how reproduction 'gets done'. In highlighting how class and gender ideologies seem to be carried and transmitted in school texts and in suggesting methods by which we can explore how teachers and pupils *receive or reject* such ideologies, she seeks to investigate how the relationship between education and the political-economic system can be conceptualised in less mechanistic ways.

Whilst, in their paper in this collection, Gintis and Bowles offer a number of self-criticisms of (their) earlier work, unlike some of the analyses we have considered so far, they defend this insistence that our main investigatory concern in attempting to discover the nature of the relationship between education and the political formation in which it is located must be directed towards the *form* educational arrangements and encounters take. They admit that a major weakness of the original version of the correspondence theory is that, if we assume a fairly unproblematic correspondence between schooling and the social order, it is difficult to account for those aspects of schooling which appear to stand in contradiction to dominant theories and practices. Yet, as they illustrate, such contradictions palpably exist and find forms of expression in school which would seem to pose quite direct threats to the legitimacy of the prevailing relations and mode of production. Therefore, in this paper, they offer a possible theoretical framework for coping with the capacity schooling has to reproduce patterns of social relations which both legitimate and contradict ideological conditions of the social totality. By using the notion of 'sites', that is, of cohesive areas of social life in which situationally relevant practices and rules are created, they seek to show that sets of rules governing social relations, which are quite different in terms of how basic concerns are defined, can be developed in three distinguishable areas of social experience – the state site, the family site and the site of production. The forms of discourse and the ideological rules employed in any of these sites *can be* different, depending on the history of that site. Gintis and Bowles argue that because education is located in close relation to two major sites in society, the state site and the site of production, the form it will take comes under two constraining influences. In capitalist society, education

> ... forms in general a subsystem of the state site, and therefore is directly subject to the principle of rights vested in persons. Second, education plays a central role in reproducing the political structure of the capitalist production process, which in turn is legitimated in terms of rights vested in property. Thus education is directly involved in the contradictory articulation of sites in advanced capitalism, and is expressed in terms of the property/person dichotomy: education reproduces rights vested in property, while itself organised in terms of rights vested in persons.

Of course, the extent to which this framework, which Gintis and Bowles offer, is directly applicable to the empirical conditions of schooling has yet to be substantially demonstrated. Interestingly, however, in their articles, both Edwards and Musgrave express some scepticism (although not of a disinterested nature) about the degree to which this requirement has been fulfilled with reference to the original version of the correspondence theory. Edwards argues that too often sociologists of education advance or accept sophisticated theorising too early and too easily in their analytical endeavour. As a result, it is either difficult to see what elements of educational actuality one would need to consider to assess the central ideas proposed in the theory or, because some theories refer only to abstractions, there is a danger of neglecting the interpretative and reactive capacities of social actors. We are left with 'tidy' theories floating free from the reality of an 'untidy' world. Edwards maintains that we can learn from the practices of historians and could strengthen our analyses by working with the recognition that the validity of any 'theory', including the correspondence theory, depends just as much upon its *demonstrated* applicability to the nature and origin of the practices of the world it seeks to describe as it does on its internal consistency. Musgrave has a different critical interest. He raises the possibility that certain aspects of schooling are not explicable in terms of ideological constraints imposed upon schooling but rather, on the contrary, seem to be evidence of a *failure* of dominant groups to achieve lasting hegemony. He seeks ways of unravelling the causes of curriculum development and change and directs our attention to crises *embedded within schools* themselves as being crucial contributory features. Once school systems and practices are established, he maintains, they generate an internal dynamic and we would do well to consider how present practices arise as results of and reactions to the sustaining ideology of this dynamic, or to crises within it, before we move outside the situation in our search for sources of determination.

The points raised by both Edwards and Musgrave are not unrelated to what we identified as a second major consideration in the debate on ideology and education. This consideration is to do with the approaches we adopt and the conceptualisations we employ in attempting to delineate the strictly educational theories on which practices in school are based and the relationship between them; in short, the empirical instances of educational belief systems and action. Four papers in this book address this question by either referring to how the writers' own empirical research relates to these issues or by proposing certain models we might use to handle the problems involved more efficiently – those by Strivens, Chessum, Meighan and Brown, and Easthope.

The approach adopted by Strivens is characterised by a desire to formulate descriptions of beliefs and practices without losing touch with the interests and perceptions of teachers and student-teachers. Thus, she grounds her own research, which she describes in this paper, upon two fairly specific issues. First, the identification of those practices which give indication of the general ideology at work within a particular school. Second, a comparison of the differences between the ways in which forms of social relations, which provide the basis for these practices, are variously managed and legitimated in different schools. This procedure is important, she suggests, because the isolation of critical differences *between* schools provides a possible point from which we can begin to determine how contradictions arise within the total schooling process as broad educational ideologies are transformed into specific sets of educational practices. Chessum is also concerned with the differences between schools. However, her particular interest is in how teachers in different institutions explain and justify their conceptualisations and actions when confronted by pupils who present 'problems' to them. She describes how the empirical work she has undertaken provides some reasons for assuming that teachers in different schools generate different theories and practices which are, in part, explicable through reference to the local, institutionalised context and established ideologies. Where such ideologies are institutionally well-defined and cohesive, reactions to 'problem' pupils were based upon a core belief system; where they were institutionally indistinct or weakly enforced by senior management, reactions were based upon more pragmatic considerations, that is, teachers would support those positions adopted towards 'problem' pupils which proved effective in 'containing' forms of resistance. The general point, then, raised in discussion developed in both these papers, is that we need to be alert to the possibility that schools have relative autonomy in *certain* areas which may well lessen their effectiveness as agencies of reproduction.

Interesting alternatives to attempts to develop our understanding of the relationship between ideology and education at the empirical level are provided in the papers by Meighan and Brown and by Easthope. Rather than confining their analysis to the beliefs and practices operating in *schooling*, the writers of both these papers offer a means by which we can reflect upon such ideologies by comparing them with the ideological foundations of educational settings which are different from traditional schooling arrangements. Both papers reveal the importance which the setting of an education form has for the kinds of practices it promotes and the belief systems used to organise and legitimate these practices. Meighan and Brown, using a model which attempts to draw together the crucial concerns of a series of endeavours to isolate core elements of educational ideologies, distinguish some central charateristics of an educational movement which has been set-up in opposition to the dominant school system. Education Otherwise, a movement organised by parents who wish to exercise their right to have their children educated in places other than school, mostly frequently in the home. They suggest that *where* education takes place, its socio-geographic or physical location, can be seen as just as important a factor in determining the nature and consequences of the experience as other features of its organisation which provide the ideological shape of the activity. Easthope uses the term 'setting' somewhat differently. He develops a model of ideal types of 'settings' in which forms of education take place. What distinguishes a type, for him, is the forms of social relations nurtured or made possible in the curriculum established by the particular agency which has control of the setting in which education is taking place. By contrasting the social relationships promoted or inhibited by the curricula processes in 'communal resocialising agencies' (for example, drug rehabilitation centres), apprenticeship schemes and schools, he seeks to focus upon how personal identities are created or changed in such different settings. He argues that the impact the beliefs and social relations encapsulated in the curricula of these formations have upon 'learners' are at least as influential as the social relations which typify direct inter-personal relations within these settings.

Although the four papers introduced above offer different and sometimes competing interpretations of aspects of the empirical conditions of the relationship between ideology, schooling and the curriculum, they all illustrate an important point to be established in the general debate. It is the point made by Edwards when he concludes that some theories about this relationship

> . . . may seem a realistic appreciation of compelling 'external' constraints, or an over-determined view which exceeds the evidence currently available. The issue is the most important facing the sociology of education, but it will not be resolved by exchanges of speculation. Marc Bloch's final words on the historian's craft are no less applicable to the practice of sociology – 'the causes cannot be assumed, they are to be looked for'.

At the beginning of this introduction we alluded to a sense of frustration as a feature of the climate which made an exploration of ideology and education an attractive proposition to sociologists of education. We will conclude by suggesting that the ways this exploration is developing provides some grounds for adopting a more optimistic view. Greater understanding of either the ideological constraints upon the education system or of the ways in which practices in schools can be demonstrated as drawing upon (or resisting) the tenets of a distinguishable belief system, provides a means for intervention. In one way or another, the writers of all the papers in this book express a desire for change. However, the last paper in this volume, by Reynolds and Sullivan, addresses the problems of justifying this desire and of making proposals for satisfying it. Whilst the various prescriptions suggested in this paper might not represent the consensus view in sociology of education, one of the issues Reynolds and Sullivan raise – that sociologists of education must come to terms with the relationship between their own beliefs and practices – is of fundamental importance. Their paper, by identifying the particular ideological associations which have provided the impetus for practices within sociology of education at various stages of its development and by isolating some of the consequences of these associations, helps locate the struggle for change within an historical perspective. It seems to us that sociologists of education have an obligation to present not only possible strategies for intervention in education but also the assumptions and beliefs upon which such suggestions are based. This book is intended as a contribution to debate on how both these obligations might be fulfilled.

Notes and References

1 This distinction is taken from GIDDENS, A. (1979) *Central Problems in Social Theory*, London, Macmillan.
2 See, for example, the discussions presented in YOUNG, M. and WHITTY, G. (1977) *Society, State and Schooling*, Barcombe, Falmer Press.
3 GAMBLE, A. and WALTON, P. (1976) *Capitalism in Crisis*, London, Macmillan.
4 See, for example, HALSEY, A.H., FLOUD, J. and ANDERSON, C.A. (Eds.) (1961) *Education, Economy and Society*, Glencoe III, Free Press. HOPPER, E. (Ed.) (1971) *Readings in the Theory of Educational Systems*, London, Hutchinson, 1971.
5 BOWLES, S. and GINTIS, H. (1976) *Schooling in Capitalist America*, London, RKP.
6 *Ibid.*, p. 265

Curricular Form and the Logic of Technical Control: Building the Possessive Individual.

Michael Apple, University of Wisconsin

Corporate Ideologies : Reaching the Teacher

It does not require an exceptional amount of insight to see the current attempts by the state and industry to bring schools more closely into line with 'economic needs'. Neither side of the Atlantic has been immune to these pressures. In the UK, The Great Debate and the Green Paper stand as remarkable statements to the ability of capital in times of economic crisis to marshall its forces. As the Green Paper notes:

> There is a wide gap between the world of education and the world of work. Boys and girls are not sufficiently aware of the importance of industry to' our society, and they are not taught much about it.[1]

It goes on, making the criterion of functional efficiency the prime element in educational policy.

> The total resources which will be available for education and the social services in the future will depend largely on the success of the Industrial Strategy. It is vital to Britain's economic recovery and standard of living that the performance of manufacturing industry is improved and that the whole range of Government policies, including education, contribute as much as possible to improving industrial performance and thereby increasing the national wealth.[2]

In the United States, where governmental policies are more highly mediated by a different articulation between the state, the economy, and schools, this kind of pressure exists in powerful ways as well. Often the workings of industry are even more visible. Chairs of Free Enterprise devoted to economic education are springing up at universities throughout the country. Teaching the message of industry has become a real force. Let me give one example taken from what is known as the Ryerson Plan, a corporate plan to have teachers spend their summers working mainly with management in industry so that they can teach their students 'real knowledge' about corporate needs and benefits.

> The anti-business, anti-free-enterprise bias prevalent in many parts of our American society today is very real and is growing. Unless we quit just talking about it – and do something about it now – it will prosper and thrive in the fertile minds of our youth. It will be nurtured and fed by many teachers who have good intentions but no real knowledge of how a free market operates in a free society.
>
> American business has a very positive story to tell and one of the most important places to start is with the youth of our country. The last four thousand years of recorded history proves the interdependence of economic freedom and personal freedoms of all civilisations, countries and societies. We have a perfect example in a present day test tube. Take a look at Great Britain's decline over the last thirty years.
>
> Our response is simple and effective. Reach the high school teachers of America with the true story of American business and they will carry the message to their students and their fellow teachers. The message, coming directly from the teacher, rather than books, pamphlets or films, will have a far more telling and lasting effect. Convince one teacher of the vital importance of our free enterprise system and you're well on your way to convincing hundreds of students over a period of years. It's the ripple effect that anti-business factions have been capitalising on for years.[3]

It is an interesting statement to say the least and one that is being echoed throughout advanced corporate economies. While it seems rather blatant, to say nothing of being historically inaccurate, we should be careful of dismissing this kind of program as overt propaganda that is easily dismissed by teachers. As one teacher said after completing it,

> My experience with the steel industry this summer has given me a positive and practical introduction to the business world that I might never had had, had it not been for the initiative of Ryerson management. Now I can pass a more positive portrayal of the industry on to my students; students who are usually very critical, very distrustful, and basically ignorant of the operation of big industry today.[4]

This is, of course, only one of many plans for getting the ideological message across. In fact, though there has been serious resistance to this kind of material by progressive forces in the United States, the movement to 'teach for the needs of industry' is growing rapidly enough so that a clearinghouse, appropriately named The Institute for Constructive Capitalism, has been established at the University of Texas to make the material more available.[5]

Now I do not want to minimise the importance of such overt attempts at influencing teachers and students. To do so would be the height of folly. However, by keeping our focus only on these overt attempts at bringing school policy and curriculum into closer correspondence with industrial needs, we may neglect what is happening that may be just as powerful at the level of day to day school practice. One could fight the battles against capital's overt encroachments (and perhaps win some of them) and still lose within the school itself. For, as I shall argue here, some of the ideological and material influences of our kind of social formation on teachers and students are not most importantly found at the level of these kinds of documents or plans but at the level of social practice *within* the routine activities in schools.[6]

In essence, I want to argue that ideologies are not only global sets of interests; things imposed by one group on another. They are embodied by our commonsense meanings and practices.[7] Thus, if you want to understand ideology at work in schools, look as much at the concreta of day to day curricular and pedagogic life as you would at the statements made by spokespersons of the state or industry. To quote from Finn, Grant, and Johnson, we need to look not only at ideologies 'about' education but ideologies 'in' it as well.[8]

I am not implying that the level of practice in schools is fundamentally controlled in some mechanistic way by private enterprise. As an aspect of the state, the school mediates and transforms an array of economic, political and cultural pressures from competing classes and class segments. Yet we tend to forget that this does not mean that the logics, discourses, or modes of control of capital will not have an increasing impact on everyday life in our educational institutions, especially in times of what has been called 'the fiscal crisis of the state'.[9] This impact, clearly visible in the United States (though I would hazard a guess it will become more prevalent in Europe and Latin America as well), is especially evident in curriculum; in essence in some very important aspects of the actual stuff that students and teachers interact with.

In this essay, I shall be particularly interested in curricular *form*, not curricular content. That is, my focus will not be on what is actually taught but on the manner in which it is organised. As a number of Marxist cultural analysts have argued, the workings of ideology can be seen most impressively at the level of form as well as what the form has in it.[10] As I shall argue here, this is a key to uncovering the role of ideology 'in' education. In order to understand part of what is occurring in the school and the ideological and economic pressures being placed upon it and which work their way through it, we need to situate it within certain long term trends in the capital accumulation process. Recently these trends have intensified and have had a rather major impact on a variety of areas of social life. Among these trends we can identify certain tendencies such as:

> the concentration and centralisation of capitals; the expansion of labor processes that are based on production-line technologies and forms of control; the continuing decline of 'heavy industry' and the movement of capital into modern 'lighter' forms of production, most notably the production of consumer durables; and major shifts in the composition of labor power – the secular tendency to 'de-skilling', the separation of 'conception' from 'execution' and the creation of new technical and control

skills, the shift of labor out of direct production and into circulation and distribution, and the expansion of labor within the state.[11]

As we shall see, the development of new forms of control, the process of de-skilling and the separation of conception from execution are not limited to factories and offices. These tendencies intrude more and more into institutions like the school. In order to unpack this, we shall have to examine the very nature of the logic of corporate de-skilling and control.

De-skilling and Re-skilling

At first, let me speak very generally about the nature of this kind of control. In corporate production, firms purchase labor power. That is, they buy the capacity one has to do work and, obviously, will often seek to expand the use of that labor to make it more productive. There is an opposite side to this. With the purchase of labor power goes the 'right' to stipulate (within certain limits) how it is to be used without too much interference or participation by workers in the conception and planning of the work.[12] How this has been accomplished has not stayed the same, of course. Empirically, there has been a changing logic of control that has sought to accomplish these ends. Given this history, it is helpful to differentiate the kinds of control that have been used. I shall simplify these around basic ideal types for ease of understanding.

We can distinguish three kinds of control that can be employed to help extract more work – simple, technical, and bureaucratic. Simple control is exactly that, simply telling someone that you have decided what should go on and they should follow or else. Technical controls are less obvious. They are controls embedded in the physical structure of your job. A good example is the use of numerical control technology in the machine industry where a worker inserts a card into a machine and it directs the pace and skill level of the operation. Thus, the worker is meant to be simply an attendant to the machine itself. Finally, bureaucratic control signifies a social structure where control is less visible since the principles of control are embodied within the *hierarchical* social relations of the workplace. Impersonal and bureaucratic rules concerning the direction of one's work, the procedures for evaluating performance and sanctions and rewards are dictated by officially approved policy.[13] Each of these modes of control has grown in sophistication over the years though simple control has tended to become less important as the size and complexity of production has increased.

The long period of experimentation by industry on the most successful modes of controlling production led to a number of conclusions. Rather than simple control, where control is openly exercised by supervisors or persons in authority (and hence could possibly be subverted by blue or white collar workers), power could be made 'invisible' by incorporating it into the very structure of the work itself. This meant the following things. The control must come from what seems to be a legitimate overall structure. It must be concerned with the actual work, not based on features extraneous to it (like favoritism and so on). Perhaps most importantly, the job, the process, and the product should be defined as precisely as possible on the basis of management's, not the worker's, control over the specialised knowledge needed to carry it out.[14] This often entailed the development of technical control.

Technical control and de-skilling tend to go hand in hand. De-skilling is part of a long process in which labor is divided and then redivided to increase productivity, to reduce 'inefficiency' and to control both the cost and the impact of labor. It usually has involved taking relatively complex jobs (most jobs are much more complex and require more decision-making than people give them credit for), jobs which require no small amount of skill and decision-making, and breaking them down into specified actions with specified results so that less skilled and costly personnel can be used or so that the control of work pace and outcome is enhanced. The assembly line is, of course, one of the archetypical examples of this process. At its beginnings, de-skilling tended to involve techniques such as Taylorism and various time and motion studies. Though these strategies for the division and control of labor were less than totally successful (and in fact often generated a significant amount of resistance and conflict),[15] they did succeed in helping to legitimate a style of control based in large part on de-skilling.

One of the more effective strategies has been the incorporation of control into the actual productive process itself. Thus, machinery in factories is now often designed so that the machinist is called upon to do little more than load and unload the machine. In offices, word processing technology is employed to reduce labor costs and de-skill women workers. Thus, management attempts to control both the pace of the work and the skills required, more effectively to increase their profit margins or productivity. Once again, as the history of formal and informal labor resistance documents, this kind of strategy – the building of controls into the very warp and woof of the production process – has been contested.[16] However, the growing sophistication by management and state bureaucrats in the use of technical control procedures is apparent.[17]

I have mentioned that de-skilling is a complex process as it works its way through a variety of economic and cultural institutions. Yet it really is not that hard to grasp one of its other important aspects. When jobs are de-skilled, the knowledge that once accompanied them – knowledge that was controlled and used by workers in carrying out their day to day lives on their jobs – goes somewhere. Management attempts (with varying degrees of success) to accumulate and control this assemblage of skills and knowledge. It attempts, in other words, to separate conception from execution. The control of knowledge enables management to plan;[18] the worker should ideally merely carry these plans out to the specifications, and at the pace, set by people away from the actual point of production. De-skilling is, however, accompanied by something else, what might be called re-skilling. New techniques are required to run new machines; new occupations are created as the redivision of labor goes on. Fewer skilled craftspersons are needed and their previous large numbers are replaced by a smaller number of technicians with different skills who oversee the machinery.[19] This process of de-skilling and re-skilling is usually spread out over the landscape of an economy so it is rather difficult to trace out the relationships. It is not usual to see it going on at a level of specificity that makes it clear since while one group is being de-skilling another group, often separated by time and geography, is being re-skilled. However, one particular institution – the school – provides an exceptional microcosm for seeing these kinds of mechanisms of control in operation.

In examining this we should remember that capitalist production has developed unevenly, so that certain areas of our social institutions will vary in the kind of control being used. Some institutions will be more resistant than others to the logic of corporate rationalization. Given the relatively autonomous nature of teaching (one can usually close one's door and not be disturbed) and given the internal history of the kinds of control in the institution (paternalistic styles of administration, often, in the USA, based on gender relations), the school has been partially resistant to technical and bureaucratic control, *at the level of actual practice*, until relatively recently. This 'relative autonomy' may be breaking down today.[20] For just as the everyday discourse and patterns of interaction in the family and in, say, the media are increasingly being subtly transformed by the logic and con-tradictions of dominant ideologies,[21] so, too, is the school a site where these subtle ideological transformations occur. I shall claim that this goes on through a process of technical control. As we shall now see, these logics of control can have a rather profound impact on schools.

Controlling Curricular Form

The best examples of the encroachment of technical control procedures is found in the exceptionally rapid growth in the use of pre-packaged sets of curricular materials. It is nearly impossible now to walk into an American classroom, for instance, without seeing boxes upon boxes of science, social studies, mathematics and reading materials ('systems', as they are sometimes called) lining the shelves and in use.[22] Here, a school system purchases a total set of standardised material usually one which includes statements of objectives, all of the curricular content and material needed, pre-specified teacher actions and appropriate student responses, and diagnostic and achievement tests co-ordinated with the system. Usually, these tests have the curricular knowledge 'reduced' to 'appropriate' behaviors and skills. Remember this emphasis on skills for it will become rather significant later on.

Let me give one example actually taken from one of the better of the widely used curricular systems, of the numerous sets of materials that are becoming the standard fare in American elementary schools. It is taken from *Module One* of *Science: A Process Approach*. The notion of module is important here. The material is pre-packaged into cardboard boxes with attractive colors. It is divided into 105 separate modules, each of which include a set of pre-given concepts to teach. The material specifies all of the goals. It includes everything a teacher 'needs' to teach, has the pedagogical steps a teacher must take to reach these goals already built in, and has the evaluation mechanisms built into it as well. But that is not all. Not only does it pre-specify nearly all a teacher should know, say, and do, but it often lays out the appropriate student responses to these elements as well. To make this clear, here is one sequence taken from the material which lays out the instructional procedure, student response, and evaluative activity. It concerns colors.

> As each child arrives at school, fasten a red, yellow, or blue paper rectangle on the child's shirt or dress ... Comment on the color of the paper and ask the child to say the name of the color he or she is wearing ...
>
> Put thirty yellow, red, and blue paper squares in a large bag or small box. Show the children three paper plates: one marked red, one yellow, and one blue. (See *Materials* for suggestions on marking). These colors should closely match those in the bag. Ask the children to come forward, a few at a time, and let each child take one square from the bag and place it on the plate marked with the matching color. [A picture of this with a child picking out paper from a box and putting it on a plate is inserted here in the material so that no teacher will get the procedure wrong]. As each child takes a colored square, ask him to name the color of that square. If the child hesitates, name it for him.[23]

In the curricular material, everything except the bag or box is included – all the plates and colored paper. (The cost by the way is $14.00 for the plan and the paper).

I noted that not only were the curricular and pedagogical elements pre-specified, but all other aspects of teachers' actions were included as well. Thus, in the 'Appraisal' of this module, the teacher is asked to:

> Ask each of six children to bring a box of crayons and sit together ... Ask each child to point to his red crayon when you say the word red. Repeat this for all six colors. Ask each child to match one crayon with one article of clothing that someone else is wearing ... Before each group of children leaves the activity, ask each child individually to name and point to the red, blue, and yellow crayon.[24]

Even with this amount of guidance, it is still 'essential' that we know for each child whether he or she has reached the appropriate skill level. (The APU is a step in this direction in the UK). Thus, as the final element, the material has competency measures built into it. Here the specification reaches its most exact point. giving the teacher the exact words he or she should use:

> Task 1: Show the child a yellow cube and ask, What is the color of this cube?

This is done for each color. Then, after arranging orange, green, and purple cubes in front of a child, the material goes on.

> Task 4: Say, Put your finger on the orange cube.
> Task 5: Say, Put your finger on the green cube.
> Task 6: Say, Put your finger on the purple cube.[25]

I have gone on at length here so that you can get a picture of the extent to which technical control enters into the life of the school. Little, in what might be metaphorically called the 'production process', is left to chance. In many ways, it can be considered a picture of de-skilling. Let us look at this somewhat more closely.

My point is not to argue against the specific curricular or pedagogical content of this kind of material, though an analysis of this certainly would be interesting.[26] Rather, it is to have us focus on the form itself. What is this doing? For notice what has happened here. The goals, the process, the outcome, and the evaluative criteria for assessing them are defined as precisely as possible by people external to the situation. In the competency measure at the end of the module this extends to the specification of even the exact words the teacher is to say. Notice as well the process of de-skilling at work here. Skills that teachers used to need, that were deemed essential to the craft of working with children (such as curriculum deliberation and planning, designing teaching and curricular strategies for specific groups and individuals based on intimate knowledge of these people), are no longer as necessary. With the large scale influx of pre-packaged material, planning is separated from execution. The planning is done at the level of the production of both the rules for use of the material and the material itself. The execution is carried out by the teacher. In the process, what were previously considered valuable skills slowly atrophy because they are less often required.[27]

But what about the element of re-skilling that I mentioned earlier as essential to the understanding of how ideological forms can penetrate to the heart of institutions like the school? Unlike the economy, where de-skilling and re-skilling are not usually found operating at one and the same moment with one and the same people, in the school this seems to be exactly the case. As the procedures of technical control enter into the school in the guise of pre-designed curricular/ teaching/evaluation 'systems', teachers are being de-skilled. Yet they are also being re-skilled in a way that is quite consequential. We can see signs of this at both teacher training institutions, in in-service workshops and courses, in the journals devoted to teachers, in funding and enrollment patterns, and not least in the actual curricular materials themselves. While the de-skilling involves the loss of craft and the on-going atrophication of educational skills, the re-skilling involves the substitution of the skills and ideological visions of management. The growth of behavior modification techniques and classroom management strategies and their incorporation within both curricular material and teachers' repertoires signifies these kinds of alterations. That is, as teachers lose control of the curricular and pedagogic skills to large publishing houses, these skills are replaced by techniques for better controlling students.

This is not insignificant in its consequences for both teachers and students. Since the material is often organised around and employs specified outcomes and procedures and these are built into this kind of material itself (with its many work-sheets and frequent tests), it is 'individualised' in many ways. Students can engage in it themselves with little overt interaction on the part of the teacher or each other as they become more used to the procedures, which are usually highly standardised. The students' progress through the system can be individualised (at least according to speed) and this focus on individualising the speed (usually through worksheets and the like) at which a student proceeds through the system is becoming even more pronounced in newer curricular systems. Since the control is technical – that is, management strategies are incorporated into it as a major aspect of the pedagogical/curricular/evaluative 'machinery' itself – the teacher becomes something of manager. This is occurring *at the same time* that the objective conditions of his or her work are becoming increasingly 'proletarianised' due to the curricular form's logic of technical control. This is a unique situation and certainly needs further thought. The possible effect of these forms of technical control on the students is just as serious and is something to which I shall return shortly.

Yet there are important consequences besides the de-skilling and re-skilling that are occurring. As the literature on the labor process reminds us, the progressive division and control of labor also has an impact, at the level of social relations, on how the people involved interact. While this has had a momentous effect in factories and offices, its effects will undoubtedly be felt in the school too. And, as in the workplace, the impact may have contradictory results. Let me be more specific here. With the increasing employment of pre-packaged curricular systems as the basic curricular form, virtually no interaction between teachers is required. If nearly everything is rationalised and specified before execution, then contact among teachers about actual curricular matters is minimized.[28]

If such technical control is effective, that is, if teachers actually respond in ways that accept the separation of planning from execution, then one would expect results that go beyond this 'mere' separation. One would expect, at the level of classroom practice, that it will be more difficult for teachers jointly to gain informal control over curricular decisions because of their increasing isolation. In essence, if everything is predetermined, there is no longer any pressing need for teacher interaction. Teachers become unattached individuals, divorced from both col-leagues and the actual stuff of their work. However, and here is part of what I mean by a contradictory effect, while this may be an accurate estimation of one of the results of technical control on one level, it forgets that most systems of control embody contradictions within themselves. For instance, while de-skilling, forms of technical control and the rationalisation of work have created isolated individuals in, say, factories, historically they have often generated contradictory pressures as well. The use of technical control has often brought unionisation in its wake.[29] Even given the ideology of professionalism (an ideology that might make it difficult for collective struggles to evolve) which tends to dominate certain sectors of the teaching force, other state employees who, in the past, have thought of themselves as professionals have gained a greater collective sense in response to similar modes of control. Thus, the loss of control and knowledge in one arena may generate countervailing tendencies in another. We cannot know yet how this will turn out. These contradictory results only emerge over long periods of time. In industry, it took decades for such an impact to be felt. The same will no doubt be true in schools.

Accepting Technical Control

So far in this essay, I have looked at teachers as if they were workers. That is, I have argued that the processes that act on blue and white collar workers in the larger social arena will, and are, entering into the *cultural forms* that are considered legitimate in schools. Yet schools, because of their internal history, are different in some very important ways from factories and offices, and teachers are still very different from other workers in terms of the conditions of their work. Products are not as visible (except much later on in the rough reproduction of a labor force, in the production and reproduction of ideologies, and in the production of the technical/administrative knowledge 'required' by an economy)[30] as in offices and factories. Teachers have what Erik Olin Wright has called a 'contradictory class location' and, hence, cannot be expected to react in the same ways as the workers and employees of large corporations.[31] Furthermore, there are children, who act back on teachers in ways an automobile on an assembly line or a paper on a desk cannot.[32] Finally, teaching does not take place on a line, but goes on in separate rooms more often than not.

All of these conditions do not mean that schools are immune or autonomous from the logic of capital. The logic will be mediated (in part due to the school as a *state* apparatus); it will enter where it can in partial, distorted, or coded ways. Given the specific differences of schools from other workplaces, a prime moment in its entry can be found less at the level of overt or simple controls ('do this because I say so') or at the level of bureaucratic form[33] (because individual teachers can still be relatively free from those kinds of encroachments). These controls will go on, of course; but they may be less consequential than *the encoding of technical control into the very basis of the curricular form itself.* The level of curricular, pedagogic, and evaluative practice within the classroom can be controlled by the forms into which culture is commodified in schools. If my arguments are correct, how are we to understand the acceptance and growth of this process of control?

These forms enter into schools not because of any conspiracy on the part of industrialists to make our educational institutions serve the needs of capital, as in the earlier quotes from the Green Paper and the Ryerson Plan. It occurs in large part because schools are a rather lucrative market. These sets of material are published by firms who aggressively market where there is a need, or where they can create needs. It is simply good business practice in terms of profit margins to market material of this type, especially since the original purchase of the 'system' or set of modules means increasing purchases over the years. Let me explain this by comparing it to another arena where similar techniques are employed to increase capital accumulation. Think of shaving. Large razor blade manufacturers sell razors at below cost, or even sometimes give them away as promotional 'gimmicks', because they believe that once you buy the razor you will continue to buy their blades and their upgraded version year after year. In the curricular systems we are considering here, the purchase of the modules (though certainly not cheap by any stretch of the imagination) with their sets of standardised disposable material means the same thing. One 'needs' to continue to purchase the work and test sheets, the chemicals, the correctly colored and shaped paper, the publishers' replacements of outmoded material and lessons, etc.. Profits are heightened with every replacement that is bought. Since replacement purchases are often bureaucratically centralised, because of budget control, in the office of the administrator, the additional material, is usually bought from the producer (often at exorbitant costs) not gotten from one's local store. Thus, as with other industries, this 'good business sense' means that high volume, the standardisation of each of the elements of one's product and of its form, product upgrading, and then the stimulation of replacement purchasing are essential to maintain profits.[34]

Another key element here is seeing the school as an aspect of the state apparatus. For the state's need for *consent* as well as *control* means that the forms of control in school will be encoded in particular ways.[35] The strategic import of the logic of technical control in schools lies in its ability to integrate into one discourse what are often seen as competing ideological movements, and, hence, to generate consent from each of them. The need for accountability and control by administrative managers, the real needs of teachers for something that is 'practical' to use with their students, the interest of the state in efficient production and cost savings,[36] the concerns of parents for 'quality education' that 'works' (a concern that will be coded differently by different classes and class segments), industrial capital's own requirements for efficient production and so on, can be joined. It is here that one can see how two important functions of the state can be accomplished. The state can assist in capital *accumulation* by attempting to provide a more efficient 'production process' in schools. At the same time, it can *legitimate* its own activity by couching its discourse in language that is broad enough to be meaningful to each of what it perceives to be important constituencies yet specific enough to give some practical answers to those who, like teachers, 'require' it. The fact that the form taken by these curricular systems is tightly controlled and more easily made 'accountable'; that it *is* usually individualised, that it focuses on skills in a time of perceived crisis in the teaching of 'basic skills', etc., nearly guarantees its acceptability to a wide array of classes and interest groups. Thus, the logic of control is both mediated and reinforced by the needs of state bureaucrats for accountable and rational procedures and by the specific nexus of forces acting on the state itself. The curriculum form will take on the aspects which are necessary to accomplish both accumulation and legitimation.[37] As Clarke puts it:

> Even where institutions meet a logic required by capital, their form and direction are never the outcome of a simple unidirectional imposition by capital. They involve a complex political work of concession and compromise, if only to secure the legitimacy of the state in popular opinion.[38]

This is exactly what has occurred in the use of this kind of curricular form.

The Possessive Individual

So far I have examined the encroachment into the work of teachers of the technical control systems embodied in curricular form. Yet, teachers are not the only actors in the setting where we find this material. There are the students as well.

A number of writers have noted that each kind of social formation 'requires' a particular kind of individual. Williams and others, for instance, have helped us trace the growth of the abstract individual as it developed within the theoretic, cultural, and economic practices of capitalism.[39] These are not simply changes in the definition of the individual, but imply changes in our actual modes of material and cultural producing, reproducing, and consuming. To be an individual in our society signifies a complex interconnection between our day to day meanings and practices and an 'external' mode of production. While I do not mean to imply a simple base/superstructure model here, it is clear that in some very important ways there is a dialectical relationship between economic and ideological form. As Gramsci and others would put it, ideological hegemony sustains class domination; subjectivities cannot be seen as unrelated to structure. Yet the questions remain: How are they related? Where are the sites where this relationship is worked out? The school provides a critical point at which one can see these things working out. As Richard Johnson notes, 'It is not so much a question that schools . . . *are* ideology, more that they are the sites where ideologies are produced in the form of subjectivities'.[40]

But what kind of subjectivity, what kind of ideology, what kind of individual may be produced here? The characteristics embodied in the modes of technical control built into the curricular form itself are ideally suited to reproduce the possessive individual, a vision of oneself that lies at the ideological heart of corporate economies. The conception of individualism located in the material we have been examining is quite similar to those found in other analyses of aspects of the cultural apparatus in our society. As Will Wright has demonstrated, for example, in his recent investigation of the role of cultural artifacts, like film, as carriers and legitimators of ideological changes, important aspects of our cultural apparatus represent a world in which the society recognises each member as an individual; but that recognition is dependent almost entirely upon technical skills. At the same time, while heightening the value of technical competence, these films direct the individual to reject the importance of ethical and political values through their form. They portray an individualism, situated in the context of a corporate economy, in which 'respect and companionship are to be achieved only by becoming a skilled technician'. The individual accepts and does any technical job that is offered and has loyalty only to those with similar technical competence, not primarily 'to any competing social and community values'.[41]

An examination of these curricular 'systems' illuminates the extent to which this kind of ideological movement is occurring in increasingly dominant curricular forms. Here, the *rate* at which a student proceeds is individualised; however, the actual product as well as the process to be accomplished are specified by the material itself.[42] Thus, it is not 'just' the teacher who faces the encroachment of technical control and de-skilling. The students' responses are largely pre-specified as well. Much of this growing arsenal of material attempts as precisely as possible to specify appropriate student language and action as well, often reducing it to the mastery of sets of competencies or skills. Here Wright seems correct. The notion of reducing curriculum to a set of skills is not unimportant in this regard since it is part of the larger process by which the logic of capital helps build identities and transforms cultural meanings and practices into commodities.[43] That is, if knowledge in all its aspects (of the logical type of that, how, or to – that is, information, processes, and dispositions or propensities) is broken down and commodified, like economic capital it can be accumulated. The mark of a good pupil is the possession and accumulation of vast quantities of skills in the service of technical interests. As an ideological mechanism in the maintenance of hegemony this is rather interesting. In the larger society, people consume as isolated individuals. Their worth is determined by the possession of material goods or, as Will Wright noted, of technical skills. The accumulation of such goods or of the 'cultural capital' of technical competence – here atomistic bits of knowledge and skills measured on pre-tests and post-tests – is a technical procedure, one which requires only the mastery of the prior necessary technical skills and enough time to follow the rules, at one's own pace, to their conclusion. It is the message of the new petty bourgeoisie writ large on the ideological terrain of the school.

In fact, one might hypothesize just this, that this kind of movement speaks to the increasing importance in the cultural apparatus of the ideologies of class segments with contradictory class locations, in particular what I have called the new petty bourgeoisie – those groups who make up middle management and technical occupations.[44] The particular kind of individualism we are witnessing here is an interesting shift from an ideology of individual autonomy, where a person is his, or her, own boss and controls his, or her, destiny, to a careerist individualism. Here the individualism is geared towards organisational mobility and advancement by following technical rules. As Eric Wright puts it, for the new petty bourgeoisie, 'individualism is structured around the requirements of bureaucratic advancement'.[45] It may also be a coded 'reflection' of the increasing proletarianisation of white collar work. For, while, previously, individualism signified some serious sense of autonomy over how one worked and what one produced, for a large portion of white collar employees autonomy has been trivialised.[46] The rate at which one works may be individualised, but the work itself, how it is accomplished, and what the exact specifications of the final product will be, are increasingly being specified.

At this stage, we are left with many questions. When technical control means that the form that the curriculum takes is highly specified, that it is individualised to such an extent that there is little required interaction among the students so that each activity is by necessity viewed as an individual intellectual act of skill, that answers often take the form of simple physical activities (as we saw in the module I discussed earlier), that answers are either correct or incorrect based on the application of technical rules, and this kind of form is what one follows throughout one's elementary school life, what impact does it have on the teachers and students who interact with it at the level of practice each day? This clearly points to the significance of engaging in analyses of what actually happens within the black box of the school. Do teachers and students accept this? Will the gradual introduction of the logic of technical control generate resistances, if only on a cultural level? Will class and work cultures contradict, mediate, or even transform the expected outcomes?[47] It is to this that we shall now turn.

Resistances

I have not presented an optimistic appraisal here. As the activities of students are increasingly specified, as the rules, processes, and standard outcomes are integrated through, and rationalised by, the materials themselves, so, too are teachers de-skilled, re-skilled, and anonymised. Students work on material whose form both isolates individuals from each other and establishes the conditions of existence for the possessive individual; the form of the material and the embedded nature of the technical control process does nearly the same for the teacher. Surrounded by a specific logic of control, the objective force of the social relations embodied in the form itself tends to be quite powerful.

Yet I am not arguing for a crude kind of functionalist perspective, where everything is measured by, or is aimed toward, its ability to reproduce an existing static society. The creation of the kind of ideological hegemony 'caused' by the increasing introduction of technical control is not 'naturally' pre-ordained. It is something that is won or lost in particular conflicts and struggles.[48] On the one hand, teachers will be controlled. As one teacher said about a set of popular material even more integrated and rationalised than the ones I have pointed to here:

> Look, I have no choice. I personally don't like this material, but everyone in the district has to use this series. I'll try to do other things as well, but basically our curriculum will be based on this.

On the other hand, resistances will be there. This same teacher, who disagreed with the curriculum but used it, was also partially subverting it in interesting ways. It was employed only three days a week instead of the five days which were specified. As the teacher put it:

> Listen, if we worked hard we'd finish this stuff in two or three months and besides it's sometimes confusing and boring. So I try to go beyond it as often as possible, *as long as I do not teach what is in the material to be covered by this series next year. (my italics)*

Thus, as we can see from this last part of her comment, internal conditions make such overt resistances more difficult.

Yet these internal conditions need not preclude teachers from also making these commodified cultural forms their own, to generate their own creative responses to dominant ideologies, in a manner similar to what the counter-cultural groups, studied by Marxist ethnographers, have done to commodified culture. These groups transformed and reinterpreted the products they bought and used so that they became tools for the creation of alternative pockets of resistance.[49] Students and teachers may also find ways of creatively using these systems in ways undreamed of by state bureaucrats or corporate publishing. (I must admit, however, that my repeated observations in classrooms over the last years make me less than totally optimistic that this will always or even very often be the case).

Other elements in the environment may provide the site for different meanings and practices to evolve, even within the curricular form itself. For we should remember that there may be progressive elements within the *content* of the curriculum that contradict the messages of the form.[50] And it is in the interaction between the content, the form, and the lived culture of the students that subjectivities are formed. No element in this set of relations can be ignored. This last point about the lived culture of the actors, the students themselves, needs to be stressed. One would expect resistances on the part of students as well, resistances that will be *specific by race, gender, and class*. My earlier quote from Johnson is correct here. The formation of ideologies – even those of the kind of individual I have examined in this analysis – is not a simple act of imposition. It is produced by concrete actors and embodied in lived experiences that may resist, alter, or mediate these social messages.[51] As Willis demonstrates, for instance, segments of working class youth partially defeat the ideology of individualism. The same may be true for many women and 'minority' students. While we can, and must, focus on these resistances, their actual meaning may be unclear. Do they, like those of the lads in Willis' book, also reproduce at an even deeper level ideological meanings and practices that provide quite powerful supports to relations of domination?[52] Take teachers, for example. While technical controls could possibly lead to unionisation, within the school most resistances that occur will be, by necessity, on an individual not a collective level because of the very social relations generated by the curricular form itself.[53] The effects, hence, can be rather contradictory.

When all this is said, however, we must recognise that these powerful social messages, while embedded in the actual experiences of teachers and students as they go about their day to day lives in classrooms, *are* highly mediated by other elements. The fact that individual teachers, like most other workers, may develop patterns of resistance to these patterns of technical control at the informal cultural level alters these messages. The contradictory ideologies of individualism and co-operativeness that are naturally generated out of the crowded conditions of many classrooms (you can't be an isolated individual all the time when there are twenty or thirty other people around with whom one teacher must cope) also provide countervailing possibilities. Lastly, just as blue and white collar workers have constantly found ways to retain their humanity and continually struggle to integrate conception and execution in their work (if only to relieve boredom) so too will teachers and students find ways, in the cracks so to speak, to do the same things. The real question is not whether such resistances exist – Aronowitz, myself, and others have claimed at length elsewhere that they are never far from the surface[54] – but whether they are contradictory themselves, whether they lead anywhere beyond the reproduction of the ideological hegemony of the most powerful classes in our society, whether they can be employed for political education and intervention.

Our task is first to find them. We need somehow to give life to the resistances, the struggles. What I have done here is to point to the terrain within the school (the transformation of work, the de-skilling and re-skilling, the technical control, and so on) over which these struggles will be fought. The resistances may be informal, not fully organised or even conscious; yet this does not mean that they will have no impact. For as Gramsci and Johnson remind us, hegemony is always contested.[55] Our own work should help in this contestation.

Notes and References

1 Quoted in DONALD, J. (1979) 'Green Paper: Noise of a Crisis', *Screen Education*, 30, Spring, 44.

2 *Ibid.*, pp. 36–7.

3 'The Ryerson Plan: A Teacher Work-Learn Program', (Chicago, Joseph T. Ryerson and Son, Inc., no date). I wish to thank McNEIL, L. for bringing this material to my attention.

4 *Ibid.*

5 See, for example, DOWNING, D. (1979) 'Soft Choices: Teaching Materials for Teaching Free Enterprise', (Austin, Texas, The Institute for Constructive Capitalism, The University of Texas). April mimeo.

6 This is not to deny the importance of analyzing official documents, especially those emanating from the state. Donald's article (see Note 1) provides an excellent example of the power of discourse analysis, for example, in unpacking what these documents mean and do.

7 WILLIAMS, R. (1977) *Marxism and Literature*, (New York, Oxford University Press).

8 FINN, D., GRANT, N. and JOHNSON, R. (1978) 'Social Democracy, Education and the Crisis', Birmingham, University of Birmingham Centre for Contemporary Cultural Studies, pp. 3–4.

9 O'CONNOR, J. (1973) *The Fiscal Crisis of the State*. (New York, St. Martin's Press).

10 See, for example, JAMESON, F. (1971) *Marxism and Form*, Princeton, Princeton University Press; WILLIAMS, R. *op. cit.*, (Note 7), and APPLE, M. (1978) 'Ideology and Form in Curriculum Evaluation', in WILLIS, G. (Ed.) *Qualitative Evaluation*, Berkeley, McCutchan Publishing Corp.

11 CLARKE, J. (1979) 'Capital and Culture: The Post-War Working Class Revisited' in CLARKE, J., CRITCHER, C. and JOHNSON, R. (Eds.) (1979) *Working Class Culture: Studies in History and Theory*, London, Hutchinson, p. 239. See also the impressive discussions in BRAVERMAN, H., *Labor and Monopoly Capital*, New York, Monthly Review Press (1974); and BURAWOY, M. (1979) 'Toward a Marxist Theory of the Labor Process: Braverman and Beyond', *Politics and Society*, 8, Number 3–4.

12 EDWARDS, R. (1979) *Contested Terrain: The Transformation of the Workplace in the Twentieth Century*, New York, Basic Books. p. 17.

13 *Ibid.*, pp. 19–21.

14 *Ibid.*, p. 110.

15 NOBLE, D. (1977) *America By Design: Science, Technology and the Rise of Corporate Capitalism*, New York, Alfred A. Knopf; and BURAWOY, M. *op. cit.*, (Note 11).

16 APPLE, M. (in press) 'The Other Side of the Hidden Curriculum: Correspondence Theories and the Labor Press', *The Journal of Education*. See also ARONOWITZ, S. (1978) 'Marx, Braverman and the Logic of Capital', *The Insurgent Sociologist*, 8, Fall 126–146.

17 EDWARDS, R. *op. cit.*, (Note 12).

18 I have discussed the school's role in producing this knowledge in APPLE, M. (1979) 'The Production of Knowledge and the Production of Deviance' in BARTON, L. and MEIGHAN, R. (Eds.) *Schools, Pupils and Deviance*, Driffield, England, Nafferton Press. pp. 113–131.

19 See, for example, BARKER, J. and DOWNING, H. 'Word Processing and the Transformation of Patriarchal Relations', unpublished paper, Birmingham University, England.

20 DALE, R. (1979) points this out in 'The Politicization of School Deviance' in BARTON, L. and MEIGHAN, R. (Eds.) *Schools, Pupils and Deviance*, Driffield, England, Nafferton Press, pp. 95–112.

21 GITLIN, T. (1979) 'Prime Time Ideology: The Hegemonic Process in Television Entertainment', *Social Problems*, 26, February pp. 251–266. The work of WEXLER, P. of the University of Rochester on the commodification of intimate relations is important here, especially his work in progress, *Critical Social Psychology*.

22 This is not only an American phenomenon. The foreign subsidiaries of the companies who produce these materials are translating and marketing their products in the Third World and elsewhere as well. In many ways it is similar to the cultural imperialism of Walt Disney Productions. See, for example, DORFMAN, A. and MATTELART, A. (1975) *How to Read Donald Duck*, (New York, International General Editions).

23 (1974) *Science . . . A Process Approach II, Instructional Booklet: Module 1*, Lexington, Ginn and Co., pp. 3–4.

24 *Ibid.*, p. 7.

25 *Ibid.*

26 See, for example, my analysis of science curricula in APPLE, M. (1979) *Ideology and Curriculum*, Boston, Routledge and Kegan Paul.

27 I do not mean to romanticize the past, however. Many teachers probably simply followed the textbook before. However, the level of specificity and the integration of curricular, pedagogical, and evaluative aspects of classroom life into *one* system is markedly different. The use of the system brings with it much more technical control of every aspect of teaching than previous text-based curricula. Obviously,

some teachers will not follow the system's rules. Given the level of integration, though, it will un-doubtedly be much more difficult to ignore it since many systems constitute the core or only program in that curricular area in the entire school or district. Thus, accountability to the next grade level or to administrators makes it harder to ignore. I shall return to this point later on.

28 This may be similar to what happened in the early mills in New England, when standardized production processes drastically reduced the contact among workers. See EDWARDS, R. *op. cit.*, (Note 12), p. 114.

29 *Ibid.*, p. 181.

30 See APPLE, M. *op. cit.*, (Note 18), APPLE, M. *op. cit.*, (Note 26), and NOBLE, D. *op. cit.*, (Note 15). One could also claim that schools operate to produce use value not exchange value. WRIGHT, E. personal conversation.

31 WRIGHT, E.O. (1978) *Class, Crisis and the State*, London, New Left Books, pp. 31–110.

32 Therefore, any outcomes of schooling must be analyzed as the products of cultural, political, and economic resistances as well as determinations. See WILLIS, P. (1977) *Learning to Labour*, Westmead, England, Saxon House; and APPLE, M. (1980) 'Analyzing Determinations: Understanding and Evaluating the Production of Social Outcomes in Schools', *Curriculum Inquiry*, 10, Spring.

33 I do not want to ignore the question of the relationship between capitalism and bureaucracy. Weber and others were not wrong when they noted that there were needs for rationalization specific to bureaucratic forms themselves. However, neither the *way* bureaucracy has grown in corporate economies nor its effects have been neutral. This is treated in considerably more detail in CLAWSON, D.C. 'Class Struggle and the Rise of Bureaucracy', unpublished doctoral dissertation, State University of New York at Stony Brook, 1978. See also WRIGHT, E.O. *op. cit.*, (Note 31).

34 BARKER, J. and DOWNING, H. *op. cit.*, (Note 19), p. 20. See also NOBLE, D. *op. cit.*, (Note 15) for his account of standardization and its relationship to capital accumulation.

35 DONALD, J. *op. cit.*, (Note 1), 44.

36 This is not meant to imply that the state always directly serves the needs of industrial capital. It in fact does have a significant degree of relative autonomy and is the site of class conflict as well. See DONALD, J. *op. cit.*, (Note 1) and WRIGHT, E.O. *op. cit.*, (Note 31).

37 We should remember, however, that accumulation and legitimation may be in conflict with each other at times. See WRIGHT, E.O. *op. cit.*, (Note 31) for a discussion of these possible contradictions and for an argument about the importance of understanding the way the state and bureaucracies mediate and act back on 'economic determinations'.

38 CLARKE, J. *op. cit.*, (Note 11), p. 241.

39 WILLIAMS, R. (1961) *The Long Revolution*, London, Chatto and Windus, and MACPHERSON, C.B. (1962) *The Political Theory of Possessive Individualism*, New York, Oxford University Press.

40 JOHNSON, R. (1979) 'Three Problematics: Elements of a Theory of Working-Class Culture' in CLARKE, J. CRITCHER, C. and JOHNSON, R. *op. cit.*, (Note 11), p. 232.

41 WRIGHT, W. (1975) *Sixguns and Society*, Berkeley, University of California Press, p. 187.

42 Bernstein's work on class and educational codes is interesting here. As he notes, '. . . The pacing of educational knowledge is class based'. It is based upon middle class views of socialisation. BERNSTEIN, B. (1977) *Class, Codes and Control, Vol. 3*, London, Routledge and Kegan Paul, p. 113.

43 See ARONOWITZ, S. (1973) *False Promises*, New York, McGraw-Hill. p. 95.

44 WRIGHT, E.O. *op. cit.*, (Note 31). p. 79.

45 *Ibid.*, p. 59.

46 *Ibid.*, p. 81. See also BRAVERMAN, H. *op. cit.*, (Note 11).

47 I have suggested elsewhere that this will be the case. See APPLE, M. *op. cit.*, (Note 16) and APPLE, M. *op. cit.*, (Note 32).

48 JOHNSON, R. 'Histories of Culture/Theories of Ideology: Notes on an Impasse' in BARRETT, M., CORRIGAN, P., KUHN, A. and WOLFF, J. (Eds.) (1979) *Ideology and Cultural Production*. New York, St. Martin's Press, p. 70.

49 WILLIS, P. (1978) *Profane Culture*, London, Routledge and Kegan Paul.

50 Geoff Whitty has been particularly helpful in enabling me to see this point.

51 See JOHNSON, R. *op. cit.*, (Note 48).

52 WILLIS, P. *op. cit.*, (Note 32).

53 Compare here to EDWARDS, R. *op. cit.*, (Note 12), p. 154.

54 See, for example, ARONOWITZ, S. *op. cit.*, (Note 16), APPLE, M. *op. cit.*, (Note 16), and BURAWOY, M. *op. cit.*, (Note 11).

55 JOHNSON, R. *op. cit.*, (Note 48).

Schooling and the Reproduction of Class and Gender Relations

Madeleine MacDonald, Open University

In 1967, Quintin Hoare wrote,

> British education is from a rational point of view grotesque, from a moral one, intolerable and from a human one tragic . . . Predictably, the Labour Party has at no time offered a global challenge to the present system. It has at most stood for its expansion and the elimination of some of its most flagrantly undemocratic features. It has never seriously threatened the most important of these: the continued existence of the public schools and sexual discrimination against girls in every type of school. Above all, it has never attacked the vital centre of the system, the curriculum, the *content* of what is taught.[1]

In 1980 these remarks are still valid not just for the Labour Party, but also for sociologists of education. This may seem a curious statement to make, particularly given the development of sociology of the curriculum over the last decade and the more recent flowering of feminist analyses of schooling within the discipline. However, whilst the diversity and range of material is considerable and its critical stance not disputed, I shall argue in this paper first, that what is still lacking in the studies of the curriculum is that 'vital centre' – the *content* of school subjects. The sociology of school texts has been left a minimal element, squeezed between the blocks of macro and micro studies of school structures and processes. The analyses of the ideology of textbooks and of the visual and literary resources teachers daily refer to and use in the classroom have been left with little critical evaluation, apart from that of journalists concerned about the bias in such material. Second, although there is now more research on patterns of sexual discrimination in schools, this research still retains a marginal status. By and large, it has not been integrated into the 'radical' critiques of schooling which tend to weight theories of education towards class analysis. There has been a noticeable neglect of race and sexual structures in schooling, as integral and not subsidiary elements of capitalism. Interestingly, it is only when these latter hierarchies and inequalities are referred to, that there seems to be any need for the investigation of school texts. In these contexts, educational materials are studied as potential sources of ideological representations and prejudice.

My concern in this paper with these two 'forgotten' subjects of school analysis is part of an attempt to answer the same central theoretical question. I am interested in the ways schooling may be involved in the processes of legitimation and hence of reproduction of class and gender relations under capitalism. (The complications which an analysis of racial hierarchies brings, requires another article). Here, I shall focus specifically on the structure and content of school culture as represented by the curriculum. The position I shall take is, first, that one cannot isolate out one sex or one social class. One has to remember that these categories exist within a set of social relations. In particular, the category of gender, which is socially constructed, only has meaning when the concepts of masculinity and femininity are recognised as a pair which exist in a relationship of complementarity and antithesis.

Simone de Beauvoir[2] describes this relationship by using a Hegelian distinction between Subject and Other. Man is the Subject, the absolute and woman is the Other. Within this duality, the definition of woman is constructed *relative* to man

> The terms *masculine* and *feminine* are used symmetrically only as a matter of form, as on legal papers. In actuality the relation of the two sexes is not quite like that of two electrical poles, for man represents both the positive and the neutral, as is indicated by the common use of *man* to designate human beings in general, whereas woman represents only the negative, defined by limiting criteria, without reciprocity.[3]

The assumption I hold is that both class relations and gender relations, while they exist within their own histories, can nevertheless be so closely interwoven that it is theoretically very difficult to draw them apart within specific historic conjunctures. The development of capitalism is one such conjuncture where one finds patriarchal relations of male dominance and control over women buttressing the structure of class domination. In a wide variety of 'sites' such as the work place, the family, the law and the educational system, there are the hierarchies of class and also of sex. Further, in so far as class relations (in other words the division between capital and labour) constitute the primary element of the capitalist social formation, they limit and structure the form of gender relations, the division between male and female properties and identities. I do not believe that one can dis-associate the ideological forms of masculinity and femininity, in their historical specificity, from either the material basis of patriarchy nor from the class structure. If one definition of femininity or masculinity is dominant, it is the product of patriarchal relations and also the product of class dominance, even though these two structures may exist in contradiction.

Within capitalism, the relations of class and gender take a unique form. They are brought together, for example, in the maintenance of capitalist social relations of production – where male dominance reinforces the authority of supervisors, managers and experts.[4] At a more fundamental level, the coincidence of these two structures facilitates the reproduction of the work force required by that mode of production. Biological reproduction of workers occurs within a particular family mode, which is characterised in capitalism by a patriarchal household, monogamy, and a domestic sexual division of labor which delegates to woman the prime responsibility for child care and early education. Social reproduction of the work force occurs through the extension of this domestic division of labour (supposedly derived from the biological role of woman in childbearing) to the division, within capitalism, between social production and the domestic sphere. A correspondence is maintained between the public and male worlds and between the private and female realms. This coincidence, I would argue, is one of the major factors in the reproduction of the male and female work force which, in the capitalist mode of production, is organised largely along the lines of sex segregation. The division between work and the family represents a 'split' or separation between production of commodities for exchange and the production of use values such as food, garments etc., for consumption in the family. However, this becomes 'misrecognised' or falsely perceived when it appears that the division is based upon the 'natural instincts and interests' of men in work and women in the family. Thus, the usefulness for capital of this division, and the additional superior status attributed to productive work because of its 'masculine' association, is hidden in the ideology of sex differences.

What it is important to recognise is that the congruence of these two structures is not natural but socially imposed and, as a result, has to be continually reinforced through the legal, political and educational agencies of the state, if it is to be maintained.[5] The context of this imposition is that of bourgeois hegemony; of the attempt by the bourgeoisie to gain the consent of women to a definition of femininity which locates their primary role as keepers of the home with only secondary involvement in waged work. Also the consent of men has to be won to a definition of masculinity which involves their leaving their homes to go out to work and to be responsible for the family income. If such consent can be won, the ideological conditions are more likely to be ensured for the daily and generational reproduction of the wage labour force through the unpaid work of the wife and mother.[6] Also, the recruitment of working class women is facilitated because of their domestic commitments, into those occupations which require little skill, are badly paid, are often part-time and normally lack any prospects. Other advantages for capital also arise from this sexual division of labor across the divide of work and family life. Zaretsky[7], for instance, suggests the psychiatric advantages of the family to capital by the alleviation of class aggression and alienation, through the 'hiving off' of the world of personal relations from the materialistic and harsh world of work. Women in the family become either a stabilising emotional force or alternatively the victims of male violence. Further, the State can be relieved of the responsibility of catering for such functions as early childhood care and education, sick nursing, care of the aged etc.. These can be delegated to the family and especially to women.

It is therefore within the context of bourgeois hegemony that we can understand the dominant pattern of state education where women have been implicitly oriented, if not overtly prepared, for domesticity and men for the world of work.[8] Whilst schooling, for men, has been directed largely towards the discipline of the work place, the development of mass schooling for women has taken a different direction. As Davin[9] argues, if state education developed solely as a result of a need for a skilled work force or alternatively to educate a newly franchised working class politically, this could only explain the establishment of schools for men, as women did not fall into either category. Extending Johnson's[10] argument, that the school was meant to compensate for a morally deficient family (held responsible for the decay in society), Davin presents the view that,

> a further aim of schooling was to impose on working-class children the bourgeois view of family functions and responsibilities. Education was to form a new generation of parents (especially mothers) whose children would not be wild, but dependent and amenable . . . [11]

The bourgeois form of family which schools were to establish as a 'stabilising force' was composed of the male breadwinner, the dependent housekeeping wife and dependent children. In her analysis of Board School readers of the turn of the century, Davin concludes that,

> . . . it is worth noticing that their tendency, both through the behaviour they advocated – unselfishness, compassion, devotion to housewifely industry and family duty – and through the situations which they presented as natural to women, was to direct girls towards an exclusively domestic role, even at the expense of school.[12]

We can understand the social relations of schooling not just as attempts to prepare for class obedience but also to prepare women for their role, subordinate to men. In both the reproduction of the social relations of production and the work force, we must therefore recognise the *dual* locations of family and work, not just for women but for men as well. Education for one sphere has implications for men and women's roles within the other. For working class men the contradictions between these two worlds are clear: at school they learn to expect forms of control and discipline when they become workers but they also learn about the expected dominance of men in the home. In some way they have to balance and contextualise these two different behavioural repertoires. Working class women on the other hand experience dual forms of control, both as workers and as women, and also the contradictions of trying physically and emotionally to cope with both domestic and wage work. The role of schooling in the reproduction of the capitalist mode of production, I believe, is not therefore just to do with the reproduction of a work force through basic skill training, nor is it just to do with reproduction of the social relations of production through the hidden curriculum of discipline and authority. The work of the school facilitates the maintenance *in the long run* of the work force and the social relations of production through the transmission of a set of gender relations, its association with the division between domestic and waged labour, and all the contradictions this entails.

Care must be taken however, when generalising this to all stages of capitalist development. With the growth of corporate capitalism and the emergence of the welfare state we can see an increased intervention of the state and the economy into the privatised world of the family. Patriarchy, as a set of power relations, may well conflict with the structure of advanced capitalism. This can be seen in the case of Sweden where the State has attempted, and yet failed, to combat sexual discrimination in families, the communities and the schools. The advantages to be gained by capital in the breakdown of patriarchical families would lie in the 'releasing' of married women from the home and domestic chores for waged work in the commodity production system.[13] Patriarchal structures in the families of different social classes, also may have different relations to the labour process and capital. Dorothy Smith[14], for example, argues that the family of the managerial classes has been incorporated into the bureaucracies of corporate capitalism. The family of the business executive (and in particular his wife) now stands in what she called a 'subcontractual' relationship to the corporate enterprise, transmitting its culture and values and reflecting its authority structures. Humphries[15], on the other hand, argues that historically the working class family stood in opposition to capital because in the protected world of home life the working class could maintain and transmit its own culture and values. The weakening not only of the boundaries between the family and the economy but also of the domestic division of labour amongst the middle classes has to some extent heralded in attempts to break down sex segregation in the schools and to construct and transmit a new set of gender relations, more appropriate for corporate capitalism.

The impression we have to keep is of the dynamics of class and gender relations through the development of capitalism but, more than that, it is also important to remember the existence of class and sexual struggle. The dualities of capital and labour and male and female, constitute not only social dichotomies but also hierarchies upon which both material and symbolic power is based. Inside these hierarchies the dialectics of class and sexual struggles are waged. If we wish to understand the role of schooling as one site of the reproduction of the socio-sexual division of labour, we must also be aware of the stakes of these *two* forms of struggle and their interrelations. Certainly there is now an interest in the forms of popular struggle over and in education, in forms of class resistance and the nature of the final compromises. However, this perspective has not really affected feminist analyses. There seems to be little recognition of sexual struggle particularly in the educational arena. If the history of education concerns winning the consent of women to their position in society, then surely there must also be a history of their dissent. There must be a history of women's fight for education not merely as a means of social mobility but also of sexual liberation. More than that, there must be a 'hidden' history of women's class struggle in and outside the classroom to resist and reject bourgeois definitions of femininity transmitted with such persistence through every cultural agency.

The analysis of class and gender relations requires, I believe, a theory of 'identity formation' – the patterns and processes which define, limit and transmit the range of models available to individuals to identify with. I make no assumption however that these structures will necessarily describe individual or group identities but I do assume that they will represent social priorities and the cultural framework within which individuals acquire a sense of themselves. The mistake, I believe, that many theories of education make, is they assume that social identities are formed through the experience of cultural forms without ever testing this. The experience can be as little as 'contact', as active as 'consumption' such as the buying of a book or a record, or as deep as the process of 'unconscious internalisation' or 'acquisition' of structural principles. It is at this point that our theories of education are at their most deterministic and make their greatest theoretical leaps. The learner is either assumed to be passive or 'naked' in the sense of being unaffected or unformed by any previous experience, and therefore incapable of resisting social pressures. Further, what is noticeable is how often these theories assume that individuals are what they are supposed to become. The working class are often talked of as passive, quiescent, docile or uncritical because educationalists since the nineteenth-century have argued for such, or because the school is seen to be a place of discipline and control. Yet as Willis[16] so succinctly puts it, 'merely because capital would like to treat workers as robots does not mean they are robots'.[17] Similarly women in feminist accounts, whether they are sociological or historical, tend to take on the mantle of femininity and passivity without any stuggle. In attempting to move away from biological determinism in the explanation of sex differences, such theories often fall into the trap of *social* determinism. There is a sense in which, in feminist writings, women are 'oversocialised'. Take for example, this statement by Simone de Beauvoir,

> The passivity that is the essential characteristic of the 'feminine' women
> is a trait that develops in her from the earliest years. But it is wrong to assert
> a biological datum is concerned; it is in fact a destiny imposed upon her by
> her teachers and by society.[18]

The formation of identity is a highly complex process which cannot be *assumed* to be successful at either the conscious or unconscious levels of learning. Ideally what we need is an analysis not just of the production and transmission of cultural messages but also the reception of cultural messages before we can judge the impact of these forms. Further, it is important to understand the part played by school culture in a wider context. In an age of mass media and a wide variety of cultural agencies, we can no longer justify concentrating upon schools, in isolation, as the sole or even dominant creator of meanings, class and sexual identities and consciousness. We need to investigate the relationship between 'external' cultural resources and internal school culture in both its complementary and antagonistic aspects. As Bernstein[19] has already pointed out, the consciousness of the ruling class and the consciousness of the working class are less likely to be dominated by the mode of education than by the mode of production. In contrast it is the conscious-ness of the new middle classes (called by Bernstein the agents of symbolic control) which is constituted by the mode of education and only indirectly by the mode of production. This view is supported by Willis who argues that the distinction between work and culture must be broken down particularly in the analysis of male working class indentities. He claims,

> . . . not only can work be analysed from a cultural point of view, but it must
> occupy a *central* place in any full sense of culture. Most people spend their

prime waking hours at work, base their identity on work activities and are defined by others essentially through their relation to work.[20]

To recap: I have argued, first, that any analysis of class and gender relations in schooling must recognise the historical specificity of definitions of masculinity and femininity. They are socially constructed categories and power relations which are contained within, and defined by, the structure of class relations. In educational institutions one is likely to find, therefore, the imposition of gender definitions which are integral to the culture of the ruling class (e.g. aristocractic or bourgeois concepts of masculinity and femininity). These definitions represent one aspect of their effort to exert hegemonic control through schooling. Second, I have argued that there must be recognition of the forms of class and sexual struggle in terms of educational provision and in the processes of class and sexual identity formation through culture. Third, I have argued that one of the ways class and gender relations are produced under capitalism is through the separation of domestic and wage labour and its reproduction in schools.

In the next section of this paper, I shall go back to the sociology of the curriculum to try and draw out elements of a theory of class and gender relations. The analysis will be of necessity, exploratory. I shall concentrate on the structure of school culture first, and then move on to school texts.

The first body of theory I shall look at is that of cultural reproduction, to see what a structuralist account of class and gender relations in schooling could look like. Within this category one can place Basil Bernstein's theory of educational codes and Pierre Bourdieu's work on cultural codes.[21] The theme here, is that culture has, through education, been divided into two categories – the legitimate and the illegitimate. This dichotomy also reflects the division between public and private knowledge, between culture and common sense, between school knowledge and family and community experience. Further, the transmission through educational institutions of specific forms of culture not merely ensures the reproduction of that culture but also of the class structure it supports. Culture according to Bourdieu symbolically

> reproduces in transfigured and therefore unrecognisable form, the structure of prevalent socio-economic relationships – it produces a representation of the social world immediately adjusted to the structure of socio-economic relationships which are consequently perceived as natural, so contributing to the symbolic buttressing of the existing balance of forces.[22]

The structural division and relations between forms of knowledge, according to Bourdieu and indeed Bernstein as well, is a far more significant aspect of the formation of social identities than the *actual* selection of knowledge and *its* hidden message. What is important is the acquisition of the rules and principles which govern the structural hierarchies of culture. Indeed for Bernstein[23] the word 'content' signifies merely how a period of time is filled in the school timetable. Thus a curriculum is defined 'in terms of the principle by which certain periods of time and their contents are brought in to a special relationship with each other'.[24] What is central to Bernstein's analysis is whether a school subject has high or low status, whether it is compulsory or optional and what relation it bears to other subjects in terms of the strength or weakness of its boundaries.

In both Bernstein's and Bourdieu's structuralist accounts of schooling, social identities are formed through a process of internalisation of three core classifications – those of age, sex and social class. The structures of age relations, sex relations and class relations are to be found, for example, in the family, the school and the work place. While their analyses of these classifications and their interrelations remain underdeveloped, one can still see what direction that analysis might take if we look at Bourdieu's *Outline of a Theory of Practice*.[25] In this study of the Kayble society, in Algeria, Bourdieu identified structural correspondences between the sexual division of labour and symbolic oppositions.[26] The categories of masculine and feminine were found *objectified* in the dichotomies of the right and left hands or the division between religion and magic, between external space such as the market and the fields and internal space – the home. When the child learns to use these structural divisions of gender and their objectified form in the divisions of time, space and objects, according to Bourdieu, he or she also constructs his or her social identity. This social identity is composed first of a sexual identity which is learnt through simultaneously experiencing the mother's and father's body as well as the sexual division of labour within the home. It is also made up by a whole system of social meanings and values, a body language of gestures, postures, and a physical bearing (what Bourdieu calls body hexis), a form of speech and a language. The child experiencing the structural organisation of the economic, the social and the cultural, will learn to relate to his or her own body, to other individuals and to nature according to the same principles. For the female child among the Kayble for example the experience is one of learning 'inner-directedness' or what Bourdieu called a *centripetal* orientation. The male child, by contrast, will be outer-directed – he will have a *centrifugal* orientation which will be expressed in the outward displays of virility and by his involvement in work, politics and war. The process is what Bourdieu called *embodiment*, which determines not merely the child's social identity but also his or her physical and sexual presence.

In terms of the relevance of this account for an analysis of institutionalised education, we need to ask the following questions. Is it possible to identify similar *dialectics of embodiment and objectification* in the culture of a class society? Is there any reality in talking of correspondences between the structure of gender relations, of masculinity and femininity and the divisions of school knowledge? In the world of formal education, it is certainly not difficult to identify numerous sets of oppositions which divide and distance forms of knowledge and their associated activities. For example, we can find the dichotomies of public and private knowledge, politics and psychology, reason and emotion, science and art, technology and nature, reality and fantasy. Further, as Spender[27] has noticed, there are also the methodological distinctions between hard and soft data, objectivity and subjectivity. The difficulty is of judging, at more than a common sense level, the relationship of these classifications to the social definitions of masculinity and femininity. As Roberts put it,

> How polarisation and dichotomisation affect thought systems is still open to much consideration. The 'we and they', the 'foe and friend', the 'reward and punishment' – the ubiquitous and fallacious paired opposites are obvious. What is unclear is the extent to which social sex polarisation provides the basis of such dualistic thinking.[28]

Certainly much of the literature on school subjects and sex segregation within the school, places great emphasis on the fact that some subjects are perceived of as either masculine or feminine. The 'masculinity' of science or the 'femininity' of domestic science can be seen as contributing to the unwillingness of girls to choose the former and of boys to study the latter.[29] The question is, how does such characterization occur which limits the range of choice of school subjects for the different sexes? Is it purely through the unconscious manipulations of teachers using restricted gender definitions or is it the effect of the different patterns of men and women's employment? Certainly both might enter the hidden curriculum of the school and affect the students' choice of subject. Bourdieu[30] suggests that the process of gender attribution to both students and academic disciplines is dialectical. The transference of femininity, for example, from the student to the school subject and back again to the student exemplifies the dialectic of objectification and embodiment.

> ... the objective mechanisms which channel girls preferentially towards the Arts faculties and within them, towards certain specialities (such as modern languages, art history or French) owe part of their effectivity to a social definition of the 'feminine' qualities which they help to form; in other words, to the internalisation of the external necessity imposed by this definition of feminine studies. In order for a destiny, which is the objective product of the social relations defining the female condition at a given moment in time, to be transmuted into a vocation, it is necessary and sufficient that girls (and all those around them, not least their families) should be unconsciously guided by the prejudice ... that there is an elective affinity between so-called 'feminine' qualities and 'literary' qualities such as sensitivity to the imponderable nuances of sentiment or a taste for the imprecise preciosities of style.[31]

In this description of the process, women's educational route becomes a self-fulfilling prophecy once one has imposed a specific definition of femininity. The question which one has to ask is, 'How do academic disciplines or school subjects change their gender?'. Why do some subjects change from appearing as masculine to being viewed as essentially feminine (such as the social sciences) or alternatively change in the other direction (for example, education)? The answer must lie, to a great extent, in the pressures exerted on the school and universities by the changing pattern of employment of men and women in the labour force. However, the attribution of gender to specific subjects is also part of class culture and its operation in the school is, I shall argue, one of the means for legitimating the structure of class domination.

In the family, the child learns the class-based definitions of masculinity and femininity, as well as a certain sexual division of labour. When the child enters the school this experience is challenged by a very specific set of gender relations – what I shall call, following Bernstein, a gender code.[32] The school's gender code sets up the categories of masculine and feminine as well as the boundaries and relations of power between them. While variations of the dominant gender code are possible in different types of school,[33] what is transmitted is essentially the form of gender relations which is specific to the ruling class. It represents the morality of the bourgeoisie, it legitimates in its ideal family form, as Davin[34] argued, the bourgeois family. In this sense, we can see the work of the school as involving the process of what Bernstein called *re-contextualising*, where the familial form of gender relations is converted into that of the dominant class. Because of this process the concepts of masculinity and femininity can be found to vary in different historic periods within schooling, affecting both the provision and the 'image' of school subjects. According to Bernstein, the informal everyday experience and everyday communication within the family and peer groups which shape social identities feed into and 'create procedures and performances fundamental to formal education. However, formal education also selects, and re-focusses and abstracts from such experiences and in so doing de-contextualises it'.[35] The process begins with this de-contextualising of the behaviours and competences invoked in the contexts of the home and community. They are thus freed from their dependence on these evoking contexts and, through a process of re-contextualising, become generalisable and abstract. Thus the 'practical mastery'[36] acquired through imitation of actions in the home, is converted, if the process is successful, into 'symbolic mastery' of the school discourses. One of the aspects of this process in the context of class society, is the re-contextualisation of definitions of masculinity and femininity into the class-based, and hence arbitrary, classification of school knowledge. The notions of appropriate behaviours for each sex is converted into the appropriate academic disciplines. Despite the actual availability of all subjects, girls and boys of different classes learn the new ideology of sex differences which mixes a theory of biological sex differences with expected gender differences of intelligence, ability, interests and ambitions, making it appear 'natural' that boys and girls should study different school subjects.

The process of re-contextualising, even of de-contextualising, may, however, not always be effective, especially where the family structure and culture differs considerably from the school. Let us look for a moment at the distinction between mental and manual labour which is integral to the capitalist labour process. In bourgeois culture it is transposed with the hierarchy of male over female – in other words mental labour is equated with the masculine and manual work or practical skills with the female. The dominant gender code within school is likely to transmit this pairing of two hierarchies. However, as Willis[37] has shown in *Learning to Labour*, working class boys confronted with this dual structure have two choices – either they conform, with the result that they lose credibility with their own class and deny their masculine sexuality or, they can reject the message of the school. Significantly, the conformist or 'ear'ole' is labelled as effeminate or cissy. The 'lads' on the other hand, in their resistance to bourgeois culture, invert the school hierarchy of mental over manual, celebrating the manual and physical working class masculinity. This inversion is in line with the 'lads', family culture and in particular with that of their fathers. Thus, in resistance, 'manual labour is associated with the social superiority of masculinity, and mental labour with the social inferiority of femininity.[38] On the shop floor, as well, this convergence of manual labour with masculinity has political repercussions.

> ... where the principle of general abstract labour has emptied work of significance from the inside, a transformed patriarchy has filled it with significance from the outside. Discontent with work is turned away from a political discontent and confused in its logic by a huge detour into the symbolic sexual realm.[39]

The failure of the school to 're-contextualise' the masculinity of these 'lads' into academic rather than physical displays, has reinforced the probability of their occupational destiny and the diffusion of their class discontent. On the other hand, those 'ear'oles' who conformed have been swept into acceptance of bourgeois culture. In both cases, the resolution of the conflict between sexual and class identities and school culture helps contain opposition to school order and, later, to the class divisions of the mode of production.

In the case of working-class girls, the classification of mental work as male and manual work as female, is less problematic as it is often reinforced rather than resisted by the family culture. We must however, be careful to distinguish between the application of the 'manual' category to working class and middle class women. In the case of the working class, manual labour either refers to the form of waged labour practised by this group of women or alternatively to their unpaid domestic labour. In this case the school will legitimate the equating of domesticity, of marriage and of motherhood with femininity. For the middle class girl, manual labour can either mean skilled work in secretarial or administrative occupations or alternatively the more 'practical' professions such as social work or nursing. The forms of class resistance to the imposition of bourgeois definitions of femininity by working class women takes the form of exaggerated celebration of domestic life and the over-emphasis of 'female' interests. Paradoxically the work of Willis, McRobbie and Sharpe[40] has shown that these forms of class resistance to the school, which involve the celebration of working class definitions of masculinity and femininity, have confirmed rather than broken down the cycle of class reproduction. *They undermine neither the sexual nor the social division of labour*. In both cases, mental labour and the high status and high income professions, are delegated and legitimated as the preserve of the male bourgeoisie and to a lesser extent the female bourgeoisie. The formation of sexual identities in the home and the school are therefore critical elements of the reproduction of the class structure.

In summary, I have argued in this section that specific sets of symbolic classifications represent the essence of bourgeois culture. Further underlying these hierarchies of knowledge, together with their associated 'gender', is the attempt by that class to 'win the consent' through schooling of the working class to the dominance of capital, and to win the consent of women to the sexual division of labour in which men dominate.

Let us now turn to the analysis of school texts. These texts represent a system of choices from the 'external' culture – whether we are talking about a body of literature, a range of photographs, a set of experiments drawn from the science departments of universities, or history textbooks produced by educational publishers. Despite the diversity of resources available to teachers, the research on school texts reveals a pervasive ideology – that of legitimacy of the *status quo*. This message, according to Gerard MacDonald[41] has become hidden in school textbooks which once were the vehicle for an overt ideology of conservatism based on religion.

> Textbooks present a particular ideological position which can best be described as the politics of stasis. The existing order, whether natural or social, is presented as what Marx calls an 'exterior fatality'. Textbook knowledge glosses or ignores the extent to which our world is a human project. It does not help towards either real understanding or real alternatives. Resigned quiescence is no longer an overt message in textbooks. Instead it has become their hidden agenda.[42]

School texts are characterised by their 'untouchable' and apolitical nature. They are received as the truths of a 'declassed' cultural heritage. Whether we are talking about science (Young)[43] or social science (Whitty)[44] or literature (Hand)[45] or music (Vulliamy)[46], the analyses show the uncritical orientation of texts towards both the selection of 'facts' and their presentation within an ideology which leaves unchallenged the *status quo*. Children, if working-class, are faced with a presentation of the real world which does not correspond to their 'lived' experience or alternatively with a view of the world as far too stable to be amenable to active reform.

What characterises most of the literature in the politics of school knowledge, is the examination of the social relations of learning in which school texts are employed. The effect of such texts is found to lie in the alienation of the working-class child not merely from the school and the realms of high culture but also from his or her own lived experience outside the school. When the music, the literature and the insights learned from the family and community are given secondary status within the school, when the child's language and culture are treated as 'illegitimate' and the message of the classroom is that there is only one definition of truth and that is to be found in the textbooks, then class domination is at its strongest. Through the authority of teachers, the legitimacy of examination syllabuses and the social and material rewards which accompany scholastic success, the child, it is argued, learns the reality of a class society, even if unconsciously. Yet while the force of these analyses makes disbelief difficult, what one must ask, is the nature of the ideology which is transmitted through these texts? Is there no attempt to form social identities? Is it really the case that the working class child is unlikely to acquire any sense of identity – only alienation – from school? There is little analysis of the actual representations of social class in texts which makes it extremely difficult to answer this question. Even Hardy's article on *Textbooks and Classroom Knowledge*,[47] is more concerned with the changing *form* of textbooks which have moved from presenting a body of knowledge to be taught to a new emphasis on the teaching of concepts and the development of understanding and activities. Most of the research on the content of school texts (rather than the form) has aimed at identifying potential sources of sexism and racism.

In terms of sexism, there are a number of studies of school and university texts which use several different methodologies – some quantitative and some qualitative. What they have in common is their interest in identifying the ways in which gender, and in particular women, are represented. If anything, most of the studies, especially the quantitative research, tend to assume the existence of a sexual division of labor and look for its representation in the subject matter. Also they search for consistency, rather than diversity, of images of women with the result that they identify the existence of sex role stereotypes and gender stereotypes. In addition, there is little concern with class analysis so that the overall impression is that cultural forms exist purely within a patriarchal society without any impact from capital's involvement and control over agencies of cultural production. Whereas the sociology of school knowledge, described above, has neglected, by and large, this source of cultural domination and sexual oppression, feminist analysis of school culture and the mass media has, to a considerable extent, neglected the forms of class control in the production and transmission of knowledge.

The picture which emerges from these exploratory and rather descriptive studies is, nevertheless, not only interesting but also very depressing. While we might have thought that the gains won by women in political, economic and sexual spheres would be reflected in the cultural media, if anything, this research shows just how deeply embedded are sexual ideologies and how 'conservative'. The impression gained is one of women's inferiority, her domesticity, her lack of intelligence, ability, sense of adventure or creativity. In the studies undertaken in the United States (where the majority of content analysis is found) and Britain, the analyses of school texts in, for example, domestic science,[48] history,[49] and literature[50] are complemented by those at university level in such disciplines as sociology,[51] anthroplogy,[52] psychology,[53] political science,[54] and community studies.[55] The message is still the same – there is a consistent distorted model of woman which not merely misrepresents her activities in social life but does nothing to correct the social patterns of discrimination. From the fantasy world of children's books[56] to the male bias of academic disciplines which purport to be 'value-free', one finds a persistent pattern of representations of women which can only be construed as the ideological wing of patriarchy. This pattern has three basic elements:

1. Women suffer from invisibility – which one author called her 'symbolic annihilation'. Women are absent actors in the histories of Western civilisation. They do not appear as active participants in such diverse fields as history, politics, literature, drama or art. Except for the heroine who portrays the individualised

rather than the collective struggles of women, most women are present in passive roles.

2. When women do appear, they are generally in low status or 'second-rate' jobs. The occupations they fill are most likely to be traditional, limited in prospect and narrow in range. Even in children's reading schemes, in the world of fantasy, women's prospects are not much better. Lobban,[57] for example, found in her study of children's readers that, in contrast to the thirty-three occupations shown for adult men, only eight were available for adult women – mum, granny, princess, queen, witch, handywomen about the house, teacher and shop assistant, However, what is more important is that women do not appear in employment nor in typically female jobs in the ratio in which they are actually found in the economy. If anything there is an under-representation of women in paid work with an over-representation of their financial dependence on men. Spence[58] noticed this in the case of British magazine photographs:

> The visual representation of women as not having to work, as the glam-
> orous property of men, harks back to the tradition of bourgeois painting.
> It effectively displaces the idea that women *do* work, and so inhibits their
> sense of themselves as workers. In fact according to the Equal Oppor-
> tunities Commission, women make up 37 per cent of the paid work force.[59]

The image of the female is no less arbitrary and distorted. What is interesting is that the differences between the sexes appears to increase as they move from child-hood to adulthood. Take for example Dohrmann's conclusions[60] from a study of children's educational television programmes:

> The male child is accorded the most laudable pattern: ingenuity, achieve-
> ment, bravery-rescue. The female child, while rewarded and achieving, is
> also a follower, an object of insult, and helpless. The adult female is even
> more uniformly passive, adding routine service, incompetence, and admira-
> tion of others to her behavioural repertory. The adult male excels in reward-
> ing, performing occupationally-related tasks, putting others down and
> picking them up in the rescue role.[61]

3. There is an over-riding emphasis on women's domesticity. The message comes across not as any subtle or hidden code but rather with a degree of repetition that can only be described as ideological bombardment. The assumption first of all appears to be that women have never left the home and, if they had, it must have been unwillingly. This is then limited even further by the portrayal, for example, of women in advertisements selling the products of those two 'feminine' locations in the home – the kitchen and the bathroom.[62]

This pattern can be traced from television drama to commercials, from news-papers to magazines to comics.[63] Against this background of cultural invasion into the home and the community, the school takes its place as just one competitor for the right to present the legitimate gender model which the child is encouraged to follow. In the United States, it is already the case that young children spend more time watching television than in school. Thus we cannot say that the message of the school is the only source of class and sexual identity formation nor, indeed, necessarily the dominant one. Yet the amount of time and effort spent on school texts is considerably greater than that spent on a short television programme, a once read magazine, a glanced at advertisement in the street. What we can suggest is that the message of school texts is most likely to represent in its purest form the ideological statement of the ruling class or, at least, those values which it considers essential to transmit. Because of this, I believe, it is extremely important that we analyse school texts in all their variety.

The tools for such analysis are being developed to a large extent outside the sociology of education. It is impossible to delve too deeply here into the vast body of literature which covers content analysis, semiotics, cultural histories etc. However, what I would like to do is to make some observations and draw some conclusions from this research. First, what is interesting about this research on culture is that it reveals a considerable split between the world of the family and that of work. Certainly, the equation between women and the home and men and public life appears to be carried in most media. If any message exists, it is the ideology of this division. Cultural texts are therefore, a further 'site' for the reproduction of the 'dual spheres', reinforced not just by the ascription of gender to each sphere but also by the re-contextualising of masculinity and femininity in each setting. For example, the image of the women in the daytime serial in the United States was found to be different to that shown in the evenings. The image offered to the housewives in the day time represented one of the strongest characterisation of women on television.

> The woman of the daytime serial is above all a human being. She is liked and respected by her male acquaintances not merely sought as an adjunct to male activities and interest. She is a responsible member of a family struc-ture, exercising judgement and offering support to parents and children alike. Her opinions are solicited and acted upon. She enjoys the friendship of other women.[64]

In television commercials in the States, another difference was noticed in the portrayal of masculinity. In this vivid description, one finds the distinction between the image of the man at home and the man in the world outside.

> The image of the American man in TV commercials as muscular, knowl-edgeable, dominating, independent, sexy, cosmopolitan, athletic, authori-tative and aggressive exists only when he is seen away from his family. In embarrassing contrast the American father and husband is portrayed as passive and stupid, infantile and emasculated ... But outside the house, trouble is what he is looking for. Swift as a panther, stealthy as a cougar, free as a mustang he speeds to his rendezvous with status, independence and violence.[65]

The definitions of femininity and masculinity which we find in cultural texts are not then simple, homogenous stereotypes but rather ideological products which, if they are pulled together with all their contradictions into a coherent pattern, represent one aspect of bourgeois hegemony. The existence of a dominant gender code does not however rule out the possibility of dominated or subordinated codes which reshape the dominant message of patriarchy into the requirements of specific audiences. This process of re-contextualising *within* one cultural form can be seen most clearly in Frith and McRobbie's research[66] into popular forms of music. Here, without all the statistical manipulations of content analysis, they identify two 'ideological' models of gender relations. The first exists in rock music primarily for a male audience. Masculinity is portrayed by the 'rampant destructive male traveller, smashing hotels and groupies alike . . .'. Women, in the eyes of these men, are

> either sexually aggressive and therefore doomed and unhappy or else sexually repressed and therefore in need of male servicing. It's the woman, whether romanticised or not, who is seen as possessive after a husband, anti-freedom the ultimate restriction.[67]

Teenybop music in contrast, played to a largely female audience of housewives and female factory workers, presents a different model of sexuality. As the authors argue,

> If cock rock plays on conventional concepts of male sexuality as rampant, animalistic, superficial, just-for-the-moment, teenybop plays on notions of female sexuality as being serious, diffuse and implying total emotional commitment . . . It is men who are soft, romantic, easily hurt, loyal and anxious to find a true love who fulfils their definition of what female sexuality should be about?[68]

Frith and McRobbie argue that within each musical form one can find a range of models or definitions of sexuality, mediated by the words of the song, the rhythms and beat of the music, the packaging and image of the singer or group. What their analysis reveals is the complexity of the ideological struggle to define and contain sexual identities within the framework of class culture.

This complexity can also be found in McRobbie's[69] analysis of the school girl magazine *Jackie*. Here she uses semiology to provide a method for such research, a form of analysis which has become increasingly popular in cultural studies. The advantages of this form of analysis are that it has

> more to offer than traditional content analysis if only because it is not solely concerned with the numerative *appearance* of content, but with the messages which such 'contents' signify . . . Quantification is therefore rejected and replaced with understanding media messages as *structured wholes* and conbinations of structures, polarities and oppositions are endowed with greater significance than their mere numerative existence.[70]

As a result, she is able to draw out five different subcodes of femininity which relate to beauty, fashion, popmusic, personal/domestic life and romance. What is important here is that the magazine is examined not just as a social product but also as an active agent in the *production* of new meanings. The problem therefore is not one of trying to fit these representations of women to the realities of their lives but rather to recognise the ideological 'work' carried out by these texts in the *reconstruction* rather than the reproduction of gender definitions and relations.

By analysing the combinations of various representations of femininity or masculinity within one set of texts, one is also more likely to be made aware of the contradictions which can arise between different gender definitions. Take for example, the contradictory sets of female ideals; the capable consumer housewife versus the dependent incapable wife; the insatiable temptress and the passive sex object; the all embracing earth mother versus the childlike doll. Another example can be found in the excellent analysis of 1950s texts in three domains of motherhood, education and sexuality by the Birmingham Feminist History Group.[71] Here they located the ideological struggle between the liberal concept of equal opportunity and the bourgeois ideal of separate spheres for each sex, which was resolved in the 1950s in the ideology of the two sexes being 'equal but different'. Further they identified the contradictory pressures upon married women both to return to work and to act as efficient and dedicated wives and mothers. Thus the apparent 'unity' of the 1950s under their scrutiny, collapsed into 'contradictions, tensions and divisions'. They found that

> ... There was no one representation of women; but the struggle for primacy of one set of representations concerned with marriage, home and family, is systematically victorious throughout our period.[72]

What I have argued is that not only must we be aware of the complexity of definitions of gender relations in culture but that we must recognise the role of culture within hegemony. The question I believe we should be asking is not just what relation do the representations found within texts bear to 'lived' relations but also what is the relevence of that message for capital. The struggle to define and contain sexuality, is no less a problem for capital than containing the force of class opposition and preparing the working class for the rigours of the work place. Indeed, as Gramsci[73] argues in the notes on 'Some aspects of the sexual question', the two facets of hegemony are often inextricably linked. Sexual relations, the definitions of morality, of masculinity and femininity are historically constructed under immense odds. First, according to Gramsci,

> The history of industrialism has always been a continuing struggle (which today takes an even more marked and vigorous form) against the element of 'animality' in men. It has been an interrupted, often painful and bloody process of subjugating natural (animal and primitive) instincts to new more rigid norms and habits of order, exactitude and precision which can make possible an increasingly complex form of collective life which are the necessary consequence of industrial development.[74]

Sexual instincts have undergone the greatest degree of repression from society, according to Gramsci. Within this history, the 'aesthetic' ideal of women has oscillated between the concept of 'brood mare' for reproduction and 'dolly' for sport and pleasure. The biological reproduction of the work force necessary to support an 'unproductive' sector of the population (due to age and ill health) is one of the problems connected with women's position. If this ratio is unbalanced, then a further problem for hegemony is posed.

The history of hegemonic control over relations between the sexes, has been fraught with crises which have affected mainly the middle classes and sectors of the ruling class. After each period of puritanism, Gramsci argues, there is a crisis of libertinism which only marginally affects the working class – through the depravement of their women. However, what is important in Gramsci's argument is that gender relations, or more specifically sexual relations, are linked to the methods of production and patterns of work within a mode of production. For example, he links the relative stability of sexual unions among the peasants to the system of agricultural work in the countryside. With the introduction of Fordism, the rationalisation of work, Gramsci argued, made it important that the working class hold a new sexual ethic – that of monogamy.

> The truth is that a new type of man demanded by the rationalisation of production and work cannot be developed until the sexual instinct has been suitably regulated and until it too has been rationalised.[75]

Rigorous discipline of work demands discipline of the sexual instincts and with it, according to Gramsci, comes the strenthening of the ideology of the family and the stability of sexual relations. The reason for the 'puritanical' initiatives of the industrialists, such as Ford, into working class families (controlling the consumpton of alcohol and 'womanising') could be found in the necessity of reproducing the work force in fit-state for the discipline of the new work methods. Capital needed to preserve 'outside of work, a certain psycho-physical equilibrium which prevents a physiological collapse of the worker, exhausted by the new methods of production'.[76]

In these brief notes Gramsci argues that not only are the relations between the sexes historical products, related to the development of capitalism, but also that these relations are areas in which consent has to be won. To create and make new moralities 'second nature', to win consent for the arbitrary division of social life into male and female worlds of public and private activities is no easy task and perhaps that is why there is such ideological bombardment from educational and cultural agencies of the state. It is not that capital has *succeeded* in creating classed and sexed subjects, suitably adjusted to the rigours of work in the home and the work place, but rather that no day can go by without it *trying*.

Notes and References.

1 Hoare, Q. (1967) 'Education: Programmes and Men', *New Left Review*, Vol. 32, pp. 40–52. *Ibid.*, p. 40.
2 De Beauvoire, S. (1972) *The Second Sex*, London, Penguin edition.
3 *Ibid.*, p. 15.
4 See Hartman, H. (1976) 'Capitalism, Patriarchy and Job Segregation by Sex', *Signs: Journal of Women in Culture and Society*, Vol. 1. No. 3 pt. 2 Spring p. 137–69 and Gee, M. (1978) 'The Capitalist Labour Process and Women Worker'. Paper given at the Conference of Socialist Economists Annual Conference, Bradford.

5 See LAND, H. (1978) 'Who cares for the Family', *Journal of Social Policy*, Vol. 7, No. 3 pp. 257–284.

6 For a brief summary of the 'domestic labor debate' which analyses the economic implications and advantages to capital of women's household work see FEE, T. 'Domestic Labor: an analysis of housework and its relation to the production process', *Review of Radical Political Economics*, Vol. 8, No. 1 Spring p. 108.

7 ZARETSKY, E. (1973) '*Capitalism, the Family and Personal Life*', New York, Harper Colophon Books.

8 DYEHOUSE, C. (1977) 'Good Wives and Little Mothers; Social Anxieties and School Girl's Curriculum 1890–1920', *Oxford Review of Education*, Vol. 3 No. 1 pp. 21–36; SHARPE, S. (1976) *Just Like a Girl*, Harmondsworth, Pelican; DEEM, R. (1978) *Women and Schooling*, London, Routledge and Kegan Paul; WOLPE, A.M. (1977) *Some Processes of Sexist Education*, London, WRRCP pamphlet, and (1976) 'The Official Ideology of Education for Girls' in FLUDE, M. and AHIER, J. (Eds.) *Educability, Schools and Ideology*, London, Croom Helm; articles by DELAMONT, S. in DELAMONT, S. and DUFFIN, L. (Eds.) (1978) *The Nineteenth Century Women*, London, Croom Helm.

9 The 1869 Franchise Act created approximately a million new voters none of which were women see DAVIN, A. (1979) 'Mind you do as you are told, reading books for Board School Girls', *Feminist Review*, No. 3, pp. 89–98.

10 JOHNSON, R. (1970) 'Educational Policy and Social Control in Early Victorian England, *Past and Present*, No. 49.

11 DAVIN, A. *op. cit.*, (Note 9) p. 90.

12 *Ibid.*, p. 98.

13 The State also acted against patriarchal family structures during the two world wars, by encouraging the employment of women in wage labour. The child care facilities established during this period were later to be closed down when women were directed back to the home.

14 SMITH, D. (1975) 'Women, the Family and Corporate Capitalism', *Berkeley Journal of Sociology*, Vol. XX, pp. 55–90.

15 HUMPHRIES, J. (1977) 'Class Struggle and the Persistence of the Working Class Family', *Cambridge Journal of Economics*, No. 3, Vol. 1 pp. 241–258.

16 WILLIS, P. (1979) 'Shop Floor Culture, Masculinity and the Wage Form' in CLARKE, J. CRITCHER, C. and JOHNSON, R. (Eds.) *Working Class Culture*, London, Hutchinson.

17 *Ibid.*, p. 187.

18 DE BEAUVIOR, S. quoted in FREEMAN, J. (1970) 'Growing up Girlish', *Trans-Action*, Vol. 8, November –December, pp. 36–43.

19 BERNSTEIN, B. (1977) 'Aspects of the Relation between Education and Production', in *Class, Codes and Control*, Vol. III, Routledge and Kegan Paul, 2nd edition.

20 WILLIS, P. *op. cit.*, (Note 16) p. 186.

21 For a critical analysis of the work of BERNSTEIN, B. and BOURDIEU, P. see, MACDONALD, M. (1977) *Curriculum and Cultural Reproduction*, E202 Block 3 Bletchley, Open University Press.

22 BOURDIEU, P. (1971) 'The Thinkable and the Unthinkable', *Times Literary Supplement*, 15 October. p. 1255.

23 BERNSTEIN, B. (1977) 'On the Curriculum', in *Class, Codes and Control*, Vol. III, London, Routledge and Kegan Paul, 2nd. Ed.

24 *Ibid.*, p. 79.

25 BOURDIEU, P. (1977) *Outline of a Theory of Practice*, London, Cambridge University Press.

26 For an outline of this theory see MACDONALD, M. 'Cultural Reproduction: The Pedagogy of Sexuality', *Screen Education*, Autumn/Winter No. 32/33 1979 pp. 143–153.

27 SPENDER, D. (1978) 'Educational Research and the Feminist Perspective', Paper presented at the British Educational Research Association Conference Leicester University April.

28 ROBERTS, J. quoted in SPENDER, D. *Ibid.*

29 See, for example, KELLY, A. (1975) 'A Discouraging Process: How Girls are eased out of Science'. Paper presented at the Conference on Girls and Science Education, Chelsea College, March 19–20th; WYNN, B. (1977) 'Domestic Subjects and the Sexual Division of Labour', in WHITTY, G. *School Knowledge and Social Control*, E202 Block 3 Bletchley, Open University Press.

30 BOURDIEU, P. (1977) *Reproduction in Education, Society and Culture*, London, Sage.

31 *Ibid.*, p. 78.

32 For a description of gender codes see MACDONALD, M. (1980) 'Socio-cultural Reproduction and Women's Education' in DEEM, R. (Ed.) *Schooling for Women's Work*, London, Routledge and Kegan Paul.

33 CLARRICOATES, K. (1980) 'The importance of being earnest ... Emma ... Tom ... Jane ... The Perception and Categorisation of Gender Conformity and Gender Deviation in Primary Schools' in DEEM, R. *op. cit.*, (Note 32).

34 DAVIN, A. *op. cit.*, (Note 9).

35 BERNSTEIN, B., *Class, Codes and Control*, *op. cit.*, (Note 19) p. 30.

36 For the distinction between practical and symbolic mastery see BOURDIEU, P. *op. cit.*, (Note 25 and Note 30).

37 WILLIS, P. (1978) *Learning to Labour*, Farnborough, Saxon House.

38 *Ibid.*, p. 148.

39 WILLIS, P. *op. cit.*, (Note 16) p. 198.

40 WILLIS, P. *op. cit.*, (Note 37); McROBBIE, A. (1978) 'Working Class Girls and the Culture of Femininity', in *Women Take Issue*, Women's Studies Group, Center for Contemporary Culture Studies, London, Hutchinson; SHARPE, S. *op. cit.*, (Note 8).

41 MacDONALD, G. (1976) '*The Politics of Educational Publishing*' in WHITTY, G. and YOUNG, M. (Eds.) *Explorations in the Politics of School Knowledge*, Driffield, Nafferton Books.

42 *Ibid.*, p. 223.

43 YOUNG, M. (1976) 'The Schooling of Science', in WHITTY, G. and YOUNG, M. (Note 41) *op. cit.*

44 WHITTY, G. (1976) 'Studying Society: for social change and social control' in WHITTY, G. and YOUNG, M. (Note 41) *op. cit.*

45 HAND, N. (1976) 'What is English', in WHITTY, G. and YOUNG, M. (Note 41) *op. cit.*

46 VUILLIAMY, G. (1976) 'What Counts as School Music', in WHITTY, G. and YOUNG, M. (Note 41) *op. cit.*

47 HARDY, J. (1976) 'Textbooks and Classroom Knowledge: The politics of explanation and description', in WHITTY, G. and YOUNG, M. (Note 41) *op. cit.*

48 See WYNN, B. *op. cit.*, (Note 29).

49 TRECKER, J.L. (1971) 'Women in US History High School Textbooks', *Social Education*, March, pp. 249–260, 338. ANYON, J. (1979) 'Ideology and United States History Textbooks', *Harvard Educational Review*, Vol. 49 No. 3 August, pp. 361–386.

50 WOLFF, C.G. (1972) 'A Mirror for Men: Stereotypes of Women in Literature', *Massachusetts Review*, Vol. 13, pp. 205–218', see also articles in STACEY, S., BEREAUD, S. and DANIELS, J. (Eds.) (1974) *And Jill came Tumbling After*, New York, Dell.

51 EHRLICH, C. (1971) 'The Male Sociologist's Burden: The Place of Women in Marriage and Family Texts', *Journal of Marriage and the Family*, Vol. 33 August, pp. 421–30.

52 SLOCUM, S. (1975) 'Women the Gatherer: Male Bias in Anthropology', in REUTER, R. (Ed.) *Toward an Anthropology of Women*, New York, Monthly Review Press.

53 WEISSTEIN, N. (1971) 'Psychology Constructs the Female', in GORNICK, V. and MORAN, B.K. (Eds.) *Women in Sexist Society*, New York, Basic Books.

54 BOURQUE, S. and GROSSHOLTZ, J. (1974) 'Politics as Unnatural Politics, Political Science Looks at Female Participation', *Politics and Society*, Winter pp. 225–66.

55 FRANKENBERG, R. (1976) 'In the production of their lives, Men (?) Sex and Gender in British Community Studies', in BARKER, D.L. and ALLEN, S. (Eds.) *Sexual Divisions and Society*, London, Tavistock.

56 See, for example, LOBBAN, G. (1975) 'Sex Roles in Reading Schemes', *Educational Review*, Vol. 27 No. 3, June, pp. 202–10; WEITZMAN, L. J. *et al*, (1976) 'Sex Role Socialisation Picture Books for Pre-School Children', in *Sexism in Children's Books*, Children's rights workshop No. 2 London, Writers and Readers Publishing Co-op; DIXON, B. (1977) *Catching Them Young (No. 1) Sex, Race and Class in Children's Fiction*, London, Pluto Press; WOMEN ON WORDS AND IMAGES (1975) *Dick and Jane as Victims*, 1975 edition, P.O. Box 2163, Princeton NJ 08540.

57 LOBBAN, G. (1978) 'The Influence of the School on Sex Role Stereotyping in CHETWYND, J. and HARTNETT, O. (Eds.) *The Sex Role System*, London, Routledge and Kegan Paul.

58 SPENCE, J. (1978) 'What do people do, all day; Class and Gender in Images of Women', *Screen Education*, Winter, No. 29, pp. 29–45.

59 *Ibid.*, p. 31.

60 DOHRMANN, R. (1975) 'A Gender Profile of Children's Educational T.V.', *Journal of Communication*, Vol. 25, No. 4, pp. 56–65.

61 *Ibid.*, pp. 62–3.

62 See, for example, COURTNEY, A.E. and WHIPPLE, T.W. (1974) 'Women in T.V. Commercials', *Journal of Communication*, Vol. 24, No. 2, pp. 110–8.

63 For good summaries of research see BUSBY, L.J. (1975) 'Sex Role Research on The Mass Media', *Journal of Communication*, Vol. 25, No. 4, pp. 107–31 and UNESCO (1979) 'Mass Media: The Image Role and Social Conditions of Women', *Reports and Papers on Mass Communication*, No. 84.

64 DOWNING, M. (1974) 'Heroine of the Daytime Serial', '*Journal of Communication*', Vol. 24, No. 2, p. 137.

65 BARDWICK, J.M. and SCHUMANN, S.I. (1975) Portrait of American Men and Women in T.V. Commercials, *Psychology*, IV (4) pp. 18–23, quoted to BUSBY, L.J. *op. cit.*, (Note 63) p. 116.

66 FRITH, S. and McROBBIE, A. (1978) 'Rock and Sexuality', in *Screen Education*, No. 29 Winter, pp. 3–20.

67 *Ibid.*, p. 7.

68 *Ibid.*, p. 7.

69 McRobbie, A. (1978) 'Jackie: an ideology of Adolescent Femininity' CCCS Stencilled Occasional Paper No. 53.

70 *Ibid.*, p. 11, For other example of semiotics see CCCS Women's Studies Group, 'Images of Women Women in the Media' CCCS Occasional Paper No. 3.

71 Birmingham Feminist History Group, 'Feminism as Femininity in the nineteenth fifties', *Feminist Review*, No. 3, 1979 pp. 48–65.

72 *Ibid.*, p. 64.

73 Gramsci, A. (1971) *Selections from the Prison Notebooks*, translated by Hoare, Q. and Nowell-Smith, G., London, Lawrence and Wishart.

74 *Ibid.*, p. 298.

75 *Ibid.*, p. 296.

76 *Ibid.*, p. 303.

Contradiction and Reproduction in Educational Theory

Herbert Gintis
Samuel Bowles
University of Massachusetts

We are often asked how our ideas on education have developed since the publication of our book, *Schooling in Capitalist America.*[1] More specifically, what would we change if we had it to do over again? We must confess that, due to competing research commitments, we have not submitted this issue to a sustained investigation. Thus in this paper we will limit our treatment to a single question: that of our handling of contradictions within education and contradictions in the capitalist social formation resulting from the specific nature of the educational system. This question is absolutely fundamental. For as we suggested in our book, creating a truly egalitarian educational system geared toward the full development of students' cognitive, critical, and personal powers requires fundamental social change. But such fundamental social change, involving as it does overcoming the inertial tendencies in social development, can be achieved only by understanding and exploiting the contradictions already present and operative in society.[2] We feel that one of the weaker aspects of our book lies in its weak and possibly voluntaristic political prescriptions for educational change. This weakness flows from an inadequate treatment of the systemic contradictions of advanced capitalism. We shall here sketch how this fault might be repaired.

The Correspondence Principle

In *Schooling in Capitalist America* we began by asking what might be expected of an adequate educational system. We found that three goals were central to the traditional liberal conception of the social role of schooling. First, education should be *egalitarian* in the sense of acting as an effective force for overcoming the natural, social and historical inequities that tend inexorably to arise in society. Second, education should be *developmental* in the sense of providing students with the means to develop the cognitive, physical, emotional, critical, and aesthetic powers they possess as individuals and as human beings. Third, education should be a means of what John Dewey has called the 'social continuity of life'.[3] That is, education should promote the smooth integration of individuals as fully functioning members of society. We then endeavored to show, using a variety of descriptive, historical, and statistical sources that education in advanced capitalism actually *reproduced* social inequality, rather than attenuating it, and acted rather more as a force for *repressing* personal development than fostering it. By contrast, what the schools seemed to do best was precisely to produce the 'good citizen' – its integrative function.

Why this pattern of success and failure? Is it to be found in the educational system itself or in the articulation of the school system with the social structures within which the schools are located? We concluded the latter. Dewey, in *Democracy and Education*, argued that a prerequisite for education's fulfilment of its egalitarian, developmental, and integrative functions is that society be *democratic*. For in a democratic society, the requirements of the citizenry are the abilities to relate to one another equally and reciprocally in controlling their common affairs. Schools that prepare students for this task of life will be necessarily egalitarian. Moreover, full personal development involves precisely the development of those cognitive and other social powers that allow individuals effectively to participate in democratically constituted collectivities and thereby to control their lives.

The critical problem in the articulation of schooling with advanced capitalism, we suggested, lies in its undemocratic structure of control over the process of production. The capitalist enterprise is not characterised by civil liberties, due process, democratic participation, or guaranteed rights. Rather, it is characterised by rights vested in property rather than persons and the control of the production process by capitalists and managerial personnel, giving rise to a class structure quite inimical to democratic principles.

A main proposition in *Schooling in Capitalist America* held that a major objective of capital, in its interventions into the formation and evolution of the educational system, was precisely the preparation of students to be future workers on the various levels in the hierarchy of capitalist production. Given the quite significant success of capital directly and indirectly structuring schools and in the face of the undemocratic nature of economic life, schools could not fulfill their egalitarian and developmental objectives. We concluded that the only means toward the achievement of progressive educational reform is the democratisation of economic life, allowing for a democratic and emancipatory school system which does not conflict with the formation of adults capable of effective participation in the system of production.

We also argued specifically that the current relationship between education and economy is ensured not through the *content* of education but its *form*: the social relations of the educational encounter. Education prepares students to be workers through a *correspondence* between the social relations of production and the social relations of education. Like the division of labor in the capitalist enterprise, the educational system is a finely graded hierarchy of authority and control in which competition rather than co-operation governs the relations among participants, and an external reward system – wages in the case of the economy and grades in the case of schools – holds sway. This correspondence principle explains why the schools cannot at the same time promote full personal development and social equality, while integrating students into society. The hierarchical order of the school system, admirably geared towards preparing students for their future positions in the hierarchy of production, limits the development of those personal capacities involving the exercise of reciprocal and mutual democratic participation and reinforces social inequality by legitimating the assignment of students to inherently unequal 'slots' in the social hierarchy.

The correspondence principle, we believe, makes four positive contributions to progressive educational strategy. First, its explanatory value is great. Despite the considerable scepticism which greeted publication of our book, critics have made little headway in overturning our major empirical conclusions. Indeed the one major subsequent statistical investigation of sources of educational and economic success – Christopher Jencks *et al.'s Who Gets Ahead?* – dramatically confirms our own findings.[4] Second, in an era where the failures of liberal school reform have become increasingly evident to policy-makers and the public, the correspondence principle shows a positive alternative. Egalitarian and humanistic education are not unattainable due to some inherent defect in human nature or advanced industrial society, but to the undemocratic nature of participation in economic life. Educational reform requires at the same time economic transformation towards democratic socialism. Third, our formulation rectifies an earlier pre-occupation of both liberal and Marxian analysis with the overt content of schooling. By focussing upon the experience of schooling, the correspondence principle provides a consistent analytical framework for understanding the school as an arena of structured social interaction. Fourth, our formulation of the correspondence principle contributes to a more positive understanding of the goals of socialist transition. In older critiques of capitalist society, almost unique stress was laid on the private ownership of means of production. At least as far as educational reform is concerned, we have been able to show that not ownership, but *control* is central to social inequities. Merely passing from private to social ownership without challenging in any substantial way the social relations of economic life, can have no impact on the egalitarian and humanistic goals of progressive educational reform. The correspondence principle then represents a powerful antidote to the authoritarian tendencies all too often found in an otherwise progressive socialist movement.

The correspondence principle is, however, not without its problems. The most critical is simply this: by standing in our approach as the *only* structural link between education and economy and by its character as an inherently *harmonious* link between the two, the correspondence principle forced us to adopt a narrow and inadequate appreciation of the *contradictions* involved in the articulation of the educational system within the social totality. Yet as we have stressed, no political strategy can be developed without due attention to the systemic contradictions that can be exploited towards effective and progressive intervention. It is perhaps for this reason that our approach has been variously termed as 'radically functionalist' and imbued with 'missionary pessimism'.

This is not to say that our educational theory has been devoid of principles of contradiction. Indeed, we went to great lengths to demonstrate the 'lack of fit' between education and society at large. Our major contribution in this respect was what we termed the contradiction between *reproduction* and *accumulation* in advanced capitalism. The educational system, we suggested, contributes to the reproduction and legitimation of the social relations of capitalist production. Yet at the same time the tendency of capitalist production is accumulation – the expansion of the wage labor system and the eclipse of older forms of production. This movement leads inevitably to a re-structuring of the social relations of production and a consequent change in the requirements for their reproduction. The contradiction between reproduction and accumulation thus takes the form of the educational system periodically falling *out of harmony* with the evolving structure of capitalist production relations. We do not think the contradiction between reproduction and accumulation is incorrect. Indeed, it is capable of aiding our understanding of both the striking periodicity of educational reform and of the major periods of educational change – such as the Common School Movement, the Progressive Education movement, and most recent the movement for the reform of higher education in the United States. Let us take the latter case as an example.

Many have wondered why such intense opposition to dominant social institutions in the decade of the 1960s occurred predominantly among students in higher education. Our answer, which we still believe correct, ran as follows. The social relations of higher education were laid down in the United States early in the twentieth-century to train a professional, managerial, and propertied élite capable of controlling their own lives as well as the lives of others. With the vast increase in the economy's demand for skilled white collar labor after World War II and popular demand for access to higher education, however, higher education had to fill the gap in training students who, far from constituting a quasi-independent élite, were destined to staff the relatively powerless middle levels of the capitalist hierarchy of production. The norms of liberal education, critical thought, and free space for personal expression, all fostered by higher education, clearly failed to provide an adequate affective, normative, or even cognitive preparation for students *en route* to the fragmented, routinized and closely supervised work life of the salaried worker. Whence the material basis for their revolt: a discrepancy between the social relation of education and social relations of production. Indeed, our analysis of the contradictions of higher education has been substantiated by subsequent events. In the United States the response to the student movement in the decade of the 1970s was the move towards the *vocationalisation* of higher education: raising tuitions, promoting two-year vocational as opposed to four-year liberal arts schools, redesigning the curriculum to eliminate 'critical thought' in favor of 'occupational skills', and stressing the commuter campus in contrast to the resident university where an oppositional 'youth culture' might develop.[6]

So-called 'back to basics', while having little rationale in terms of either pedagogical or technological reason, may be understood in part as a response to the failure of correspondence between schools and capitalist production brought about by the dynamics of the accumulation process confronting the inertia of the educational structures. This principle of contradiction, however, is clearly insufficient for effective political intervention. For it is purely inertial and passive: education merely *lags behind* a developing economic system. Such a mode of analysis provides no reasons why anything other than a periodic lagging-followed-by-catching-up dynamic might be present in the educational system. This dynamic is hardly absent: indeed it provides a compelling basis for identifying the quite distinct major epochs of educational reform in the United States. Yet it fails to elucidate the dynamic of change internal to the school system. For this reason it provides no clear-cut method for political intervention in the process we have theoretically isolated.

The task of searching for an adequate principle of contradiction between education and economy to supplement the correspondence principle is hampered, we now believe, by the very methodological stance we adopted in analysing social life. We found ourselves much impressed with the classical Marxian paradigm of base/superstructure, according to which the economic system forms a base of material relations defining the essence of social life, with respect to which such institutions as the family, the state, the educational system, the communications media, and cultural relations in general, appear as mere superstructural reflections. According to this approach, contradictions in the economic system can have reverberations in other spheres of social life, but the latter cannot impart any autonomous contradictory effects to the reproduction process as a whole, save the inertial non-correspondence which then formed the basis of our reasoning. It is hardly surprising, then, that we failed to locate a central contradiction in the education/economy relationship.

Sites and Practices

If a social formation is not to be viewed as an economic 'base' with a series of social levels successively stacked on top, how should it be conceived? We suggest that society be treated as an ensemble of structurally articulated *sites of social practice*. By a *site* we mean a cohesive area of social life characterised by a specified set of characteristic social relations or structures. These distinct 'rules of the game' regulate the manifold social practices at each site. Thus the state, the family system, and capitalist production are all sites in a capitalist social formation. Briefly speaking, the site of capitalist production is characterised by private property in the means of production, market exchange, wage labor, and capitalist control of production and investment. The state is characterised by the institutions of liberal democracy and the family site by the structure of power and kinship known as patriarchy.

These three sites – state, family, and site of capitalist production – we take as fundamental to the dynamics of advanced capitalist social formations. In the first instance, they define the three major relations individuals have *vis-à-vis* their society; each person has at the same time a specific citizenship, gender, and class status, and none of these can be understood as flowing simply from the others. Again, each of these sites is independently capable of supporting relations of dominance and subordinacy. Indeed, we would characterise the site of capitalist production as the site of dominance of capital over labor and the family as the site of dominance of men over women. By contrast, the state in its liberal democratic form, while required to reproduce the conditions of domination and subordinacy in family and economy, is not itself necessarily a site of domination. This observation will be important for our analysis of contradictions in the educational system.

The dynamics of a site cannot be deduced from its structure – its characteristics social relations – either alone or in relation to the structure of other sites. Rather, we must view sites as merely *structuring the practices occuring within them*. Practices, in turn, must be seen as neither the effects nor the reflection of structures, but fundamental and irreducible elements of social dynamics. The relation of a site to practices occurring with it is analogous to the relation between a language and a conversation: the language *structures* the conversation in terms of syntax and grammar, while exercising only partial control over the content of communicative exchange. But we must be more precise concerning our use of the term 'practice'. By a *practice* in general we mean a social intervention on the part of an individual, group, or class, whose *object* is some aspect of social reality, and whose *project* is the transformation (or stabilisation) of that object. We will lay stress on four basic types of practice – appropriative, political, cultural, and distributive. By an *appropriative practice* we mean labor in its usual sense of transforming nature; its object is the natural world and its project is the creation of useful products. By a *political practice* we mean a social intervention geared to changing the social relations of a site – the 'rules of the game'. The object of a political practice, then, is the structure of a site, or its articulation with other sites, and its project is the transformation of these social relationships. By *culture* we mean the ensemble of tools of discourse that a group employs towards exchanging information, expressing states of consciousness, forming bonds of solidarity, and forging common strategies of action. A *cultural practice*, then, is one whose object is culture and whose project is the transformation of the tools of discourse on the basis of which the formation and co-ordination of all group practices can be undertaken. Finally, the object of a *distributive practice* is the distribution of power, income and other desirable social prerogatives, and whose object is effecting a change in this distribution.

In summation, then, a social formation is a structural articulation of sites, and a site is a structure articulating the appropriative, political, cultural, and distributive practices occurring within it.

Our next goal will be to argue that in view of the particular nature of state, family, and economy in an advanced capitalist social formation, these sites articulate as a *contradictory totality*, and that the dynamics of the whole derive from the contradictory nature of this totality.

We may characterize the interaction of sites in general in terms of two dynamic principles: *structural delimitation* and the *transportation of practices across sites*. By delimitation we refer to the constraints placed on the development of a site by the very nature of its articulation with environing sites. By the tranportation of practices we refer to the fact that groups, in their struggle and confrontations, do not always limit themselves to practices characteristic of the site in which these struggles occur but will, under specific circumstances, attempt to 'transport' practices characteristic of other sites. These two processes, we suggest, account for the possibility of sites articulating as a contradictory totality. An example from the education/economy interaction will serve to clarify these two dynamics. First, it is well known that funding for the educational system and willingness of students to participate depend significantly on its ability to enhance the economic status of its graduates. Thus the requirements for economic success, determined within the site of capitalist production, *structurally delimit* the forms of change open to the educational system, whatever the desires of educational reformers. Indeed, this in part accounts for the very existence of the correspondence principle in education. Conversely, educators intent on improving support for educational expansion, have consciously *transported political practices* from the site of capitalist production to restructure the social relations of education.

These two mechanisms account for the structure of education. We have not characterised the educational system as a site, because rather than exhibiting a uniform set of social relations, schools participate both in the state site and the private economy. By and large, however, the educational system is a sub-site of the state but with radically different principles of internal organisation and participation. While the state, in general, is organised according to the principle of majority rule, the schools are organised according to that of top-down control. The mechanism of structural delimitation penalises forms of educational change which expose students to political relations not compatible with their future positions as workers by ensuring a limited range of job opportunities for these students. In addition, as Raymond Callahan has shown in *Education and the Cult of Efficiency*[7] educators have not merely passively followed the dictates of structural delimitation, but have actively undertaken the transportation of capitalist practices: they have drawn on the literature and philosophy of business organisation to mold the schools into forms favorable to the needs of capital accumulation and reproduction of the subservient position of workers at the site of capitalist production.

These examples, however, take the form of *reproductive* delimitation and transportation. We may equally validly speak of these mechanisms as *contradictory*. In terms of delimitation, contradiction takes the form of distinct sites, developing according to their own internal principles, changing so as to *undermine* the reproduction of the social processes of other sites. Contradictory delimitation in the educational system accounts for many of the concrete ways in which the schools fail to conform to the dictates of the capitalist economy. Let us cite three examples. Two of these relate to the critical location of education as *within* the state yet *serving* the site of capitalist production. First, the formally equal status of women as citizens, gained early in the Twentieth-Century, virtually ensures that the state political mechanism will come to supply relatively equal education to men and women. Yet the reproduction of hierarchical relations in the capitalist enterprise has depended on the subordination of women to men. The outcome of this discrepancy is either a delegitimation of the educational system or a delegitimation of the economic sub-ordination of women to men in the economy. Second, a parallel development with respect to blacks and minorities has occurred over the past two decades: their relatively equal position as citizens has produced a great deal more educational equality than the capitalist economy, whose hierarchical relations depend in part on the maintenance of the inferior position of blacks, is capable of matching. Once again, delimitation acts *contrary* to the requisites for reproducing the social relations of capitalist production. A third example of contradictory delimitation has been previously mentioned. The expansion of higher education in the post-World War II period, while serving the needs of the site of capitalist production for white collar wage-labor, has still taken the *form* of traditional liberal arts, quite incompatible with the social relations of the capitalist enterprise. This mechanism, which we previously thought of as simply an inertial dynamic of the educational system, now can be more comprehensively described as a form of contradictory delimitation.

The transportation of practices can also take a contradictory form, through their possible effect of the superposition of practices within a site. In terms of education, as we shall stress in the next section of this paper, contradictory transportation often takes the form of imposing forms of democratic participation in education which have been lifted from the state site, of which the educational system is a sub-site with a distinct structure of social relations.

Before returning to a direct treatment of education, we shall elucidate the two principles of contradictory delimitation and contradictory transportation in terms of the notion of the rights characteristic of the three major sites of advanced capitalist formation.

Political practices at the site of capitalist production are characterized by *rights vested in property*, the rights being exercised by individuals only insofar as they own property or represent those who do. By contrast, political practices in the liberal democratic state are characterised by *rights vested in persons*, according to which all individuals, as citizens, participate equally (though indirectly through representatives) in the determination of state decisions. Again by contrast, the family site is characterised by *rights vested in adult males* to control the labor and reproduction of women.

The articulation of sites in advanced capitalism as a contradictory totality flows, we maintain, from the discrepancies among these forms of vesting of rights of political participation. This is most evident in the case of the transportation of practices. For instance women, having gained the status of full citizenship in the state site, have struggled in recent years to *extend* rights vested in persons to the family site – in the form of the demand for full equality in family life – where they come into direct confrontation with the principles of patriarchal domination.

Another important instance of the transportation of practices has taken the form of workers demanding, and often succeeding in attaining, the precedence of person rights over property rights at the site of capitalist production. We may cite several types of demands that illustrate this process in the history of the workers' movement from the Nineteenth-Century, when even full citizenship rights were only extended to the propertied, to the present. The first is the clear and insistent demands of workers for suffrage: full political participation on the basis of person rather than property or estate. The second is the right of workers to associate and organise common representation *vis-à-vis* employers, superseding the market-mediated confrontation of capital and labor. Third, and manifestly unrealisable under capitalism, is the right to employment, negating the market-determination of rates of unemployment. Fourth, and increasingly important since World War II, has been the demand that the civil rights of equal treatment and due process apply to, and hence dominate, market transactions. Thus the Civil Rights Movement in the United States in the 1960's demanded the equal treatment of blacks and whites by merchants and employers, limiting thereby their powers of unrestricted use and free contract. Similarly, the women's movement in the United States and Europe has demanded equal treatment in the capitalist economy in an attempt to weaken the free exercise of property rights on the part of discriminatory employers. Even workers' struggles for decent occupational safety and health conditions have taken the form not primarily of agreement through collective bargaining but of state regulations governing and restricting all contractual relations. Finally, the increasingly popular social goal of equality of opportunity is simply the application of the liberal concept of equality before the law, but now applied to the capitalist economy itself, where it is manifestly unrealisable within the context of the capitalist class structure.

The positive rights to full participation on the basis of person rather than property has involved as well the demand for *the extension of the spheres of social life governed by formally democratic procedures.* The possibility of popular participation in politics in nineteenth century Europe and the United States rested upon the *laissez-faire* state – the state whose concrete practices and interventions were strictly limited to a restricted range of social decision-making. Indeed, for the 'late developers' in Europe – such as Germany, Italy, and Russia – the reliance on a state actively intervening in the process of capital accumulation increased the stakes involved in the granting of democratic forms tremendously – a fact amply reflected in their twentieth century histories. Yet the *laissez-faire* state could not be contained. In part, of course, capitalists themselves demanded extensions towards economic stabilisation and the building of the social infrastructure of capital accumulation. But equally important, citizens have demanded extensions of state practices to cover what were traditionally market-governed determinations.

Three dominant trends have been evident in recent decades. While these recent trends are virtual extensions of the historical logic of transportation of practices, their substance is qualitatively distinct. The first involves the transportation of civil equality to the economic sphere. Equality before the law has been a bourgeois demand since the French Revolution but the right to equal treatment in economic relationships directly expresses the dominance of person over property rights. Yet such have been the explicit demands of women, racial and religious minorities, and immigrant workers. Equally potent, but quite unrealizable under capitalism, have been the demands for substantive equality of economic opportunity. A second dominant trend has involved the extension of the concepts of positive right from suffrage and association, won by women and the working-class through struggle, to a comprehensive set of minimum rights due an individual by the very fact of citizenship. These demands, which may be called an Economic Bill of Rights, include state-provided services, such as health, education and social security, as well as interventions into private economic transactions, as in the case of occupational health and safety regulations, consumer protective laws, and life-line utility guarantees. Finally, demands for the extension of democracy have taken the form of struggles over the transportation of parliamentary democratic practices to those most sacrosanct arenas of capitalist control – the production and investment processes. While support for due process and constitutional guarantees have always formed part of twentieth century worker demands, rebellion against 'checking your civil rights at the factory gate' has in recent years blossomed into increasingly self-conscious demands for full work-place democracy and control of investment.

Capitalist social formations, then, are inherently contradictory systems, faced with the difficulty of maintaining the reproductive boundaries between the spheres of application of property rights, person rights, and male prerogatives. Nor has it done an acceptable job of maintaining these boundaries. If our analysis of social struggles presented above is correct, an Achilles heel of the capitalist system lies in its characteristic articulation of the state, economy, family totality. The liberal democratic state is at once the citadel of private property and the instrument of incursions upon this venerable institution. What E.P. Thompson has called the 'logic of the process' of social struggles has taken, in part, the form of the demand for the dominance of person rights over property and male privilege.[8] These struggles have complemented direct confrontation in family and production sites and can be expected to form an integral element in any effective socialist movement of coming years.

Before turning to the implication of this analysis for education, we must stress one aspect of this dynamic of social struggle: its occurrence wholly *within* the liberal discourse of natural rights. Workers have opposed the domination of capital not by moving outside liberal discourse, but by turning one of its internal principles against another. Socialists have often lamented this tendency of the workers' movement, seeing in it a lack of workers' consciousness of their class condition. Were workers adequately attuned to the true nature of their social condition and aware of their objective interests, it is argued, they would reject liberal discourse in favor of a Marxian analysis of social life. Workers would then demand an end to exploitation and alienated labor and strive for a classless society.

This interpretation of liberal discourse is, however, quite inappropriate and, indeed, idealistic. Liberal discourse is not a coherent political philosophy or a set of ideas. Nor was it the creation of the leading classes in society bent on the legitimation of the exploitation of labor.[9] Liberal discourse is the structure of cultural practices in advanced capitalist social formations. As a real ensemble of social relations, it is no more capable of being 'false' or 'true' than is a political or appropriative structure. Rather than reflecting or embodying ideas, it is simply a medium of communication. Like other structures, it in no way determines the acts of communication which occur through it, though it may delimit the range of communicative forms capable of expression within it. Finally, while liberal discourse may be criticized, it can only be transformed *internally*, through the conscious cultural practices of contesting groups. Indeed, this is exactly the way in which liberal discourse has developed through time. To view this fact in proper perspective, we must reject the notion that terms of discourse have 'meanings' in favor of the more operational notion of their having concrete *social uses* and specific *ranges of application* determined by modifiable social conventions.[10]

After a certain point in the industrial revolution, workers ceased operating outside the structure of liberal discourse, and rather began to contest the *use* and *range of application* of its fundamental terms. The conditions surrounding this transformation of discourse varied from country to country, but they generally coincided with workers receiving concrete gains in the form of political rights and rights of association in return for their acquiescence to the employment of the liberal tools of communicative discourse. They did not, however, leave these tools intact in their bourgeois form. Thus contemporary liberalism, far from being a unified expression of a political philosophy, is itself an internally contradictory system incapable of reproducing the boundaries between the major sites of the advanced capitalist social formation – state, family, and site of capitalist production. In particular, the essence of the demands for democratic socialism are partly expressible through the tools of liberal discourse. Socialism is in part the application of the principle of rights vested in persons to the major institutions of economic life. Its fulfilment involves two major elements. First, the replacement of the political structure of the production process by a fully democratic system of participation and control. Second, in place of capitalist control of investment and growth, a democratic decision process controlled by the groups and communities affected by investment decisions. Similarly, the essence of the demands for women's liberation are easily expressible through the tools of liberal discourse. The subordinate economic position of women can be overturned by applying the principle of the equal rights of citizens to the area of hiring and promotion, in place of the property norms of free contract and hierarchical authority. Similarly, the principle of democracy and reciprocity in personal relations is quite adequate to express the basis for a non-patriarchal reorganisation of family life.

What then are the limitations of operating within liberal discourse? By couching its fundamental concepts in terms of *person* rights, liberal discourse has difficulty in expressing issues of solidarity and co-operation as goals of political practices. The only generalisable form of bonding recognised in liberal discourse is that of nationality based on common citizenship and culture. Similarly, by relying on concepts of rights, whose use is virtually restricted to procedural issues, any assessment of the *substance* of democracy and participation lies outside its purview. For this reason appeals for solidarity and co-operation must, and do, transcend liberal discourse, drawing on the discourse of co-operative, family, brotherhood, and community. The actual discourse of socialism is thus an amalgam of liberal discourse and these expressions of bonding normally banished to the hinterlands of the political idiom.

Education and the Contradictions of Social Life

The central contradiction in the educational systems of advanced capitalist society derives from two aspects of its location in the social totality. First, it forms in general a subsystem of the state site, and therefore is directly subject to the principle of rights vested in persons. Second, education plays a central role in reproducing the political structure of the capitalist production process, which in turn is legitimated in terms of rights vested in property. Thus, education is directly involved in the contradictory articulation of sites in advanced capitalism and is expressed in terms of the property/person dichotomy: education reproduces rights vested in property while itself organised in terms of rights vested in persons.

We have emphasised that it is the *form* of the educational encounter – the social relations of education – that accounts for both its capacity to reproduce capitalist relations of production and its inability to promote domination and healthy personal development. The actual *content* of the curriculum has little role to play in this process. The contradictory location of the educational system can also be described in terms of its characteristic *form* of discourse, as opposed to the actual *content* of the curriculum. The form is that of the cultural structure of liberal discourse.

The liberal discourse has become the predominant cultural-structural form for the constitution of class and gender demands can certainly not be attributed to the educational system alone. Indeed, we have elsewhere argued that the hegemony of liberal discourse in class and gender struggles depended on an historically specific 'accord', arriving at different times in different countries. By an accord, we mean a mutually accepted joint redefinition and consequent reconstitution of political reality by antagonistic classes or class fragments. Through an accord, class interests are redefined. Class identities are respecified so as to produce a novel logic of social action. An accord is a reorganisation of society on two levels: institutions and communicative tools of political discourse. On the institutional level, the accord results in the admission of a new set of organisational forms (associations, unions, commissions, electoral laws and practices, etc.) and corresponding to these a new specification of organisational legitimacy. On the communicative level, the accord results in the creation of new communicative tools which (a) provide a common framework for political discourse across contending groups, (b) express the moral legitimacy of the newly created institutional nexuses, (c) are admitted by speakers and hearers as intelligible and worthy of affirmation, and (d) are affirmed in all the major formal institutions of daily life (media, political speeches, educational institutions, churches, law). In short, it is the coming into being of a new set of 'rules of the game' of political discourse and struggle.

An accord is likely to set into motion a totally new logic of social action and class struggle. On the institutional level, the existence of new organisations implies a redefined distribution of political power and a consequently redefined constellation of viable political strategies available to social groups. The new set of tools of communicative discourse, endowed with a new effectiveness by the very institutional forms they express and legitimate, will tend to force out of the political arena older forms of discourse (in the case of the capital/labor accord, for instance, theological and socialist forms) and the organisations that support them. These new tools will in turn represent the only available means of political communication and, thus, will be the basis for any future expression and organisation of political demands (until, of course, the accord is destroyed).

The accords giving rise to the current logic of class struggle in advanced capitalist countries occurred in the first decades of the twentieth century, and took distinct forms in each social formation concerned. In nearly all cases the working class was granted suffrage and the right to form workers' associations; in turn, elites have isolated and eliminated revolutionary socialist alternatives. The results were as varied as the conditions giving rise to the heightening of class confrontation. In Northern Europe, the smooth transition to social democracy resulted; in Germany, Italy, and Eastern Europe, the result was the total rupture of political life and the rise of fascism. In the United States, the Progressive Era witnessed the transition from *laissez-faire* to monopoly capitalism, the rise of 'safe' unionism and the squelching of hitherto growing socialist and populist movements.

Thus, while the educational system cannot be cited as the source of the near universality of liberal discourse, it certainly has played a central role in its reproduction. Whatever the actual content of the political philosophy and social theory presented in schools, the educational system in the twentieth century surely has provided students with little facility in any but modes of discourse based on natural rights. This contradictory position of education explains its dual progressive/reproductive role (promoting equality, democracy, toleration, rationality, inalienable rights, on the one hand, while legitimating inequality, authoritarianism, fragmentation, prejudice, and submission on the other) and is, in part, a reflection of the stress in liberal discourse on procedure over substance. But it provides as well the tools by means of which it can be transformed into an instrument in the transition to socialism: the exploitation of the contradictions that have come to inhere in the tools of liberal discourse. The goals of progressive educational reform must be framed within the structural boundaries of liberal discourse, and can be simply expressed as the full democratisation of education. These goals can be divided into two complementary projects: the democratisation of the social relations of education, and the reformulation of the issue of democracy in the curriculum.

We have stressed in *Schooling in Capitalist America* that the transformation of the schools cannot proceed without parallel developments at the site of capitalist production. Demands for the democratisation of the social relations of education therefore are likely to be effective only in the context of workers' demands for the democratisation of the production process – in short, for the full development of workers' control. The first step in the democratisation of education is a similar move toward teachers' and parents' control of the educational process. For teachers, as workers, will surely be involved in the movement for the democratisation of economic life and parents, as community members, will similarly be involved in the extension of the powers of local community decision-making.

Beyond this, the philosophy of education must develop in the direction that personal development through schooling be geared toward rendering students capable of controlling their lives as citizens, family members, workers, and community members. In particular, the educational process must be structured so that students gradually come to control increasingly substantial spheres of their education as they move from early to later levels of schooling. Current theories of progressive education stress that students be given free rein to develop their individual personalities, to be self-motivated and self-actualising. While the substance of such educational reforms must be conserved, they can be criticised in general for their failure to recognize the inherently *social* character of educational formation. As we emphasized in our book, there is no 'true self' to emerge prior to the concrete social interactions that individuals experience. This is not to say that individuals are infinitely malleable or that they should be subjected to a rigidly conformist schooling. Rather, it is to say that the ineluctably social impact of education cannot be ignored.

The admirable quality of the self-development philosophy of education lies in the power it draws from embracing a central category of the discourse of rights: the right to freedom from unwarranted interference, of which John Stuart Mill was the most eloquent exponent. Its draw-back, of being incurably a-social, is easily remedied by recourse to the communitarian emphasis on joint democratic control of conditions of social life by affected groups and individuals. No doubt there are formidable obstacles in the development of such a philosophy of educational structure and we are not personally equipped to meet this task. But it remains central to the growth of an effective movement toward socialist education.

Finally, progressive educators must exploit the internal contradictions of liberal discourse by developing curricula which dramatise the major oppositions inherent in the joint advocacy of rights vested in persons and property. Moreover, it must emphasise the sub-ordination of property and gender rights to person rights in a just society. This of course does not preclude some emphasis on the proper role for property and gender rights as adjuncts and supports for rights vested in persons – for instance a woman's right to choose when to conceive and bear a child independent of the preference of the natural father, or an individual's rights to personal (not productive) property free from social interference.

Liberalism puts forth a promise it cannot make good. The promise it extends is that of democracy, equality, liberty, and personal fulfilment for all, within the context of capitalism. Unlike traditional theology's balm of beatific after-life, this promise is in the here and now and it is the codification of two centuries of struggles, ideals, and aspirations by oppressed groups in capitalist society. The emptiness of its promise must be exposed and this, indeed, has been the project of socialists over the years. Socialism, should it come to pass in the advanced capitalist countries, will however have little to do with the inevitable process of advancing forces of production bursting asunder their capitalist shackles. Rather, it will be the real fulfilment of the liberal promise, and with it the transformation of tools of communicative discourse of capitalism. Our arguments in this paper are no doubt sitting ducks for misinterpretation and calumny. Are we not justifying liberalism? Are we not advocating socialism as its logical culmination? No. We are arguing that liberal discourse is a fact not a defeat. It is a site of intervention and it embodies the emancipatory achievements of the popular classes. The logical culmination, if it have any, is its own demise. In what way, depends on conscious choices of political actors. 'As soon as democracy shows a disposition ... to become an instrument of the real interests of the people', as Rosa Luxemburg has noted, 'the democratic forms themselves are sacrificed by the bourgeoisie and their representative'. Yet for all that, socialism remains the extension of democratic freedoms from civil and political life to economic life itself.

1 BOWLES, S. and GINTIS, H. (1977) *Schooling in Capitalist America*, London, Routledge and Kegan Paul.
2 *Ibid.* Chapter 11.
3 DEWEY, J. (1966) *Democracy and Education*, New York, The Free Press.
4 JENCKS, C., BARTLETT, S., CORCORAN, M., CROUSE, J., EAGLESFIELD, D., JACKSON, G., McLELLAND, K., MUESER, P., OLNECK, M., SCHWARTZ, J., WARD, S. and WILLIAMS, J. (1980) *Who Gets Ahead?* New York, Basic Books.
5 See especially BOWLES and GINTIS, *op. cit.*, Chapters 9 and 11 (Note 1).
6 THE CARNEGIE COMMISSION ON HIGHER EDUCATION, (1963) *Priorities for Action*, New York, McGraw-Hill Book Company. KENISTON, K. AND THE CARNEGIE COUNCIL ON CHILDREN, (1977) *All Our Children*, New York, Harcourt, Brace, Jovanovich.
7 CALLAHAN, R. (1962) *Education and the Cult of Efficiency*, Chicago, University of Chicago Press.
8 THOMPSON, E.P. (1979) *The Poverty of Theory and other Essays*, London, Merlin Press.
9 The analysis of liberal discourse as the outcome of class struggles in the early stages of capitalist development is made in GINTIS, H. (1980) 'Theory, Practice, and the Tools of Communicative Discourse,' *Socialist Review*, Spring.
10 This type of analysis of social discourse was first developed by the philosopher Ludwig Wittgenstein, and has never been adequately developed in social theory. See GINTIS, *op. cit.*, (Note 9).

Schooling for Change: Function, Correspondence and Cause

Tony Edwards, University of Newcastle-Upon-Tyne.

Variations on the theme of schooling as a conservative force have dominated recent sociology of education, and are well represented in this book. My own purpose is not to question the theme but rather the process of composition. I want to explore the difficulty of moving such analyses from mere assertion to some load-bearing empirical ground, and then to consider the advantages of enlarging the historical dimension which many of these accounts already display.

The theme itself is too familiar to need more than the briefest recapitulation. What is learned in schools is a necessary contribution to the process by which industrial societies recreate the material, normative and cognitive conditions of their existence and by which hierarchies of wealth and power are 'legitimately' reproduced. Schools will, therefore, have whatever characteristics are needed to shape social identies and social relationships into the appropriate forms. Opportunities for reform will be strictly limited because there will be 'a prevailing type of education from which we cannot deviate without encountering that lively resistance which restrains the fashions of dissent'.

Although those last words are Durkheim's, the summary which preceded it deliberately mixes items from the sociological vocabularies of order and control.[1] It does so because theories of education as a source of social order and theories of schooling as an instrument of social control display important similarities in method, despite the political gulf between them. Both make frequent reference to 'social imperatives' and 'underlying purposes', and both face the problem of *showing* how these 'deep' processes are realised in actual events. It is not unreasonable, then, to detect in the work of Bowles and Gintis a 'flamboyant functionalism' in which, like some extravagant piece of Gothic architecture, the strengths and weaknesses of the style are clearly in view.[2] The particular weakness which concerns me here is the practice of constructing a description of how things 'are' from a theoretical analysis of how things 'must be' to maintain the social system, thereby avoiding the chore of observation. But that practice is itself a consequence of a complementary strength – the refusal to treat any social institution out of context. It may then be assumed that an analysis of the whole will simultaneously outline the parts or that the superstructure can be predicted from a careful study of the base. Both functionalist and correspondence theories of schooling refuse to understand an education system as that system may ask to be understood; the 'real' determinants of curriculum and pedagogy are seen as lying elsewhere. Indeed, education systems are regarded, from both perspectives, as unusually vulnerable to 'external' demands and constraints and the sociological task is defined as being that of identifying the connections. If the analysis begins with classroom practices, how are 'the structural features which they embody' to be recognised?[3] Alternatively, if the researcher starts on the theoretical heights and then descends to engage in 'detailed observation of school routines', how are the results of that observation to be incorporated into the larger analysis?[4]

If the recent sociological preoccupation with these questions has made it increasingly difficult to get away with 'merely' micro-studies of classrooms, it has provided few clear guidelines for what to do instead.[5] If an adequate sociological account has to integrate structural features and interactional practices (as Bernstein and others have argued so strongly), how far 'out' from the interaction can structural features be identified without losing sight of their connections with actual events?

Since my own attempts to 'move out' have been entirely tentative, they provide a convenient illustration of some of the difficulties of doing so. I have argued that the typical organisation of classroom talk can be partly accounted for by what teachers 'have to do' to maintain orderly interaction in conditions where good discipline not only requires the suppression of noticeable noise but also that large numbers of often involuntary learners are contained for long periods within a single communication system. For example, independently of the content of the lesson, and often despite the teacher's intention of opening up discussion, there are strong organisational pressures for questions to be 'closed'. By asking questions to which they clearly know the answers already, teachers retain rights to allocate, reallocate and terminate pupils' turns. To this 'managerial' explanation have to be added the consequences of transmitting knowledge. For most practical purposes, what the teacher knows has the external and constraining properties which Durkheim attributed to social facts and the complementary assumptions of pupil ignorance and teacher expertise both generate and justify highly asymmetrical rights of participation. The authority of the teacher is therefore signalled and reproduced in the routine patterns of classroom talk.[6] Now it is certainly of 'considerable sociological interest' to show in this way *how* the rules regulating teacher-pupil relationships 'generate distinctive texts'. But it may be thought of even greater sociological interest to ask – *why* those rules? Bernstein himself outlines a clear, if insubstantial, causal sequence in which the structure of classroom interaction is seen as a microcosm of the 'macroscopic orderings of society'. 'Power and control are made substantive in the classification and framing, *which then* generate distinctive forms of social relationship, *and thus* communication'.[7] From this perspective, merely microscopic explanations must be judged inadequate. My own analysis, with Furlong, of the 'language of teaching' was an attempt to trace the structure and structuring of teacher-pupil communication in one part of the curriculum in one innovative school. At least at the 'local' level, the analysis resembles Giddens' discussion of 'structuration' because it treats structure as 'both the medium and the outcome of practices'.[8] But what was the scope of that sense of structure? Our location of the teaching we observed ranged no further than the 'difficult' catchment area of the school, and we explicitly avoided any account of the teachers' innovatory purposes being unwittingly subverted by macrostructural constraints. They themselves recognised internal contradictions in the school's commitment to resource-based learning (for example, the tension between developing 'pupil autonomy' and making efficiently planned use of elaborate curriculum packages), the pressure for 'results' on a school stereotyped as being both innovative *and* disorderly, and their own professional commitment to developing literacy skills. The main teaching methods we describe are explained as ways of reconciling the tasks of maintaining classroom order, transmitting skills and information, allowing some pupil control over at least the pacing of their work, and leaving the teachers themselves plenty of room to deal with the problems of individual pupils.

That account may well appeal to the practical commonsense of teachers who read it. But is it enough? It relies on what historians often call practical inference; the explanation of actions as the outcome of what seemed to be the thing to do, given the actors' purposes, their view of the situation, and their sense of what was possible. Such an explanation is not falsified by showing those actors to have been in some respects mistaken, misguided, or blind to possibilities or constraints which were 'objectively' there. But seeking to recapture how the situation seemed to those involved is not all that historians do. They are also likely to be interested in *how* and *why* that situation was and whether it was 'really' something more. Sociologists have similar questions in mind when they refer either to the 'objective location' of classroom practices which 'are' otherwise then they 'seem' or to teachers' 'misrecognition' of the 'objective effects' of what they do.[9] From this perspective, the account of resource-based teaching, which I have outlined, is wide open to the objection which Bisseret makes to Bernstein's sociolinguistic codes (and which I have made myself to certain sociolinguistic working definitions of what constitutes the social world) – namely, that it reduces social relations to inter-personal relations and dissolves social structure into a series of settings for interaction.[10] If it deals with *social integration* as 'systemness on the level of face-to-face interaction', it ignores *system integration* which is 'systemness on the level of relations between social systems or collectivities'.[11] More particularly, it fails to show how and why a particular form of systems integration is reflected in, and reproduced by, a particular form of social integration. The only defence against that criticism might be provided by taking the argument that even in apparently innovative classrooms pupils were still learning *generalisable* lessons in how to work within a received frame of reference and defer to an accredited expert as being, at least implicitly, an explanation of why (because of society's 'need' for such lessons to be learned) classroom interaction 'must' display the working-out of a power relationship.[12]

It is precisely that *kind* of explanation which concerns me here. Typical patterns of classroom talk may be interpreted as 'creatively articulated solutions' to some of the problems posed by crowds of often involuntary learners from whom measurable learning has to be produced. The temptation to present classroom life as nothing more or less than a direct reflection of power relations in the wider society may be firmly resisted. But the question remains – how is the sociological imagination to extend beyond the school to ask why *those* are the problems with which teachers and pupils commonly have to cope without thereby exceeding its capacity to ground these larger explanations in evidence?[13]

The particular form of explanation I want to examine here is that which works back from certain 'functional requisites' or 'social imperatives' to the practices from which these necessary outcomes are produced. What is an implicitly causal sequence of this type is provided by Levin.

> It takes little imagination to see the correspondence between grades for school work and wages for work performance . . . ; to see the competition for grades parallel the competition among workers for advancement; and to see the teacher in the classroom impose his arbitrary values on his underlings just as does the boss on the job.[14]

Now insofar as the imagination referred to here is sociological, the task undertaken follows Wright Mills' prescription by revealing as public issues what would otherwise appear merely as interpersonal troubles. It is this task which is undertaken by Michael Apple in his analysis of how American classrooms have been transformed by the application of managerial processes at work in 'the larger social area' to teachers' re-skilled transmission of 'pre-packaged curricular systems'. Clearly, in so far as the 'forces' seen to be at work are not recognised (or are misrecognised) by those whose relationships are 'thereby' constrained or changed, such explanations depend on the sociologist's trained capacity to see beyond the actors' view. They therefore display the fundamental dilemma which Kingsley Davis saw in all functionalist analysis, that 'it goes against the grain of ordinary discourse' to trace the unrecognised consequences of an action 'as leading by their unrecognised effect . . . to the continuous reinforcement of that action'.[15] It was therefore extremely difficult to present the analysis as a persuasive *causal* explanation. The difficulty is recognised by Bowles and Gintis. Having explained how (for example), in the American common school, curriculum tracking and 'progressive pedagogy' developed *so as to produce* 'the new forms of motivation and discipline required in the emerging Corporate Order', they admit their failure to 'identify the mechanisms whereby economic interests are translated into educational program'.[16]

Given this problem, there are obvious analytical attractions in contexts where explicitly proclaimed economic and political purposes can be followed through into the classroom, and where the educational consequences of changes in the wider society can be readily identified. For example, the 1938 *Regulations for Secondary Education* in Germany were a direct expression of the Nazi notion of 'Gleichschaltung' – which was not a simple subjection of schooling to politics but a flamboyantly 'functionalist' assertion that 'no really essential integral branch of national life can be split off the central stock of what we call the nation's Kraft' and that education had to be 'redirected into the life stream of the people'.[17] Those regulations prescribed or authorized compulsory racial instruction 'according to National Socialist principles', historical instruction which exalted the 'volk' and revealed its enemies, and moral instruction which emphasized leadership, unity, and instinct. The teachers' authority was also diminished by having their political loyalty put on trial before parents *and pupils*, and by the equal importance given to the 'civilising' mission of the Youth Movements. I will take two further totalitarian examples. Having previously described with alarmed respect the 'making of the New Soviet Man', Urie Bronfenbrenner was a member of a multidisciplinary American delegation which observed with equally alarmed respect 'the calm, the orderliness and the apparent uniformity of the young children of China'. In a 'totally cohesive' and 'ideologically saturated' curriculum, nothing seemed to be left either to chance or to the individual choices of teacher or pupils. Tasks were closely prescribed, the achievement of *collective* solutions to cognitive and moral problems was pervasive and teachers acted as 'initiators, maintainers and terminators' of all classroom and most playground activities. The non-reflective responses of teachers to some typically Western questions about, for example, child development, individual differences and classroom management seemed to express their confident recourse to authoritative definitions of how the appropriate social character was to be formed.[18] A similarly direct progression from political and economic diagnosis to detailed educational prescription is evident in the Cuban government's implementation of school reforms as a direct expression of a revolutionary ideology, and its recognition that those reforms could not have taken root in less ideologically fertile ground.[19]

These are deliberately 'easy' examples in which the process of educational reform, and the checking of its consequences, are matters of public record. There will obviously be more challenging opportunities to bring 'news' where the record is less revealing or where it seems to be saturated with politically convenient myths. Indeed, there is a sharp contrast between Bronfenbrenner's alarm at the relatively unsystematic and incoherent socialisation process in America, and the recent insistence of sociologists and revisionist historians that children in the 'free world' are no less systematically (though more secretly) 'schooled to order'. But to reveal this otherwise hidden process is to move so hard against the tide of liberal educational discourse as to place on those who do so a formidable task of 'proving' their case. In practice, that task is often evaded. Some of the bleakest accounts of schooling as social control seem to follow the American Declaration of Independence in presenting their 'truths to be self-evident', and they deserve the charge of 'empirical irresponsibility' which Christopher Hurn has levelled against some revisionist answers to the old question – do schools ameliorate or reinforce inequality? To say this is not to deny the extraordinary difficulty of showing *how* the effects of a complex stratified society penetrate the classroom or even of defining what the evidence of that penetration might be like. Most difficult of all is the identification of mediating influences. It is altogether too easy to leap directly from macrostructural analysis to over-determined and largely inferential description of classroom practices.

My concern in the rest of this paper is with the historical refuge in which many sociologists of education have recently sought some shelter from these problems. Sometimes they have done so to display what Apple calls 'that peculiarly Marxist sensitivity to the present as history', and to the heavy weight of historical residues.[20] Thus it may be argued that an educational system presents through time only the 'illusion of change', or that the 'schooling of the people' is marked by a *persistent* tension between 'the rhetoric of democracy and the reality of a class-divided society'.[21] But with this substantive recognition of 'the present as history' goes a methodological appreciation of the historian's advantage of hindsight. A knowledge of what happened next makes it possible to detect the 'current' of events and so uncover causes and consequences of which the participants were unaware. The task of *relating* structure and action may then be more easily managed.

As a former historian, I feel a natural sympathy with Wright Mills' claim that 'all sociology worthy of the name is historical sociology', and with his advice to social scientists to use the 'productions of historians' as a 'great file' of evidence relevant to their own concerns.[22] It is advice which has been followed enthusiastically by those sociologists who have drawn much of their evidence for the repressive functions of schooling from periods when teachers were openly instructed to 'gentle the masses'. In doing so, they face an obvious temptation merely to dip into the file for convenient illustrations of a predetermined theory, as Gerald Grace recognises when he admits to having *used* history as a resource in ways 'which may have violated many of the conventions of historical scholarship'.[23] But this is not a problem I want to exaggerate. There are no conventions of scholarship which can guarantee objectivity, and the historian's *prior* sense of what really mattered in the period being studied influences not only how the data are to be interpreted but what are to count as data in the first place. Simply, what 'facts' are sponsored as fact? It would be generally admitted by historians that the record of the past is regularly revised according to the preoccupations of the present, and according to its presuppositions about human motives and behaviour.[24] 'If one starts with the assumption that this society is in fact racist . . . and institutionally structured to protect vested interests', then the past will certainly 'take on vastly different meanings'.[25] The results of starting in this way are evident in recent radical revisions of the old familiar story of educational progress and reform; revisions which depend less on new evidence than on subjecting old evidence to new questions and new analytical concepts.[26] All this can be admitted, however, without denying that it is the *pursuit* of objectivity which shapes the historian's methods. At this more modest level, the 'conventions of historical scholarship' have something to teach some sociologists about placing an excessive reliance on a few apt quotations. Horace Mann may write about the 'training of obedient workers' or Kay-Shuttleworth about diffusing that modest dose of approved information which 'tends beyond anything else to promote the security of property and the maintenance of public order' but the clarity of such particular statements does not avoid the obligation to ask how representative they were even of the individual informant (since few witnesses are so obliging as to be entirely consistent in their declared intentions) or to locate them in the discourse of their own time.[27] There is the associated problem, too, that history is often written from above, not as the outcome of Becker's hierarchy of credibility ('the bosses know best') but from an unavoidable reliance on what are often the *only* available witnesses. Thus David Tyack recognises the enormous practical difficulties of recapturing the educational experience of those 'victimised by their poverty, their color, their cultural differences' when it is the Schoolmen who are often the only regular guides to what the schools were like. There is a special problem when the researcher strongly disapproves of his key witnesses, not because he needs to empathise with them but because of 'the difficulty of maintaining a complex of suppositions ("Suppose I believed such-and-such and wanted so-and-so") in the face of a view of the world totally antipathetic to it'.[28]

I have touched briefly on difficulties encountered in using historical evidence for *any* analytical purpose. But since my main concern in this paper is with how macro-theories of schooling are to be empirically grounded, I have to consider a distinction which is often drawn between the explanations normally offered by sociologists and historians. Sociologists, it is said, seek to generalise; their interest is in regularities and patterns. To historians, however, 'a mass of apparently unique facts still offer certain undeniable delights', and their interest is in the course of particular events.[29] That conventional contrast is certainly overdrawn, though something like it seems to have been in Marc Bloch's mind when he commented that sociologists had made room for history among the sciences of man only to 'relegate it to one poor corner' in which (having reserved for themselves everything 'that appears susceptible to rational analysis') they shut up those facts 'which they condemn as the most superficial and capricious'.[30] In this context, 'rational analysis' implies the deliberate building up of empirical generalisations and explanatory theories, while mere historians are seen as offering interpretations which are both less systematic and more local in their application. If valid, that contrast would mean a high risk of methodological schizophrenia for the historical-sociologist. In practice, however, the dichotomy changes into a continuum. There are undoubtedly some historians who rarely lift their heads from the fine print of their documents and some grand sociological theorists whose enthusiasm for structures and factors leaves them no time to observe actual events. But in between these poles are innumerable sociologists with a taste for story-telling and innumerable historians anxious to combine their delight in 'the colorful, complex reality of specific episodes' with a more analytical concern 'for what is general and what is particular in historical events – and sometimes even why'.[31] A merging of methods, evident in the work of many individuals, is regularly displayed in the French journal 'Annales' (of which Marc Bloch himself was a founder) and in 'Past and Present', launched in 1949 to promote 'scientific history' and the rigorous analysis of 'the very nature' of societies and their historical development. So even the softened contrast, which I go on to draw, conveniently ignores some fierce battles over the proper resemblance of historical explanations to explanatory models found in the natural and social sciences. Having made that properly cautious point, I now want to suggest that some recent theories of schooling conform too closely to the 'covering law' model in which the events to be explained are deduced from a general law and a set of initial conditions within which that law applies; that such explanations are likely to be over-simplified and over-determined; and that they would be strengthened by adopting more of the *narrative* approach which historians more commonly employ.

A common sociological procedure is that outlined by Dore in his discussion of how far a functional analysis can provide a causal explanation. Sociologists search out regularities in the events they study, seek to induce causal laws from them, and then attempt to 'order such laws into a comprehensive theory'.[32] This is roughly the procedure which he adopts himself in his analysis of the 'diploma disease'. A large number of case-studies are used to build up and exemplify his diagnosis of education being systematically distorted by the progressively inflated importance of qualifications as 'proxy measures for the abilities which employers seek'. Examinations are therefore 'the earth around which the whole Ptolemaic system of schooling revolves', with especially grievous consequences in late-developing countries. A rather similar procedure is apparent in Carnoy's accumulation of case-studies showing how schools were used in times of social upheaval to 'hold things together' and to incorporate large numbers into the developing economic order. The 'distinct and conclusive pattern' extracted from these case-studies then supports a comprehensive theory of schooling as 'cultural and economic imperialism'.[33] I have no wish to question these particular examples, both of which rest on extensive and detailed empirical work. My target is rather the formulation of general explanations (whether in terms of function or correspondence) which are either premature or substitutions for detailed empirical work. While recognising, again, the inseparability of theory and data, I agree with Karier that if social theory is to inform historical inquiry 'it ought to emerge in transactional relationship to that inquiry' and so be both prerequisite *and* consequence.[34] Especially to be avoided are theories so general that it is impossible to define what confirming or refuting evidence would be like and theories which persistently present the 'real' story as taking place behind the backs of those whose actions give it life.

What normally holds historians back from referring explicitly to explanatory 'laws' is a fear of overriding the particularity of events. Any such 'law' is only applicable 'other things being equal' and an over-eager search for patterns may lose sight of situational differences. That was an argument used against Michael Katz' account of the development of mass schooling, an account in which he seemed to his critics to have seriously underestimated the influence of 'the individual, the accidental and the plain messy'. Katz replied to the criticism by asserting that what occurred was more than 'a series of haphazard events', and that there must have been 'general forces' at work.[35] But that defence depends on posing unrealistically sharp alternatives. An awareness of the 'plain messy' in human affairs is not incompatible with an awareness of structural constraints which severely reduce the unpredictability of events. For example, Marc Bloch illustrated the salience of *immediate* causes by the case of a man tripping to his death from a mountain path. Although the laws of gravity and the economic reasons for the existence of the path are undoubtedly among the necessary conditions for that event, 'we should give a mistep as the cause because it occurred last, was the least permanent and most exceptional in the general order of things, and so seems the antecedent which could have been most easily avoided'.[36] But, if a recent deterioration in the condition of the path could reasonably be attributed to cut-backs in public spending, Bloch would certainly have insisted on extending the scope of the explanation of the accident. What he was emphasising was the importance of identifying the connections between conditions, causes, and consequences.

In practice, then, the normal form of historical explanation is that of the *narrative*, a more or less credible story in which the sequence of events is (at least implicitly) a sequence of causes and effects, adequate as an explanation in so far as the reader is not impeded from following the story by gaps for which no plausible links have been provided.[37] The more skilful the narrative, the less need there is for a more formal explanation because at each stage the action taken seems to be the thing (or one of the things) to have done. Compared with various forms of structural explanation in sociology, the approach may well seem extraordinarily loose and unsystematic but, as Hexter comments, historians have long learned to live with it and the 'pursuit of strict causal adequacy would strike them dumb'. Indeed, too much attention to Katz' 'general forces' can lose sight of 'the inter-relations of times, places, persons and circumstances' in an analysis, the whole tendency of which is 'to dissolve and destroy these tendons and ligaments which hold historical stories together'.[38] Again it must be emphasised that nothing in this narrative approach should be taken as implying a naïve voluntarism in which historical actors are presented as having been free to take any number of paths. As was suggested earlier, historical equivalents of a 'sociology of situations' are evident in historians' frequent willingness to move away from (or beyond) even the fullest possible reconstruction of how the situation seemed at the time to identifying constraints which were 'objectively' there. If 'the escape of human history from human intentions, and the return of the consequences of that escape as causal influences on human action is a chronic feature of social life', it is also a chronic feature of historical narrative. But what Giddens goes on to argue against are forms of functionalist explanation which seem to distance themselves from any description of human action. History and sociology are only likely to be 'methodologically indistinguishable' to the extent that their practitioners display a common awareness that not even the most deeply sedimented institutional features of societies come about because those societies need them to do so. They come about historically, as a result of concrete conditions that have in every case to be directly analysed'.[39]

The dangers of excessive abstraction are apparent in those explanations of the content, form and consequences of nineteenth-century popular schooling which make often unsupported references to 'capitalist imperatives', the 'needs' of the developing corporate order, and to the correspondence between the organisation of mass schooling and the organisation of mass production. For example, there is no firm evidence that educational reformers learned directly from visits to, or even descriptions of, factories and their frequent use of the *language* of mass production may well have been no more than a tactical use of a currently persuasive rhetoric. There is evidence, however, that the overt association of ignorance with disorder led *directly* – that is, by traceable sequences of decisions and actions – to a deliberate appeal to the 'respectable' working-class for recruits to teaching; to their careful segregation during a training which stressed a moral and social concern for 'the poor' while avoiding 'politics'; to a style of school and classroom architecture which expressed and reinforced a confidence in the transmission of carefully measured remedies for 'the misery of ignorance and its attendant vices'; to the widespread use of instructional manuals as a means of controlling the activities of teachers whose technical competence was not to be trusted; and to the demand for measurable results from so prodigal an expenditure of public money. Less directly, the need to do all this cheaply for a rapidly growing school population produced some obvious 'rational' solutions to the consequent organisational problems. Those solutions in turn presented teachers with the task of producing the required results in crowded classrooms in short time and pupils with the consequent demands for stillness, attention and busyness. The strategies adopted to cope with these problems then became so institutionalised as to seem the normal forms of teaching and learning.

Even in condensed form, that narrative is not (in Katz' sense) 'haphazard'. It may be regarded as superficial in its neglect of the 'deeper' economic and political currents carrying the schools along but *how* the schools were aligned with other social institutions is a process that has to be demonstrated and the alignment may turn out to have been a rather loose fit. There is no substitute for detailed description of how educational practices emerged and became matters of routine and the temptation to present a theoretically tidy version of an untidy reality should be resisted. To reverse Merton's well-known comment, it is important that sociological accounts should not leap from remote axioms to particulars without a clear presentation of the intermediate steps and any abstractions should stay 'close enough to observed data to be incorporated in propositions that permit empirical testing'.[40]

That point has relevance for the teaching of sociology of education, especially to those coming to it for the first time. Whatever theories of educational structure and function they encounter 'must bear on the actual experience of children in schools'.[41] Students immersed in varieties of structuralist sociology are likely to encounter too much language 'at the apex of a pyramid of experience', language which conveys the analytical essence without providing much sense of the experience from which it was initially distilled. 'The vast range of human activities', details of which the student could 'respond to with comfort and interest', remain hidden from view.[42] But even the most dedicated theorist needs to make frequent descents from 'that high plateau where ideologies war and isms clash ... but no man acts or suffers or even lives'.[43]

It is also necessary to do this as a check on that sense of an *inexorable* process of domination which is so evident in recent sociology of education. The dilemma was neatly presented in *Letter to a Teacher by the School of Barbiana*. To deny the existence of a dominant group or 'interest', which has 'cut the schools' to measure, is to risk appearing a simpleton; to assert its existence is to give the account a possibly unwarranted air of mystery and conspiracy.[44] But a proper balance between naïvety and fatalism is an *empirical* matter. I have no wish to end this paper with an optimistic rhetorical flourish. I want only to argue that irrationality, delusion and helplessness should not be imputed too early and too easily in the analysis of schooling. There would be little advantage in replacing the old story of irresistible educational advance with a new story of irresistible educational coercion if both stories are presented as taking place 'behind the backs' of those whose actions gave them life. History is too easily written as the history of successes, thereby losing that vital historical sense of a time when things could have been otherwise. But even the most thorough analysis of social conditions is unlikely to indicate that there was only one possible outcome and the 'tendons and ligaments' of detailed historical narrative direct attention to those antecedents of events which could have been avoided. Some recent accounts of nineteenth-century popular schooling have emphasized both the frequent reluctance of working-class parents and pupils to receive the instruction offered to them, and their attempts to devise alternatives, and have also indicated the striking lack of evidence that the young were *in fact* 'schooled to order'. Some accounts of contemporary schooling have also described ways in which teachers and pupils seek to transform, or at least subvert, the conditions in which they work.[45] It may still be argued, of course, that such resistance is strictly limited in scope – that it may make the consequences of how schools are organised more bearable without seriously challenging their structure. At the conference on which this book is based, Herbert Gintis insisted that the schools have almost no room for manoeuvre and little capacity for change. That may seem a realistic appreciation of compelling 'external' constraints, or an over-determined view which exceeds the evidence currently available. The issue is the most important facing the sociology of education, but it will not be resolved by exchanges of speculation. Marc Bloch's final words on the historian's craft are no less applicable to the practice of sociology – 'the causes cannot be assumed, they are to be looked for'.[46]

Acknowledgements.

I am grateful to my colleagues John Beattie and Bruce Carrington for frequent arguments about and against points raised in this paper. I am also grateful to Peter Lee, of the London Institute of Education's History Department, for thoughtful and critical comments on an earlier draft.

Notes and References.

1 DURKHEIM, E. (1956) *Education and Sociology*, Glencoe, the Free Press, p. 66. The summary contains especially loud echoes of DREEBEN, R. (1968) *On What is Learned in School*, Reading, Mass., Addison-Wesley; BOURDIEU, P. (1973) 'Cultural Reproduction and Social Reproduction', in BROWN, R. (Ed.) *Knowledge, Education and Cultural Change*, London, Tavistock; CARNOY, M. and LEVIN, H. (Eds.) (1976) *The Limits of Educational Reform*, New York, McKay; and BISSERET, N. (1979) *Education, Class Language and Ideology*, London, Routledge and Kegan Paul.

2 COHEN, D. and ROSENBERG, B. (1977) 'Understanding Schools in Capitalist America', *History of Education Quarterly*, 17. 2., pp. 113–168.

3 BERNSTEIN, B. (1977) *Class, Codes and Control Vol. 3*, London, Routledge and Kegan Paul, p. 2.

4 APPLE, M. (1979) *Ideology and Curriculum*, London, Routledge and Kegan Paul, p. 16.

5 A preoccupation with the relationship between macro- and micro-level analysis is apparent in the contributions of David Hargreaves, Olive Banks, Sara Delamont and Andy Hargreaves to the first of these Westhill conferences; see BARTON, L. and MEIGHAN, R. (Eds.) (1978) *Sociological Interpretation of Schooling and Classrooms: A Reappraisal*, Driffield, Nafferton.

6 EDWARDS, A. (1980) 'Patterns of Power and Authority in Classroom Talk', in WOODS, P. (Ed.), *Teacher Strategies: Explorations in the Sociology of the School*, London, Croom Helm.

7 BERNSTEIN, B. *op. cit.*, (Note 3) pp. 11–12.

8 EDWARDS, A. and FURLONG, V. (1978) *The Language of Teaching*, London, Heinemann, pp. 96–101 and 151–155; GIDDENS, A. (1976) *New Rules of Sociological Method*, London, Hutchinson, pp. 120–125, and (1979) *Central Problems in Social Theory*, London, Methuen, pp. 60–73.

9 SHARP, R. and GREEN, A. (1975) *Education and Social Control*, London, Routledge and Kegan Paul, pp. 21–24; BOURDIEU, P. and PASSERON, J.P. (1977) *Reproduction in Education, Society and Culture*, New York, Sage, p.x.

10 BISSERET, N. *op. cit.*, (Note 1) pp. 90–106; EDWARDS, A. and SEIDEL, G. (1979), 'Social Facts and Socially-Constituted Linguistics', *Sociolinguistics Newsletter* 10. 2, pp. 18–20.

11 GIDDENS, A. (1979) *Central Problems in Social Theory*, *op. cit.*, (Note 8) pp. 76–77. The distinction is the nearest Giddens wishes to go towards 'admitting the usefulness of a differentiation between macro- and micro- sociological studies'.

12 EDWARDS, A. and FURLONG, V. *op. cit.*, (Note 8), p. 155; EDWARDS, A. *op. cit.*, (Note 6) pp. 249–50.

13 For an unusually thoughtful and empirical attempt to relate structural features and interactional practices, see HARGREAVES, A. (1978) 'The Significance of Classroom Coping Strategies', in BARTON, L. and MEIGHAN, R. *op. cit.*, (Note 5).

14 CARNOY, M. and LEVIN, H. (Eds.) (1976) *op. cit.*, (Note 1) p. 28.

15 DAVIS, K. (1959) 'The Myth of Functional Analysis as a Special Method in Sociology and Anthropology', *American Sociological Review* 24, pp. 757–72.

16 BOWLES, S. and GINTIS, H. (1976) *Schooling in Capitalist America*, London, Routledge and Kegan Paul p. 186.

17 WILHELM, T. (1939) 'Scholars or Soldiers? Aims and Results of "Nazi" Education', *International Educational Review* 8, pp. 81–102. The article is based on a paper given by Wilhelm (then head of a teachers' training college) to the Nottingham Education Society a few weeks after the Munich agreement. For the move from theory into practice, see, for example, BECKER, H. *German Youth: Bond of Free?* London, Kegan Paul 1946 and LAQUEUR, W. (1962) *Young Germany: A History of the German Youth Movement*, London, Routledge and Kegan Paul.

18 BRONFENBRENNER, U. (1970) *Two Worlds of Childhood*, New York, Sage; KESSEN, W. (Ed.) (1975) *Childhood in China*, Yale University Press.

19 CARNOY, M. and WERTHEIN, J. (1977) Socialist Ideology and the Transformation of Cuban Education', in KARABEL, J. and HALSEY, A. (Eds.), *Power and Ideology in Education*, New York, Oxford University Press.

20 APPLE, M. *op. cit.*, p. 16.

21 KATZ, M. (1975) *Class, Bureaucracy and Schools: The Illusion of Educational Change in America* (2nd Edition, New York, Praeger; NASOW, D. (1979) *Schooled to Order: A Social History of Public Schooling in the United States*, New York, Oxford University Press, p. 4.

22 WRIGHT MILLS, C. (1970) *The Sociological Imagination*, Harmondsworth, Penguin pp. 159–182. A similar case is argued at greater depth in GOLDMAN, L. (1969) *The Human Sciences and Philosophy*, London, Cape, pp. 23–33.

23 GRACE, G. (1978) *Teachers, Ideology and Control*, London, Routledge and Kegan Paul. p. 3.

24 For a lucid discussion of objectivity, see CARR, E.H. (1964) on 'The historian and his facts', in *What is History?* Harmondsworth, Penguin, pp. 7–30.

25 KARIER, C. and VIOLAS, P. (Eds.) (1973) *The Roots of Crisis*, Chicago, Rand McNally, p. 5.

26 An early example was JOHNSON, R. (1970) 'Educational Policy and Social Control in Early Victorian England', *Past and Present* 49, pp. 96–119. See also McCANN, P. (Ed.) (1977) *Popular Education and Socialisation in the Nineteenth Century*, London, Methuen; and TYACK, D. (1974) *The One Best System: A History of American Urban Education*, Harvard, Harvard University Press. There is an intriguing example of what two historians can do with the 'same' facts about the 'social control' functions of English Sunday Schools in THOMPSON, E.P. (1968) *The Making of the English Working Class*, Harmondsworth, Penguin, pp. 412–416, and LAQUEUR, W. (1976) *Religion and Respectability: Sunday Schools and Working Class*, Yale University Press. For an extended discussion of different sociological treatments of the 'same' evidence, see HURN, C. (1978) *The Limits and Possibilities of Schooling*, Boston, Allyn and Bacon.

27 The brief historical sketch in CORRIGAN, P. (1979) *Schooling the Smash Street Kids*, London, Macmillan, is particularly 'unhistorical'.

28 LEE, P. (1978) 'Explanation and Understanding in History', in DICKINSON, A. and LEE, P. (Eds.) *History Teaching and Historical Understanding*, London, Heinemann, p. 74. For an interesting discussion of how to resist writing history 'from above', see the editorial collective's introduction to the first issue of *History Workshop: A Journal of Socialist Historians* 1976.

29 HOFSTADTER, R. (1968) '*History and Sociology in the United States*; in LIPSET, S. and HOFSTADTER, R. (Eds.) *Sociology and History: Methods*, New York, Basic Books, p. 12.

30 BLOCH, M. (1965) *The Historian's Craft*, PUTNAM, P. (trans.) Manchester, Manchester University Press, p. 20.

31 TYACK, D. (1972) *op. cit.*, p. 5. See also STEDMAN JONES, G. 'History: The Poverty of Empiricism', in BLACKBURN, R. (Ed.) *Ideology and Social Science*, London, Fontana.

32 DORE, R. (1961) 'Function and Cause', *American Sociological Review* 26, pp. 843–53.

33 CARNOY, M. (1974) *Education as Cultural Imperialism*, London and New York, McKay.

34 KARIER, C. (1979) 'The Quest for Orderly Change', *History of Education Quarterly* 19. 2. pp. 159–78.

35 KATZ, M. *op. cit.*, pp. 147–50.

36 BLOCH, M. *op. cit.*, pp. 190–192.

37 VON WRIGHT, G. (1971) *Explanation and Understanding*, London, Routledge and Kegan Paul; GALLIE, W. (1964) *Philosophy and the Historical Understanding*, London, Chatto and Windus; LOUCH, A. (1969) 'History as Narrative', *History and Theory* 8, pp. 54–70.

38 HEXTER, J. (1972) *A History Primer*, London, Allen Lane, p. 118.

39 GIDDENS, A. (1979) *op. cit.*, pp. 7–8 and 113. A very similar point about the recursiveness of situations is made by CARR, E.H. *op. cit.*, p. 52. There is an intriguing discussion of the interplay of freedom and constraint in human action and in sociological theory in DAWE, A. (1978) 'Theories of Social Action', in BOTTOMORE, T. and NISBET, R. (Eds.), *A History of Sociological Analysis*, London, Heinemann.

40 MERTON, R. (1967) 'On Sociological Theories of the Middle Range', in his collected papers on *Theoretical Sociology*, Glencoe, Free Press, pp. 39–40.

41 FRITH, S. (1977) 'Socialisation and Rational Schooling: Elementary Education in Leeds before 1870', in McCANN, P. (Ed.) *op. cit.*, (Note 26) p. 88.

42 ROSEN, H. 'The Language of Text-Books', in CASHDAN, A. *et. al.* (1972) *Language in Education*, London, Routledge and Kegan Paul and Open University.

43 HEXTER, J. *op. cit.*, p. 270

44 SCHOOL OF BARBIANA (1970) *Letter to a Teacher*, Harmondsworth, Penguin, p. 62.

45 For example, WILLIS, P. (1977) *Learning to Labour*, Farnborough, Saxon House; CORRIGAN, P. (1979) *op. cit.*; WOODS, P. (1979) *The Divided School*, London, Routledge and Kegan Paul. There is an unusual contrast drawn between the ineffectiveness of nineteenth-century elementary schools and the effectiveness of the public schools as instruments of social control in MUSGROVE, F. (1979) *School and the Social Order*, London, Wiley.

46 BLOCH, M. *op. cit.*, p. 195. Bloch's analysis of the historian's craft was written as a prisoner following the collapse of the French army in 1940, and was left in mid-sentence when he died in the prison camp.

The Limits of Curricular Experience: An Analysis of Experience and Possibility[1]

P.W. Musgrave, Monash University

> ... a theory capable of interpreting educational change ... must take into account the existence of profound educational conflict without either assimilating the parties involved to conflicting social classes (Marxist tendency) or attributing to the values involved some order of ascendancy and subordination according to social needs (structural-functionalist tendency).
>
> M. Scotford-Archer and M. Vaughan.[2]

Introduction

During the last decade much analysis of education has been couched in the Marxist terminology of a capitalist ruling class trying to impose or maintain hegemony over the working class and of 'the correspondence' of the activities or the outcomes of the educational sector to the structures and processes of society in general or of the economy in particular. Theoretical disagreement has been rife and so far the detailed historical evidence adduced for such an account has not gone unchallenged.[3] Furthermore, the admission is sometimes made that the concept of hegemony is difficult to use in any closely defined way. In these cases, where the term is used in a weaker sense, the analysis tends to find a situation where members of the ruling class – although rarely succeeding, and then but briefly – constantly try to achieve a state of hegemony.[4] Such analyses may be more realistic, in their acknowledgement both of methodological problems and of the substantive difficulties for the ruling class in their efforts to solve recurring 'crises in hegemony',[5] but so far they have made no real attempt to explain the *educational* causes, if any, of their failure to gain lasting hegemony.

In this paper I propose to start from this failure and, because much recent thinking has focussed upon the curriculum, to examine as a case study certain historical evidence concerning the development of the school curriculum in England since about 1850, especially at the elementary level, in an attempt to answer two relevant important questions:

1. What limits were put during this period upon curricular freedom?
2. What general process seems to produce these limits?

Finally, I shall ask what implications this analysis has for theories of curricular development and, hence, perhaps, for the place of the concept of hegemony in such sociological thinking.

The English Curricular Experience

Beeby's Four Stages

My starting point is an *ex post facto* analysis by the New Zealander, C.E. Beeby, published in 1966 and based on his wide experience as an educational administrator in Micronesia. Beeby suggested that the educational systems of developing countries passed through four stages:

1. The Dame School Stage: ill-educated and untrained teachers taught an ill-defined curriculum in an unarticulated educational system.
2. The Stage of Formalism: teachers with some education and training taught a highly organised curriculum under close supervision, especially through examinations and inspection, using the 'one best method' and focussing upon the school class as a whole.
3. The Stage of Transition: teachers with secondary education and more training taught a less tightly specified curriculum under somewhat relaxed controls.
4. The Stage of Meaning: well-educated and highly trained teachers aimed to develop an understanding of the meaning of a very loosely specified curriculum, using materials and methods that matched individual needs, and without close external supervision.

This basically descriptive and, perhaps, Whiggish, framework has been used to order accounts of the historical development of the primary curriculum in Tasmania and of some aspects of teacher education in Australia. Furthermore, one small questionnaire study successfully used these same stages to compare administrators' perceptions of education in the mother country, Britain, and two industrialised former colonies, Australia and New Zealand, with a number of such newly independent, developing Pacific societies as Malaysia, Papua New Guinea and Western Samoa.[6] There would, therefore, seem to be some possible analytical leverage in ordering data relating to the history of the curriculum in England using these four stages but also, unlike Beeby, in asking questions about the course and directions of development, remembering that ultimately the aim is to try to explain the failure of the ruling class to achieve hegemony.

The English Evidence

Although the government began to devote public monies to elementary education through religious bodies from 1833 there was no direct public control of the curriculum until 1862. Prior to the 1830s many dame schools, often little more than child-minding establishments, existed but between 1840 and 1846 Kay-Shuttleworth initiated reforms that led to a supply of somewhat better educated and trained teachers. By 1856 one HMI rated eighty per cent of the schools that he inspected as 'fair', describing a 'fair' school in these terms:

> In the first class the children will be able to read a page of Natural History ... with tolerable fluency ... [and] answer collateral questions on this, not well, but not preposterously ill; ... have a general knowledge of the distribution and conventional divisions of land and water on the surface of the globe; ... work a sum in compound addition – two-thirds of them without a mistake; ... write a short account of any object named to them which they had seen or read about ... with trifling errors of grammar and of spelling.[7]

The teachers who taught this, on the whole formal, curriculum or the clergy responsible for them had, however, begun to be a little adventurous in some aspects of the curriculum so that in 'good schools' another HMI reported that 'physical Science, natural history, political economy and ... drawing' were taught. Indeed, the first major battle between those in schools and those in the central administration over curricular content, except in the field of Religious Instruction, occured in the 1850s about the teaching of Science. An attempt was made to base the Science curriculum on 'Common Things', a 'Science for the People', but opposition both from academics and from those with power at the centre prevented this development.[8]

By the late-1850s there was considerable disquiet amongst those in power, or those able to influence them, because they felt that the elementary schools, even though not catering well for all their pupils, were, nevertheless, too well-developed in their top classes. Comparison was made between a cheap or free elementary education (of some standard and worth) and the education coming to be called secondary (often poor and not very useful) for which the middle class had to pay. Because of such feelings the Newcastle Commission on Elementary Education was appointed; its Report (1861) recommended the adoption of a very formal control over the elementary curriculum. This was established through a system of inspection leading to payment of teachers by their results in teaching the Revised Code of 1862.

Pressure, particularly from the Inspectorate (then at odds over this matter with their political masters), but also from the teachers and their unions, now growing in power,[9] led to a gradual widening, after 1867, in the offerings earning grant under the Code. In the Code of 1871 a sentence concerning the teaching of Science, more particularly in relation to teaching through using natural objects, shows clearly that the move from the Stage of Formalism towards that of Meaning was beginning:

> Such plans would necessarily differ in town or country, and the suitability of each to the school in which it is to be adopted must be a matter of discretion.[10]

Discretion to vary materials, content and methods was beginning to be allowed to teachers.

In 1886, a Royal Commission (Cross) was appointed to inquire into the workings of the Elementary Education Acts. In their report, published in 1888, the Commissioners can be said to have considered that

> the Standards of examination in elementary subjects were too useful to be safely abandoned, but could be so modified as to permit greater freedom in classifying scholars . . .

The process of granting discretion to teachers, *but within bounds*, was continuing. Another recommendation in the same vein was that,

> while the introduction of a set of official text-books was not advisable, a more or less extended programme, showing the range of study intended to be covered by the Code, ought to be accessible to teachers and to managers.[11]

Many of the changes suggested by the Cross commissioners were embodied in the Code of 1890. 'Manual Instruction', for example, was allowed to count for 'attendance'; the pressures at work here will be seen below to be both economic and educational. In 1894, further encouragement was given to the teaching of 'Domestic Economy'. As was also true in the case of broadening the content of the 'Physical Exercises' allowable for grant, pressure came largely from those interested in the health and hygiene of the nation rather than from any idea of preparing boys and girls better for the work-force. Such forces, militarist and imperialist in aim, though usually couched in medical terms, were particuarly strong after the Boer War.[12]

The Code of 1895 marked the end of many of the remaining close controls introduced in 1862. For example,

> In this year begins the abolition of the annual examination in class subjects of schools for older scholars. This change represented a further step towards freedom and elasticity of schools for the teacher both in framing his curriculum and in carrying it out in detail.[13]

The curricular implications of the Education Act of 1902 were not great and, in the main, concerned the time-table for, and the provision for opting out of, Religious Education. Following this Act, there was a period of severe conflict between the Board of Education and some Local Education Authorities (LEAs) over this subject but, after the first world war, the system of locally agreed syllabuses, upon which the 1944 Education Act was so successfully built, developed. By this date, religion had become so much less important to most people that it was possible to make opting out of compulsory Religious Education more difficult.[14] More recently, there have been attempts in several LEAs to widen the agreed syllabus of compulsory Religious Education so that religions other than Christianity, and even such secular ideologies as humanism or Marxism, may be included. In effect, the religious and the political systems enshrined in the constitution could be seen to be under attack from the agreed syllabus of the one compulsory subject in the schools. Furthermore, the political ideology suggested for compulsory teaching was fundamentally critical of the ideology of the ruling class.

Reverting to the chronological account of the development of the Elementary Code, by 1911 the situation was that in some LEAs

> ... the question of curriculum [was seen] as a matter to be settled between the teacher on the one hand and the Inspector on the other. Others were inclined at first to require from their teachers adherence to syllabuses and time-tables made out in varying degrees of detail, but there is now a tendency to relax this stringency where it has been adopted.[15]

Variations existed and were more often coming to depend upon the initiative of the teacher. The quality of the changes can be judged by examining developments in individual subjects. In English, for example,

> where a few years (before) there would have been two lessons in Dictation to one in Composition, the proportion has been reversed.

Creativity was on its way in! In Science, and particularly in Geography, rote learning had diminished and local conditions around the school had started to influence the content of the curriculum. Furthermore, the belief of the Inspectorate was that

> one of the characteristic differences between the methods of to-day and those of a few years ago lies in the increased amount that is now left to the children to find out for themselves.

In both Geography and History there were available 'many more [text] books than there were a few years ago'.

All of these changes were summed up under two broad headings in the *Report of the Board, 1910–11*:

(i) The child's life in school is being brought into closer relation with his life out of school. [Inevitably] materials and experiences var[y] with the locality ... Hence follow[s] (a) the increasing difference between the schools in one area and those in another ... and (b) the growing divergence, after a certain stage, between the education of the boy and that of the girl.

(ii) ... the influence of the school is spreading more and more widely over the whole sphere of the child's interests and activities.[16]

We have only to consider these optimistic judgements of the, to us, illiberal Code of 1911 – more liberal though it undoubtedly was when compared with the Revised Code of 1862 – to understand how much more freedom teachers to-day have gained over the curriculum. What Beeby called the Stage of Meaning has presumably been approximated. One of the weaknesses of Beeby's account, useful as it can be in gaining analytical purchase on problems of curriculum development, is that he assumes the concept of 'Meaning' to have some absolute content though he does not define this. Beeby never asks: 'Meaning for what?' or 'Meaning in what context?'.

In this regard one instance referred to above assumes great importance. The attempt to teach a political ideology (Marxism), that was opposed to the established ideology, as part of the compulsory agreed course in Religious Education met with strong opposition in the city concerned from representatives on the local council elected to support the existing system. This incident forces us to ask: 'Can those in power in any society permit the curriculum, particularly that taught in state-provided schools, to become so wide in content that it can be seen to, be preparing future citizens to bring about the demise of the present social structure?'. Or to rephrase the question in the terms that Beeby uses: 'Which Meaning is to be transmitted in the curriculum?'.

Before trying to make any generalisations about the nature of the processes at work in the course of curricular development in any society some attention must be given to the nature of the demands for changes and the opposition to such demands.

The Process Analysed

In his inaugural lecture Dahrendorf was concerned to show the origins of material inequality in societies, but his analysis rested on the need for a hierarchy of power to preserve the norms by which any particular society was defined. Those who are seen to deviate from social norms, or to attempt so to do, will be checked. As Dahrendorf puts it:

> Society *means* that norms regulate human conduct; this regulation is guaranteed by the incentive or the threat of sanctions; the possibility of imposing sanctions is the abstract core of all power.[17]

The next step here, then, must be to examine instances of challenge to ruling curricular norms. Such challenges may bring about crises which, as Habermas notes, can be seen as objective indices of the 'unresolved steering problems'[18] of a society. Therefore, if one wants to unravel the causes of and limits to curricular development, an examination of curricular crises should be a worthwhile approach. Finally, in this section, the attempt will be made, based on the evidence so far presented, to outline a generalised account of curricular development from which can be adduced some notion, at least in theory, of the bounds of the freedom available in curricular choice.

Challenges

Here three challenges to curricular normality, that were reported in the previous section, will be considered. The main direction of the argument is that many of the influences that appear to be diverting the curricula, considered in this case study, towards the Stage of Meaning are not easily describable as economic, even interpreted in its indirect sense to include political elements.

The first challenge to normality, in the elementary school curriculum considered above, was in the field of Science and occurred before the introduction of the Revised Code. Demands for a 'Science of Common Things', which would more closely match the mind and motivation of the elementary school child, originated from an Anglican clergyman responsible for a school at King's Somborne in rural Hampshire. The logic of the Rev. Richard Dawes' case was supported by a number of eminent academics including, for example, John Henshaw, Regius Professor of Botany at Cambridge. Their challenge was defeated on two grounds. Other academics, largely under the influence of Huxley, had the power to define this version of science as contrary to ruling paradigms; the nature of physics, chemistry and botany were seen to be different from that of the suggested curriculum and support was given to a more traditional form of Science for schools, best described as a science of natural history. The other opposition case was grounded in an altogether different argument, also still heard to-day, that separate curricula, whether in Science or any subject, should not be socially divisive by reinforcing the identities of the different social classes.[19] Clearly, in the latter case, an argument about curricular change based on the political nature of capitalist society was influential but it only underpinned part of the total explanation of challenge and response and could also be applied to the situation of dominating and dominated groups in non-capitalist societies.

The second challenge to be considered relates to the introduction of hand work into the elementary school. In the years prior to the Cross Commission, considerable criticism had grown up that the elementary curriculum was becoming 'clerkly'. This tendency can probably be attributed to the contemporary feeling that such an education opened up valued avenues for social mobility and this was felt particularly strongly by teachers, that is, by those responsible for passing this curriculum on to pupils, who had also often themselves become upwardly mobile through this 'clerkly' learning. The Cross Commission took account of the demand for a more apt curriculum for future workers and circularised ten counties asking for views on manual instruction. Only between a quarter and a third of school managers and head teachers favoured its introduction; some teachers opposed it because the subject was seen as one for technical schools, whose curriculum was perforce closely tied to the economic structure. The Commissioners, however, recommended its introduction.[20] Yet the arguments used to support the content and methods eventually used in the schools were not dependent upon economic advantage, but upon the educational case made by those favouring various Scandinavian craft movements, for example, Sloyd.[21] Once again, the institutional bases of curricular challenge and response were more complex than often portrayed.

Lastly, and of great importance to the argument here, the case of Religious Instruction (later Education) also shows a very mixed pattern of institutional influences. Until the early years of the twentieth-century an explanation of the development of this subject in schools may be grounded largely in terms of, first, an aristocratic support for the established church which, secondly, yields to the assaults of the nonconformist middle *and* upper working classes. Yet, as the twentieth century advanced, the changing nature of Religious Education can be traced to the lessening salience of religion as a social institution, to the loosening paradigm of theology itself and to changes within the demographic structure, although the final challenge of converting compulsory Religious Education into, at least in part, compulsory Political Education was checked by conservative political groups.[22]

Crises

The development of Religious Education has been marked by a series of what may better be termed as crises, defined as Habermas uses this term, since *'social integration* [was] at stake'.[23] This way of viewing crises can be seen, in this context, to be an extension of Dahrendorf's concept of challenges to 'established norms'.

The introduction in 1862 of the Revised Code can be viewed as a definite response to what was seen as a crisis by those with power, largely still aristocratic in their nature, to bring the elementary school system and its curriculum back under their control. This form of schooling was to be for the lower classes and was to be minimal in content. The financial arrangements descending from Kay-Shuttleworth had permitted the uncontrolled growth of a form of education that seemed both fiscally, and educationally, inefficient and too wide in content to the rulers, the aspiring new middle classes and many of the civil servants who served these groups. Under these threatening circumstances, the growth was checked – as it had been a little earlier, in the case of the new Science curriculum, and as it was to be a hundred years later, in the case of the suggested innovations in Religious Education.

So far, mainly due to the method followed here of using successive Codes as data, the emphasis has been on the academic, not the moral, curriculum though, of course, this division is largely an analytical one. In recent times, however, many curricular crises seem to have arisen over the moral aspects of what is taught. Usually, certainly in Australia, such instances have involved a single teacher. One particular case of a secondary teacher in New South Wales who was accused by a parent of teaching 'unsuitable lessons' – in that the material he used related to sex – has been usefully analysed in sociological terms. New South Wales Education Department supported the criticism and suspended the teacher for five months whilst the matter was investigated, although ultimately the teacher was, in effect, found not guilty. The main concept used to organise the analysis of this incident was that of 'dangerous knowledge'. Such knowledge was dangerous because

> in blurring the conventional boundaries of his pedagogy, the teacher . . . dislocated the unwritten ideological consensus.[24]

Controls were successfully used by the State administration to exclude the dangerous knowledge, even though the teacher was eventually not formally disciplined.

Sometimes whole schools are seen as attempting to teach dangerous knowledge. The, by now, well known case of William Tyndale School is an example. In this primary school, a pedagogy, with its supporting organisation, was established whose aim was to transmit a certain set of moral values and behaviour, characterised, in particular, by great freedom and wide personal choice. Some parents, and others connected with the school, came to object so strongly that ultimately the LEA had to hold an official inquiry that resulted in the closure of the school.[25]

Though an argument might be mounted that this school was called to account not because it taught dangerous knowledge, but because it was inefficient, there seems no doubt that the crucial parts of the public debate were couched in terms of dangerous knowledge. Once again the moral curriculum of a school was seen to be dangerous and, in this case, a complex amalgam of those with power ultimately prevented its teaching.

The Process Itself

Once an educational system has developed beyond the Dame School Stage, teachers are trained to a level where they are able to begin to think for themselves, to question and to criticise. Like most intellectual workers they wish for autonomy. This implies that there is, within the educational system itself, a force at work that tends to encourage curricular change. Gouldner has noted that many significant social tensions derive from the conflict between the professional and the propertied fractions of the middle class.[26] Teachers, as intellectuals, do not always wish to exercise, in Gramsci's terms, 'the subaltern functions of social hegemony'.[27] There develops, therefore, within education itself great pressure towards conflict over what may be taught.

This force drives the curriculum towards, and is particularly pronounced in, what Beeby called the Stage of Meaning. Beeby appeared to assume that in this stage all would make choices that matched the liberal democratic regimes which he ideologically favoured. Yet not all teachers have seen this as a definition of meaning and, in addition, what some teachers have seen as a liberal and democratic curriculum has been defined by the general public, or by the powerful often on behalf of the general public, as dangerous knowledge. When a crisis ensues, agents of respectability respond by bringing power to bear to eliminate from the academic or moral curricula elements which they see as so dangerous that they are beyond the bounds of curricular tolerance. Such reactions may occur at the local level, as was the case at the William Tyndale School, or at the national level, as has perhaps been demonstrated by the recent discussion in the UK of a core curriculum. The process may work through adults or children; an example of the latter channel occurred when secondary pupils refused to co-operate in the Schools' Council Mathematics for the Majority Project, because they defined it as 'not proper maths'.[28] In brief, curricular innovation is as inevitable as is the occasional and limiting response by which it is defined to constitute dangerous knowledge.

Implications

Theoretical

Crisis in the curriculum may be a sign of some deeply seated societal crisis, but according to the analysis here, curricular crises are from time to time inevitable and are rooted in the schools themselves once a society has an educational system of a relatively well developed nature. Some teachers will challenge the established norms by trying to teach dangerous knowledge. Habermas has pointed out that

> improved schooling of cognitive capacities increases the probability that dissonances between proffered patterns of interpretation and perceived social reality will arise and intensify the problem of identity.[29]

It is to this social process, not to any explanation at the psychological level, to which one is appealing when one says that the educational system is marked by some tendency not to reproduce the social structure that set it up that is, not to ensure hegemony. The system has autonomy, though within certain limits; the boundaries of curricular respectability are patrolled by the powerful of various social institutions.

Furthermore, to analyse the relationships between education and other parts of the social structure in terms of a correspondence principle that focusses only on links to the economy, even when done in an extremely sophisticated manner,[30] overlooks both the complexities of the other social institutions interlocking with education and the autonomous influence of education itself. A subtle analysis of the comparative salience of various social institutions must be undertaken. Furthermore, if the focus in such an analysis is put upon challenges, responses and crises, any tendency to reify social institutions should be avoided. The direction of development in a society will be seen to depend ultimately upon those controlling its steering mechanism and this may be, for example, capitalist, socialist or, as we now once again realise, theocratic in nature, but those with power from the whole range of social institutions, and not just the economy, have here been shown to have a possible and even perhaps, from time to time, the ultimate influence upon decisions about what are acceptable curricular choices.

Practical

This theoretical position has wide implications for those wanting to make curricular changes. All in education must bear in mind that there is a socially determined range of tolerance, often not yet manifestly defined, within which curricular variation is permissible and outside of which innovators cannot trespass without some interested person or group feeling that contemporary social norms are threatened. Curricular freedom is not absolute but relative to the local and the national social structure. This very complex and, for those in the game, often extremely vexatious situation can only be described as political. In the terms used by Scotford-Archer and Vaughan, whose work was cited at the beginning of this paper, it will be marked not merely by 'domination' but by a fluid social reality born in the inevitable 'assertion' of teachers wanting to challenge contemporary curricular normality in very varied ways which are not always immediately perceived as challenges. Many humble, not practical, aspects of school curriculum can be analysed in such apparently abstract terms. As an example and in conclusion, I would cite a parent's comment on the teachers in a rural high school in Victoria:

We can't expect better dressing from kids until the teachers dress better. The meeting with staff we had last month only one teacher was in a dress. The rest were wearing blue jeans and one was wearing thongs.[31]

Notes and References

1 I wish to thank Professor R. J.W. Selleck (Monash University) and Doctor W. Taylor (University of London Institute of Education) for helpful comments on an earlier draft of this paper.

2 SCOTFORD-ARCHER, M. and VAUGHAN, M. (1971) 'Domination and Assertion in Educational Systems', in HOPPER, E. (Ed.) *Readings in the Theory of Educational Systems*, London, Hutchinson, p. 56.

3 See. for example, CARNOY, M. and LEVIN, H.M. (1976) *The Limits of Educational Reform*, New York, David MacKay; and BOWLES, S. and GINTIS, H. (1976). *Schooling in Capitalist America*, Routledge and Kegan Paul. For criticisms of the historical basis of such accounts see, for example, KAMENS, D.H. (1977) a review of Bowles and Gintis, *op. cit.*, in *American Educational Research Journal*, Vol. 14, No. 4, pp. 499–510; JOHNSON, R. (1976) in DALE, R. ESLAND, G. and MACDONALD, M. (Eds.), *Schooling and Capitalism*, London, Routledge and Kegan Paul, pp. 44–54. The following paper is also relevant: SANDERSON, M. (1972) 'Literacy and Social Mobility in the Industrial Revolution in England', in *Past and Present*, No. 56, pp. 131–154, and the subsequent exchange with LAUER, T. (1974) in *Past and Present*, No. 64, pp. 96–112.

4 See, for example, CLARKE, J. HALL, S. JEFFERSON, T. ROBERTS, B. (1976) 'Subcultures, Cultures and Class. A theoretical overview' in HALL, S. and JEFFERSON, T. (Eds.), *Resistance through Rituals*, London, Hutchinson, pp. 9–79 (espec. pp. 35–45).

5 HOARE, Q. and NOWELL SMITH, G. (1971) (Eds. and Trans.) *Selections from the Prison Notebooks of Antonio Gramsci*, London, Lawrence and Wishart, p. 210 and pp. 275–6.

6 BEEBY, C.E. (1966) *The Quality of Education in Developing Countries*, Harvard University Press; HUGHES, P.W. (1969) 'Changes in Primary Curriculum in Tasmania', in *Australian Journal of Education*, Vol. 13, No. 2, pp. 130–46; MUSGRAVE, P.W. 'After Freedom, Whither Teacher Education?' in MURRAY SMITH, S. (1976) (Ed.), *Melbourne Studies in Education*, Melbourne, Melbourne U.P., pp. 188–208; MUSGRAVE, P.W. (1974) 'Primary Schools, Teacher Training and Change: Beeby Reconsidered' in *Papua and New Guinea Journal of Education*, Vol. 10, No. 1, pp. 42–7.

7 *Report of the Board of Education*, 1910–11, British Sessional Papers, Vol. XXI, 1912–13, p. 5 (henceforth cited as *Report, 1910–11*).

8 LAYTON, D. (1973) *Science for the People*, London, George Allen and Unwin.

9 TROPP, A. (1957) *The School Teachers*, London, Heinemann.

10 *Report, 1910–11*, p. 9 (see Note 7).

11 *Ibid.*, pp. 14–5.

12 MUSGRAVE, P.W. (1977) 'Morality and the Medical Department: 1907–1974' in *British Journal of Educational Studies*, Vol. 25, No. 3, pp. 136–9.

13 *Report, 1910–11*, p. 18 (see Note 7).

14 CANNON, C. (1964) 'The influence of religion on educational policy since 1902' in *British Journal of Educational Studies*, Vol. 12, No. 2, pp. 143–60.

15 *Report*, 1910–11, pp. 22–3.

16 *Ibid.*, p. 40.

17 DAHRENDORF, R. (1968) 'On the Origin of Inequality among Men', in *Essays in the Theory of Society*, London, Routledge and Kegan Paul p. 173, (italics in original).

18 HABERMAS, J. (1976) *Legitimation Crisis*, London, Heinemann, p. 4.

19 LAYTON, D. *op. cit.*, passim.

20 *Royal Commission on the Working of the Elementary Education Act*, 1886–8, pp. 151–2.

21 MUSGRAVE, P.W. (1967) *Technical Change, the Labour Force and Education*, London, Pergamon, p. 93.

22 HULL, J.M. (1975) 'Agreed syllabuses, past present and future' in SMART, N. and HORDER, D. (Eds.), *New Movements in Religious Education*, London, Temple and Smith, pp 98–120

23 HABERMAS, J. *op. cit.*, p. 4.

24 JOHNSTON, K. (1978) 'Dangerous Knowledge: A Case Study in the Social Control of Knowledge', in *Australian and New Zealand Journal of Sociology*, Vol. 14, No. 2, p. 112.

25 GRETTON, J. and JACKSON, M. (1976) *William Tyndale*, London, George Allen and Unwin.
26 GOULDNER, A.W. (1976) *The Dialectics of Ideology and Technology*, New York, Seabury Press, p. 132.
27 HOARE, Q. and NOWELL SMITH, G. *op. cit.*, p. 12.
28 SPRADBERRY, J. 'Conservative Pupils? Pupils resistance to a curriculum innovation in mathematics', in WHITTY, G. and YOUNG, M. (Eds), *Explanations in the Politics of School Knowledge*, Driffield Nafferton Press pp. 236–243.
29 HABERMAS, J. *op. cit.*, p. 91.
30 For examples see the papers in CARNOY, M. and LEVIN, H.M. (Eds.), *op. cit.*
31 FITZGERALD, R.T., MUSGRAVE, P.W. and PETTIT, D.W. (1976) *Participation in Schools?*, Australian Council for Educational Research, p. 63.

Contradiction and Change in Educational Practices

Janet Strivens, University of Liverpool

This paper will bring together a number of issues which have concerned me in recent years, the most immediate being the present role of sociologists working in departments and colleges of education. This role is discussed in the light of the current challenge to certain areas of social science in institutions of higher education, and a reassessment of the status of social science theory in vocational training. It is argued that sociologists who work with practitioners must be more prepared to take the problems that practitioners face and involve themselves in the development of strategies. In considering the implications of such a shift in role, it is suggested that certain aspects of schooling would repay more attention than they have hitherto received from sociologists. More research is needed into differences that exist in educational practice, their location in the processes of schooling and their effects. However, it is stressed that the teaching role of sociologists is at least as important as their research role and the paper ends with a brief discussion of the problems and possibilities of working with both student and experienced teachers, bringing sociological perspectives to bear on the problems they face in schools and classrooms.

There has been a recent trend in teacher education to reassess the role of theory in vocational training.[1] The essential challenge is to the traditional status of the social sciences; questions are being raised about the relevance of theoretical studies in the social sciences on courses where time is strictly limited and the first priority should be the acquisition of practice skills. To quote the recent UCET document on the PGCE course:[2]

> ... it is now recognised that if educational theory, in any of its branches, is to influence teaching activities in schools, it must be directly related to those activities ... It is therefore important ... that within the course itself the educational theory included be put to work by students in the analysis of practice and the making of practical judgements.

It may be noted in passing that a similar trend towards 'the erosion of the theory-methods distinction' is also discernible in social work training; the CCETSW consultative document on the teaching of social work in courses leading to the

CQSW comments on 'a shift away from a traditional pattern of discrete subject contributions' with guarded approval and suggests that social work may now need to disentangle itself from sociology.[3]

It would be easy to dismiss this challenge as a reflection of political trends in the wider society, which combine a naïve technological approach to education with the slogans of accountability and the prime importance of the needs of industry. It could thus be seen as part of a broader attack on the social sciences within the academic world, reflected in such political decisions as the allocation of resources to different research councils and to specific areas of research.[4] Recent perspectives within the sociology of education whose analyses of the educational system are fundamentally critiques of the prevailing economic and political systems render this discipline peculiarly open to attack.

There is however a further challenge from within; the students themselves, faced with the immediate problems of surviving their teaching practice and probationary year, are increasingly vocal about what they see as their needs. Contemplating a job in a field where the sheer strain of maintaining control is apparently draining the energies of the most experienced teachers, their dismissal of anything in their training that does not appear to tell them what to do, or at least give them some guidance on strategies, is at the least understandable. This attitude is likely to be reinforced, as they take up their first jobs, by teachers whose contempt for 'college learning' is apocryphal and whose first advice to students may well be to forget all they have been told. Generally, then, students learn to teach from those who do it in schools and, thus, reproduce the conservatism inherent in practice.

Sociologists might well argue in reply that it is not their brief to tell teachers what to do. Their role is to provide an account of the system as it operates which might help students understand some of the conflicts, constraints or opportunities they encounter. The student will then, as teacher, be equipped to offer 'an informed commentary on, and critique of, current policies and practice'.[5] This, at least, would be the attitude of sociologists who recognise some commitment to the preparation of teachers for practice. Others, particularly those fortunate enough not to be directly involved in training courses, may well show less concern to justify their activities with reference to the effect of sociological analyses on practice.

It is understandable that sociologists should show such reluctance towards, and suspicion of, what may appear as a call to relevance. The welcome given in the early seventies to the 'new' sociology of education, with its insistence on the necessity for sociologists to 'make' their problems rather than 'taking' them from educators and policy-makers[6] was in part a reaction to the failure of the sixties optimism that sociologists and policy-makers together could bring about a new era of equality.[7] More recently, the currency gained by certain kinds of marxist analysis which demonstrate the tight links between the education system, the state and capitalist society have tended to foster the attitude that any changes in the education system are politically unimportant: '... they *only* represent changes in the tactics of the state and therefore of the ruling class in its form of ideological domination'.[8] Short-term strategies are thus counter-productive.

On the other hand some sociologists, whilst acknowledging the dangers of 'reformism', have argued for the importance of relating their analyses to 'the problem of "Monday morning"'.[9] Corrigan, for example, states that:

> ... it is imperative that sociologists not only relate their findings to the political world around them, but also try and take their problems from the day-to-day political world.[10]

This is *not* simply to take the problems as defined by those in power in the state but nor is it to withdraw into an academic kabal which refuses to dirty its hands with the problems of practitioners. Willis supports the same view with reference to theoretical arguments for the relative autonomy of the cultural from structural determinants, and his argument will be examined in more detail below.

The position taken in this paper is that the development of strategies of direct relevance to teachers in the field should constitute a central problem for sociologists in the field of education; in particular, to those teachers who would be prepared to accept many aspects of the accounts currently on offer of the intimate nature of the relationship between the educational, economic and political systems but whose problem is then to discover how these accounts may best inform and direct their practice. In the next part of this paper I will offer some suggestions for the direction of attention to areas where the contradictions within the present educational system seem to me particularly acute. The discussion makes two claims which will be taken separately: the first is that *differences* already exist in current educational practice which deserve more careful analysis than they have received hitherto; the second is that the crucial location of these differences is in the *form of social relations* between teachers and pupils. Some illustration is offered from my own recent research in comprehensive schools of the kind of effects which even minor difference in emphasis within a school's policy and practice concerning social relations might have on the experience and consciousness of teachers and pupils.

School Differences

The claim that differences exist in educational practice which have not received sufficient attention from sociologists requires some clarification. There has been a longstanding tendency among both British and American academics to accept the view that differences between schools make little or no difference to their pupils' chances in later life (excluding the private sector of course) in comparison with the overwhelming effects of influences external to the school; depending on one's perspective, these might be family, social or inherited factors. (Probably the most influential study has been that of Christopher Jencks[11] based on the *Coleman report* of 1966, *Equality of Educational Opportunity*.) This attitude has existed, in all sections of the educational establishment, alongside a recognition of the contradictions which clearly exist in educational aims and values, most noticeably in the debate about so-called 'traditional' and 'progressive' approaches in education. It is not difficult to understand why there should be such a willingness on the part of many groups, who otherwise differ widely in their social and political values, to accept research which indicates that aims and values in education apparently make little difference in practice. Such beliefs lend support to the 'British' tradition of a mixed economy in the education system and a 'healthy' heterogeneity of practice; they are acceptable to teachers' unions in that they support the autonomy of teachers, and especially heads, to do what they think best in their own schools, while absolving them from responsibility if things don't seem to go too well; they allow teacher trainers to see their role as helping the student develop whatever style and methods of teaching she or he is most comfortable with.

Those unwilling to accept this majority verdict on the relative insignificance of differences between schools are likely to argue that the variables used in such large scale studies as that of Jencks are necessarily external and concrete; while it is relatively easy to make comparisons on the basis of resources and teacher-pupil ratios, the important differences lie in attitudes and values held by teachers which influence their classroom practice. Thus, the Bennett report[12] largely assumes a correspondence between teachers' educational philosophies, whether 'traditional' or progressive, and their 'teaching style' and claims that these lead to different educational outcomes, as assessed by levels of attainment achieved by pupils under different regimes.

Bennett's report brought howls of protest from many quarters, most notably the 'progressives'[13] claiming that the educational objectives which *they* pursued were not reduceable to standardised achievement tests, and that to attempt to assess pupil progress under a progressive teaching regime in this way showed a fundamental misconception of the values of progressivism in education. However, the claims of the progressives were simultaneously being undermined in a much more serious way with the publication of a number of detailed studies, of teachers and pupils, which shared some common features in their attempts to locate the everyday experience of teachers and pupils (their actions and the accounts they give) within the wider political and economic structures of society. In the field of primary education, Sharp and Green's study *Education and Social Control* is centred around the constructs and values of teachers, and teachers who largely subscribe to a liberal-progressive ideology. By relating the statements and interpretations of teachers to a careful observation of their actual practice in the classrooms, Sharp and Green claim to show the crucial paradox of liberal ideology; that commitment to such an ideology not only fails to affect the differential outcomes of the pupils' educational experience but may actually obscure the operation of the process of differentiation. As they comment, this is because of

> the structural underpinning and determination of the teachers' practice . . . , although they appear to be satisfying their own ideological commitments, they are unconsciously accommodating to a situation which renders it impossible to realise their commitments.[14]

Constraints on the teachers' practice beyond and within the classroom make it impossible to operationalise the child-centred ideology, as the teachers understand it, yet child-centred practice masks this reality more effectively than the less subtle modes of differentiation of the traditional approach.

The studies by Willis and Corrigan concentrate on the experience of (male, white) pupils, with relatively little attention to the teachers' perspective. Corrigan intended to select pupils whose educational experience differed; the two schools he used appeared, superficially, to be very different but, he claims, the boys experienced both schools in exactly the same way. Unfortunately, too little information is given on the schools to evaluate this important claim. However, he is concerned with the possibilities: he suggests that 'given the nature of contradictions within the present educational system it *is* possible to teach in a slightly more humane way, to reach the pupils with a different view of the world',[15] though he goes on to stress the importance of teachers understanding their political position and not remaining in isolation from their necessary allies.

The analysis of contradiction is a central theme of Willis' study. Using the concept of 'partial penetration' he shows how the counter-school culture develops, in opposition to the official ideology of the school, a far more realistic, though crucially limited, understanding of the functioning of society outside school which, paradoxically, leads the 'lads' to an apparently free choice to enter the exploitative and oppressive world of manual labour. Since the focus of the study is the lads' experiences and understanding, the analysis of the school experience is relatively brief but it does make an important claim, illustrated by comments from teachers themselves, for the existence of a basic teaching paradigm, which is 'massively dominant' in our schools: knowledge held by teachers is exchanged for control, the submission of pupils to their authority. Thus the teacher's authority is legitimated morally, not through direct coercion. This paradigm can be maintained when the teachers' knowledge can be seen as related to qualifications, and these are seen as necessary to secure a desirable career. For the 'lads', however, there is increasingly a different interpretation and valuation which undermines the basic paradigm. Insofar as this basic paradigm holds in all schools, 'progressive' methods merely prolong and spread the development of the oppositional culture:

> Progressivism as it is usually practised can be seen as a continuation of traditionalism in the sense that it attempts to preserve a version of the consent which has always been at the heart of the older method.[16]

In the face of this consensus among researchers using very different methodologies and starting from very different assumptions about the nature of education and society, a few voices have persisted in arguing that differences between schools *are* important and deserving of more attention, although the ways in which, and reasons why, they differ are sometimes far from clear. Powers' report on delinquency rates among juveniles in Tower Hamlets in the 1960s made a strong claim for the role played by schools in 'protecting children from the risk of delinquency'.[17] (Unfortunately it also highlighted the special problems of confidentiality in such research and probably increased for a time the difficulties experienced by other researchers who considered these findings important and needed access to schools to explore them further). Recently the work of Reynolds in South Wales and that of the Rutter team in London have provided further evidence of the value of studying schools as a major area of influence.[18] *Fifteen Thousand Hours* includes a range of measures of both school process and outcomes and claims that differences between the schools in outcomes are systematically and stably associated with characteristics of the schools as 'social institutions', a concept operationalised as the combined measure of school process variables. They support the value of thinking of schools in terms of a school 'ethos', pointing to an analogy with studies of other relatively self-contained organisations showing how they tend to develop their own culture or set of institutionalised meanings.

The Rutter study has already attracted much comment and criticism,[19] not the least for its lack of a theoretical analysis of the role of schooling in society. Whatever its strengths and weaknesses, however, it clearly does not attempt to provide accounts or analyses of the *culture* of the school studied. The section on school processes includes measures of academic emphasis, teacher actions in lessons, rewards and punishments, pupil conditions, children's responsibilities, stability of teaching and friendship groups and staff organisation. Although interesting patterns of association emerge, the methodology adopted by the team cannot provide a means of understanding the experience of the school for its staff and pupils.[20]

A consideration of the claims and methods of the Rutter study in comparison to, say, those of Willis' study, highlight an increasingly acute research problem within the sociology of education, of the relation of the cultural to the structural analysis.[21] It presents itself as both a theoretical and a methodological problem. The theoretical problem of the relation of the cultural level to economic and political structures, as presented by Willis among others, has been referred to above. The methodological problem which runs throughout educational research is partly a question of the appropriate use of ethnographic accounts and participant observation techniques. Before discussing my own attempts to approach these problems, I want to clarify the terms of my second claim for the form of social relations in the school as the crucial location of school differences.

Social relations in the school

Probably the most influential attempt to make a theoretical link between different forms of culture and economic and political divisions in society has been Bernstein's writings, both in sociolinguistics and the sociology of education. Developing out of the controversial early work on sociolinguistic codes is an attempt to locate a crucial dimension of differentiation, the awareness of constraining and limiting effects of social conditions, in an individual's experience of social relations within the family and community. The clearest discussion of the central problems his work addresses is contained in 'Social class, language and socialisation'.[22] He states it thus:

> If we grant the fundamental linkage of symbolic systems, social structure and the shaping of experience it is still unclear *how* such shaping takes place. The *processes* underlying the social structuring of experience are not explicit.

The second difficulty is in dealing with the question of change of symbolic system.

It is clear from his argument that the use of the elaborated code is much more than a set of superficial linguistic habits. It is, crucially, the use of reflexive cognition arising out of the need to communicate particular meanings in the context of inter-personal relationships where meanings are not clearly socially defined. Its use allows the possibility of access to the grounds of one's socialisation; allows the individual to break through a sense of the inevitability of a given social arrangement to a sense 'that the world is permeable'.

Bernstein originally contended that the elaborated code was the form of language use found in schools, which created problems for the child whose experience of more bounded and delineated inter-personal relations had developed in him or her the tendency to a different kind of language use. The child who can manage the social role of pupil in relation to teacher is also likely to be able to engage in particular uses of language. She/he could, for example, know how to challenge a teacher's authority, both in disciplinary and academic matters, and have the challenge accepted. The critical examination of information, the asking of 'why' questions, the assertion of the right to be heard and to have one's views taken into consideration (and knowledge of how to do this in an *acceptable* way) are all forms of activity associated with the experience of certain forms of social relations and realised in the selection of certain linguistic forms.

Among many critics of Bernstein's work, Cooper's interesting study of language use in classrooms[23] suggested that it was highly misleading to associate the use of the elaborated code with requirements of the teacher/pupil roles. He demonstrated convincingly that the ordinary language of teachers in schools is much closer to restricted code use. This seems to me to make an important point that elaborated code use is highly unlikely to be learned in the average school because most schools do not offer the experience of the type of relationship through which such skills are developed.

This focus on the nature of the teacher/pupil relationship forms the link with Bernstein's concept of the 'framing' of educational knowledge. Almost alone among sociologists currently offering critiques of curriculum theory, he is con-cerned not merely with the classification of knowledge but the form of its transmis-sion:

> Frame refers to the specific pedagogical relationship of teacher and taught ... the strength of the boundary between what may be transmitted and what may not be transmitted, in the pedagogical relationship ... Frame refers us to the range of options available to teacher and taught in the *control* of what is transmitted and received ...[24]

A more detailed and grounded explication of the links between social control and access to knowledge may be found in the work of Douglas Barnes.[25] His argument, most fully developed in *From Communication to Curriculum* is that the style of discourse, the personal and linguistic interaction, that exists between teacher and pupil fundamentally influences the learning process. For valid learning to take place, the learner must develop experience of formulating the problem. She or he should come to regard the teacher as a resource, someone who may well possess useful information and may suggest fruitful lines of thought. But understanding comes from applying information in a flexible way to new situations and problems, testing its limits, and the learner must become aware of those limits herself. Because of this, Barnes advocates the increased use of small groups and peergroup learning as it facilitates the kind of exploratory, sometimes tentative, cognitive activity implied by this model of the process of understanding. The power differential which almost inevitably exists between teacher and pupil impedes this process by the extent to which it prompts a pupil to offer 'correct' answers in a finished form. Some examples provided by the team which worked on the 'Writing across the Curriculum' project provide the clearest illustration of the operation of such peergroup learning.[26]

What is the relevance of this work to current concerns in the sociology of education? The problems it explores are at the heart of the muddled debate on progressivism. We are constantly informed of the contradictions which exist in liberal-democratic ideology, showing nowhere more acutely than in related educational philosophies. Yet the critiques offered have generally been partial, directed at a particular aspect. While researchers may be justified in claiming that teachers hold sociologically naive and individualistic conceptions about the educational process, they generally do not seem to be making this claim from the basis of a real understanding of the ideas and thinking behind different approaches to teaching and learning. Barnes' work, through its sensitivity to the politics of communication, and its ability to demonstrate through careful analysis of teacher and pupil talk a different quality of learning in different social environments, provides a gloss on the notion of different pedagogies. In Barnes' accounts of classrooms, we can see in practice a different 'framing' of educational knowledge.

A serious problem, faced by those who might endorse in principle the concept of education proposed by Barnes, is the lack of clear empirical support for the effect of different pedagogies on educational outcomes. There are obvious practical problems, as in any research which is concerned with the effects of particular experiences over a period of time. But a more fundamental problem is the lack of an adequate conceptualisation of educational outcomes which might relate to different processes in the schools. There appears to be a gap in educational thinking precisely in that area where contradictions in values and assumptions most clearly reveal themselves. I will return to this point later, after a discussion of some of the problems of research into school differences arising from my own work.

Problems of research into school differences

It has been claimed above that a weakness of the Rutter team's study is its inability (partly as a result of the methodology adopted) to offer a cultural account of the schools they worked with. In what sense can a school be regarded as possessing a culture? To use the term is to assume that most institutions, even where membership is fluid, offer a degree of common experience which generates a taken-for-granted set of meanings shared by participants. Recent trends in classroom research,[27] sometimes explicitly identifying an 'anthropological' approach, have stressed the importance of the 'negotiated order' in the understanding of institutional life. While this is a necessary corrective to some of the naïveties of organisational approaches, and a warning to the researcher, the case may occasionally have been overstated. Systems of meaning within institutions are, typically, *not* totally implicit; new members are not born into the culture but join it as articulate beings who are accustomed to communicate meanings verbally, and may be given to formulating ideas which make sense of their individual practice and experience. In other words, the statements which members of institutions make about their actions and those of other members (including the giving of reasons in terms of principles and values) constitute a form of evidence for the meaning system of that institution. This is *not* saying that the culture of a school is accessible to the researcher through the verbal statements of its members, merely that in the 'artificial' culture of an institution there is more likely to be a recognisable relation between verbal constructions of reality and observable practice.

This is more than a methodological point. It implies, first, that institutions may vary in the strength on their institutional 'ethos', or the degree to which members experience the institution in a similar way. The degree of congruity in different members' accounts of institutional events might be an indication of this. Second, the genesis of a shared system of meanings may be partially explicable in terms of the explicitly held aims and policies of some of its members. Third, institutions have different forms of power relations; a 'shared' system of meanings in a strongly hierarchical institution may depend on the extent to which the head can enforce his authority against oppositional tendencies. It is important therefore not to make generalisations about 'schools' but to leave open the question of the explicitness and coherence of values and assumptions within any one institution. The possibility would seem to exist, however, of a school developing and possessing a 'microculture' with some limited degree of autonomy. Such a view would make sense of a number of isolated cases of experiments in alternative forms of education; these include small ventures existing precariously on the edge of the system; schools within the system which have been torn apart in conflicts between staff, parents and the LEA, and others which may have achieved a limited success if only because of committed people with power within local authorities and the chance to select a staff in basic agreement about principles.[28] The existence, and very often rapid demise, of such attempts are important in highlighting the nature of the constraints, the potentialities and limitations for present action. It is worth noting that such attempts have rarely involved individuals, more often groups or whole institutions. It is hard to conceive of an individual teacher, particularly at secondary level, establishing a mode of teaching and relating to pupils which was opposed to the dominant expectations within the school. Yet sociological analyses which have not focussed on the macro-system have tended to plunge to the level of individual classrooms.

If the notion of an institutional culture based on common experience generating shared assumptions is allowed, then insofar as experiences are *not* common, the values and assumptions of different groups will reflect this. Wide disparities in power of different groups within the institution, leading to very different ways of experiencing the institution, create discontinuities in members' interpretations and may foster the development of alternative shared accounts (which as Willis shows may owe a great deal to cultural experiences outside the bounds of the institution).

Interesting studies do, of course, exist of the differential experience of different groups inside schools.[29] But these are predominantly case-studies, and the limitation of case-study methodology is that it cannot show how variations in the power structures in schools interact with different sets of values and assumptions engendering different forms and patterns of social relations. On the other hand, comparative studies of institutions, which attempt to include the cultural level in the analysis, face highly intractable research problems. In illustrating some of these problems from my own experience I do not intend to offer solutions, rather to suggest strategies for further discussion.

The three schools I studied are purpose-built comprehensives built in three successive years by the same local authority to serve a large area of resettlement on the outskirts of a large city. The majority of housing has been built in the last fifteen years and families transferred from inner-city clearance areas. The catchment areas of the schools are geographically allocated with almost no parental choice; thus, at the outset, some of the problems faced, for example, by the Rutter team – of considering the effects of very different catchments and parental choice – are minimised, if not avoided. The schools are also very similar in their physical environment and material resources. Since it was an absolute practical necessity to focus my observations and the gathering of information on certain aspects of the schools, I felt that the decisions should be guided by the theoretical interest in the manifestations of contradiction. (These were far from *a priori* decisions; the best way of describing the process is that where a hunch that a particular area would be interesting could be made sense of in these terms, it was followed up). I will limit the discussion here to three areas; the choice of options in the Upper School, decision-making and communication among staff, and teacher-pupil relations.[30]

A superficial pattern of internal differentiation is apparent in most secondary schools in subject and 'ability' groupings. These become particularly apparent in the fourth and fifth years – the 'Upper School' in many comprehensives. The criteria which a school uses to allocate pupils to options are often highly contradictory to an extent that few staff can be completely unaware of. The most widely recognised is perhaps the problem of the 'disruptive' pupil whose low achievement is regarded as a reflection of his or her attitude rather than ability, grouped together with the low-ability child whose positive attitude may well be adversely influenced. A related problem may be what to do with those pupils from remedial (or 'progress') groups in the Lower School. None of the schools I studied explicitly provided remedial teaching in the Upper School. There was thus a conflict between the desire to be fair and allow all pupils a free choice of subjects and the unwillingness of some staff in the more 'academic' subjects to be burdened with non-examination pupils in this crucial two years before external examinations. Nor was this simply a problem for academic subjects. The limited technical and vocational resources of the schools were invariably over-subscribed and raised questions about the type of pupil they were aimed at.

Ideally one would like to observe the process of allocation at the end of the third year, in pupils' interviews with the relevant staff. I was only able to observe some curriculum meetings in each school, look at the option lists available together with comments from staff responsible for drawing them up, and discuss with fourth year pupils their memories of this process from the previous year and their present views on the curriculum they had ended up with.[31]

School A had a core of English, mathematics and one period of careers and liberal studies. The liberal studies was generally a mass lecture or film, one means of releasing staff time for small groups, whether 'O' level or remedial work. The school prided itself on not limiting the pupils' choices with option lists, but giving a free choice and arriving at a timetable with the best possible 'fit'. Pupils in the top groups expressed themselves as generally happy with the outcome. A different view arose from pupils in the 'Community Studies' option, who maintained they hadn't known what it was, hadn't wanted to do it but had been told that there was no space left in the courses they had chosen. It made sense to regard this option as a partial solution to the second problem above: although in principle it could lead to two CSEs, being a double 'option' with a double allocation of time, nobody seemed to entertain serious academic aspirations for it. It had a reputation in the school as a 'bad' course, though it was not clear whether this was a response to the teachers running it or the type of children it catered for. The two senior teachers involved complained that the course was under-resourced and nobody showed interest in it. My observations confirmed a lack of purpose and the expectation of discipline problems; although the course had extra staff these appeared to be used for patrolling the class rather than small group teaching.

The school was considering the introduction of City and Guilds Foundation courses, to increase motivation among older pupils by their clear vocational orientation. This innovation would increase the school's problem of allocating pupils to suitable courses; more 'technical' courses like typing and car maintenance were already unavailable to the pupils in lowest category of ability (or grouped with this category for other reasons), much to their disgust. The City and Guilds course was certainly not aimed at this category, but neither did staff want to see their most able pupils attracted away from traditional academic subjects.

There appeared to be profound differences in the policy and decision-making structures of the three schools. In School A power was highly centralised, with a group of senior teachers in close accord with the views and policies of the head; he, in turn, stressed the importance of delegating responsibility once a job has been given to a person – 'that's what they're paid for'. During my time there, a deputy head was being appointed; against a strong field the post was filled, in line with general expectation, by a female senior teacher already at the school. In a previous interview, discussing her pastoral role with senior girls, she had expressed her approval of the head's policies, particularly his willingness to 'delegate' to those in positions of responsibility. In fact, the hierarchy, as it was referred to by other teachers, presented a united front in support of the head's policies. In conversation with a senior teacher, I mentioned a senior appointment at another of the schools who appeared to adopt a role in deliberate contrast with the head's philosophy; his immediate comment was that such behaviour would not be tolerated at School A.

Teachers' unions were weak in the school; for example, problems over lunchtime supervision (at the forefront of people's minds since this was the winter of 1978/9) did not arise, as it was made clear to new teachers on arrival that more duties were expected of them than at other schools, to maintain high standards of discipline. Many mutterings in the staffroom concerned the amount of break and lunchtime supervision, but even junior staff were heard to agree that it was necessary really, to prevent a breakdown of discipline. Some time after I left, I heard that two of the senior teachers had resigned from the union in a dispute between the head's policy and the union's, thus further weakening its position.

I attended as many curriculum meetings as possible in all three schools. They frequently offered a revealing means of comparing statements of aims and values expressed by heads and senior staff, either in interviews or in the pages of the Staff Handbook or school prospectus for parents, with factors actually taken into consideration in allocating crucial resources like teaching time, in deciding on size of groups and on criteria for selection and allocation of pupils to different groups.

Curriculum meetings in School A were called regularly by the Director of Studies, attended by heads of departments, senior staff and head. These were well-run, with the issue to be discussed made clear in advance. In these the head would occasionally be called on to justify his allocation of resources, which he would do. In interview, the head emphasised that this was a difficult school in a Social Priority Area; it was made clear to new staff that problems in classroom management were likely to occur and they should not blame themselves nor hesitate to seek help from senior staff. He stressed the importance above all of stability and security for these children. Comments, made by several teachers on different occasions, on the children's backgrounds and the problems to be expected appeared congruent with the head's view, and I did not come across a counter-perspective.[32]

School B had adopted the more explicit policy of restricting choice of subjects for pupils of lower ability, in order to devote more time to basics. Unlike the other two schools which preserved mixed-ability tutor-groups in the Upper School, School B's policy meant that three clear bands existed; the top quarter with five options in addition to a core, the middle half with four options and the lower quarter with three. It became clear in the curriculum meetings I observed that a major obstacle in the way of changing this arrangement (which many staff felt uncomfortable about) was the position taken by several of the staff in 'academic' departments that their subject was 'unsuitable' for the lower ability child. This threw an extra burden on maths and English staff which was resented. It was also resented by many of the pupils in the lowest and middle bands, who saw the restricted choice as an injustice.

This was not an institution, however, which appeared capable of decisive change. The comparison of it by a senior member of staff to an iceberg, drifting around with the majority submerged out of vision of those on top, made much sense of the decision-making and power structure of the school. There was no clear and coherent policy, but always the possibility that a good idea would be vetoed from above; hence there was little encouragement for teachers to put effort into curriculum innovation or improved relations with the pupils. On the other hand, individual teachers had considerable freedom to develop their own styles and ideas. No clear official ideology existed which blamed the pupils for the behaviour problems of the school; the negative side of this was that even senior teachers seemed to feel that it would be to their discredit if they admitted problems, and no support from the top could be expected. Consequently morale was low, particularly among those teachers who did have disciplinary problems. A number of comments from staff on the past history of the school presented the picture of a 'weak' head who had originally been influenced by some quite progressive ideas (possibly supported by a deputy who had since left) about the aims of comprehensive schooling. He had been committed to the idea of mixed ability teaching and pupil participation, introduced social studies as a compulsory part of the Upper School curriculum and had welcomed an attempt at one time to introduce the Humanities Curriculum Project. However when things began to backfire he withdrew his support without instituting a definitely different direction. This combined account from different teachers made sense of some of the more contradictory aspects of the school.

A major theme of pupils' comments on the school, from groups across the ability range, was unease at the lack of discipline in class (blamed by one group on 'too young teachers'). While pupils in all three schools included some reference to the teacher's ability to keep control in their assessment of good teachers, it was most noticeable in this school. But the other side of this slack authority seemed to be an awareness among the pupils that teachers were human too, and a willingness to accept that some could be trustworthy, patient and sympathetic. Curriculum meetings, called by one of the deputies and open to all interested staff, contrasted sharply with School A. Few attended, but those who did were concerned about the school and its pupils. As individuals, however, with no consensus on policy, there seemed little they could do against the force of the *status quo*.

In the third school, School C, the core of the Upper School curriculum included an afternoon a week for Community Education. The head's belief in the importance of this appeared to relate to previous experience in a community school and was underlined by two key appointments, a deputy head with special responsibility for C.E. and a youth tutor who acted as a link between school work and the school-based evening youth club in the Youth Wing. The emphasis in the Community Education course was on an understanding of the genesis of problems and provision of services in the local community, and a placement for one afternoon a week during one term in some local institution was the crucial, and for obvious reasons also the most problematic, aspect of the course. Some of the top ability pupils expressed reservations about the usefulness of the experience, although it appeared to be popular further down the ability range. It became apparent that part of the dissatisfaction of the most able students was the restricted number of subjects which they could take in addition to the core, which effectively prevented, for example, an aspiring medical student from taking three sciences at 'O' level.

This problem should be understood in terms of the head's philosophy. He made it clear to staff through written statements and discussions, that he believed that the priority for the school was to establish good relationships between staff and pupils. This implied such behaviour on the part of teachers as talking reasonably to pupils and attempting to justify instructions when challenged rather than merely asserting authority. Confrontations were not sought out. No uniform was enforced, a fact much appreciated by the girls in particular (though it may seem a trivial issue, the refusal of schools to allow girls to wear trousers, and all pupils to wear jeans, is a recurrent cause of complaint and resentment. What 'school council' agenda would be complete without this issue being raised?) While staff were generally agreed that this policy had created an atmosphere of co-operation and friendliness in the school, several felt that relationships had been emphasised at the expense of academic standards, to the detriment of the brighter students. While I was in contact with the school, the policy on options in the Upper School was changed to increase the number of subjects which could be taken, and it was accepted that expectations of academic performance should be raised. Over a period, the feeling grew that it had been unwise to assume that, good relationships having been established, these could now be left to take care of themselves. Behaviour problems were increasing and teachers were less sure of the strategies they should be adopting.

This account is derived largely from observation at a general staff meeting, supplemented by comments from individual teachers. The striking aspect of this school was the relative openness of the power structure within the school which allowed freedom of discussion and the opportunity of making more explicit the assumptions underlying general policy decisions. Teachers at School C held a strong expectation that they should be kept informed of all policy-making, and that criticisms they had of any aspect of the system might be made public; when decisions appeared to have been taken in a high-handed way by senior staff, and not communicated to other members of their departments, teachers felt entitled to complain.

To substantiate the school's claim to have established good relationships between staff and pupils, or indeed to make any comparisons of this aspect of school life across institutions, presents a difficult research problem. Whereas observations of interactions between teachers and pupils provided many examples which supported the interpretation that the power differential between pupils and teachers at School C was not so extreme as in School A, and that this was a function of the school's policy rather than a breakdown of control as at School B, this could not be asserted with any validity without a much longer period in each school and in more class-rooms with a greater range of teachers than I found possible. However, some interesting corroboration of the effect of different forms of relationship in the different schools came in comments from outside agencies which had dealings with all schools; for example, the comment of a careers officer that 'at C . . . , the kids interview *you* about their jobs'.

These brief examples of areas I felt worth exploring in the three schools will,

I hope, indicate some of the problems of arriving at an account of process which does not do violence to the different experiences of its participants but at the same time isolates features in terms which make comparison meaningful. While some problems of selective attention and bias would be reduced with more time and more than one researcher, they would still be considerable. It may be the case that any account of institutions which isolates features in such terms as to make comparison with other institutions possible and useful will inevitably appear to distort reality to members of that institution; thus, to negotiate an account with members would be inappropriate. But perhaps the most serious limitation of research which attempts to look closely at school processes is the difficulty of relating even the most sensitive comparative analysis of processes to differential outcomes beyond the school. Existing research on school differences has used such immediate 'outcomes' as examination successes, attendance rates and delinquency rates of pupils. These are highly conservative ways of evaluating the school's effects and, arguably, tend to weight the evidence against the possibility of schools and teachers as agents of change. However they have the advantage of being concrete and visible, in comparison with the apparently vague and elusive aims of those liberals or radicals who seek a fundamental redefinition of the purposes of education.[33] Should a school be regarded as successful if its working-class pupils going into manual labor are prepared to fight for better pay and conditions, and have acquired in school some of the necessary skills and knowledge to do so effectively? Can schools provide such skills? Is this more important than, or compatible with, getting the maximum number of pupils through the maximum number of external examinations. Such questions may be uncomfortable for socialist and liberal teachers alike but they should not be avoided. In schools which have made possible an educational practice where neither content nor method are experienced as alienating by working-class pupils, teachers find themselves forced to recognise these conflicts in a concrete form; for example, a portion of the precious time in the final two years of school given over to non-examined activities, whatever their 'relevance' or 'educational' value, may seem hard to justify if it appears to prejudice the pupils' chances on the job market.

Although none of the schools I worked in could be regarded as an extreme case of any educational philosophy, School C (in its emphasis, for example, on good teacher-pupil relations and the status and interpretation it gave to community studies) appeared to go furthest towards a redefinition of the basic teaching paradigm as described by Willis; it was also the school in which the possibility of conflicts over aims and practices was most clearly recognised, and allowed as a legitimate subject for debate. While the relative openness of communication and decision-making appeared to be valued by the staff and to increase their commitment to the school, they also went through periods of uncertainty and confusion about the school's values and practices. In this they formed a strong contrast with the staff of School A, who experienced no such conflict of values. However, the degree of discomfort they experienced should not be exaggerated. The areas of contradiction I have drawn attention to in School C seemed explicit relative to the other two schools, but still far from developing into a major conflict, either within the staff itself or between the school, the local community and the LEA.

Nevertheless, the possibility seems to me to exist for a school or group of teachers to shift away from the traditional definition of education. Why this should occur in a particular school and what influences the extent of the redefinition are not questions I have space to discuss here, although they would constitute an essential part of any analysis. What I want to stress is that such a shift will almost inevitably generate conflicts and confusions, not only within staffs but in the experience of individual teachers.

What has the sociology of education to offer such teachers? Current Marxist perspectives can provide a means of understanding the external conditions and constraints which partially give rise to the contradictions, but they still have little to offer the teacher trying to evaluate the effects of his or her own practice and those of the institution she/he works in. A closer focus on the variations in institutional cultures and, in particular, on the relation of teacher and taught, not as separate fields of study but in elaboration of the broader analysis, might suggest the necessary links.

Summary:

In conclusion, the problem discussed in this paper could be restated. Is it possible to have an *applied* sociology of education which is not reformist? If so, in which crucial areas do we need to increase our understanding of the system as it operates now, and how can this understanding inform practice?

An argument has been presented for directing attention in research to the analysis of differences in current educational practice, taking the school as the unit of analysis. The theoretical basis for the argument rests on the possibility of viewing any given school as a cultural system with some limited degree of autonomy. It is recognised that such research presents highly intractable problems in epistemology and methodology. The strategy which began to emerge out of this researcher's experience was to focus observations on those aspects of school life which seemed to display most clearly the contradictions in aims and practices inherent in the dominant educational ideology. In other words, observation was explicitly informed by theoretical considerations, which also suggested the central importance of the form of relations between teachers and pupils.

Two important issues are recognised which it was not possible to include within the scope of this initial research; these are the need for more adequate conceptualisation of educational outcomes, and the conditions influencing the development and extent of divergence of an institutional culture which runs counter to the dominant educational tradition.

Finally, if it is accepted that educational practice is not monolithic and that some schools have developed or begun to move towards a form of educational practice which makes contradiction more explicit, we have a role, as sociologists and teachers ourselves, in offering an analysis which can relate to the teachers' dilemmas as they are experienced. This does not mean the provision of facile solutions, but it does mean a recognition of the problems and potentialities of alternatives available to teachers. It should be possible to 'take' the problems of teachers while maintaining a critical and theoretically informed perspective, and rather than imposing sociological analyses from without, or above, to work with teachers in considering how these could and should inform the teachers' practice.

Acknowledgements

I am grateful to Len Barton, Steve Walker and David Reynolds for their helpful comments on an earlier draft of this paper.

Notes and References

1 See, for example, McNamara, D. (1977) 'A Time for Change', *Educational Studies*, Vol. 3, No. 3 pp. 179–183; Gould, J. (1977) *The Attack on Higher Education*, London, Institute for the Study of Conflict.

2 Universities Council for the Education and Training of Teachers Consultative Report, *The PGCE course and the training of specialist teachers for secondary schools* (January 1979) p. 11.

3 In 'Expectations of the teaching of social work in courses leading to the Certificate of Qualification in Social Work', Central Council for the Education and Training of Social Workers Consultative Document No. 3, March, by Wright, R. (1977); see also the report by CCETSW (July 1979) 'Analysis of responses and some policy issues arising from the Consultation'. A similar report on responses to the UCET document should be forthcoming.

4 See, for example, 'Sociology under attack' by Leonard, D. in the British Sociological Association bulletin *Network* (September 1979); also the lead article on big cuts in postgraduate training in the social sciences in the *Times Higher Educational Supplement* (January 4th, 1980).

5 Hartnett, A. and Naish, M. (1980) 'Technicians or social bandits?' in Woods, P. (Ed.), *Teacher Strategies*, London, Croom Helm.

6 Young, M.F.D. (1971) (Ed.) *Knowledge and Control*, London, Collier-Macmillan.

7 As argued, for example, in Bernbaum, G. (1977) *Knowledge and Ideology in the Sociology of Education*, London, Macmillan.

8 This comment on the 'ultra-left double bind' is taken from Corrigan, P. (1979) *Schooling the Smash Street Kids*, London, Macmillan, p. 149. This position is not of course peculiar to the sociology of education; a clear expression of and justification for the rejection of short-term solutions can be found in the introduction to Hall, S. *et. al.* (1977) *Policing the Crisis*, London, Macmillan, an important study of the social phenomenon of 'mugging'.

9 The phrase is taken from Willis, P. *Learning to Labour* (1977) Farnborough, Saxon House, chapter 9. which contains the following comments:

> If we have nothing to say about what to do on Monday morning everything is yielded to a purist structuralist immobilising reductionist tautology: nothing can be done until the basic structures of society are changed but the structures prevent us making changes. There is no contradiction in asking practitioners to work on two levels simultaneously – to face immediate problems in doing 'the best' (so far as they can see it) for their clients whilst appreciating all the time that these very actions may help to reproduce the structures within which the problems arise . . .
> To contract out of the messy business of day-to-day problems is to deny the active, contested nature of social and cultural reproduction . . . (p. 186).

10 Corrigan, P. *op. cit.*, p. 143.

11 Jencks, C. (1975) *Inequality*, Harmondsworth, Penguin.

12 Bennett, N. (1976) *Teaching Styles and Pupil Progress*, London, Open Books.

13 See, for example, Harry Pluckrose's comments in the *Sunday Times*, 2nd May 1976, and by Adam Hopkins in the *Education Guardian* of 4th May 1976, which also carried a number of letters on the subject.

14 SHARP, R. and GREEN, A. (1975) *Education and Social Control*, London, Routledge and Kegan Paul.

15 CORRIGAN, P. *op. cit.*, p. 152.

16 WILLIS, P. *op. cit.*, p. 83.

17 POWER, M.J., ALDERSON, M.R., PHILLIPSON, C.M., SHOENBERG, E. and MORRIS, J.N. (1967) 'Delinquent Schools?' *New Society*, 19th October; POWER, M.J. BENN, R.T. and MORRIS, J.N. (1972) 'Neighbourhood, School and Juveniles before the Courts', *British Journal of Criminology*, Vol. 12, No. 2, pp. 111–132.

18 REYNOLDS, D. (1976) 'Schools DO make a difference' *New Society*, 29th July; RUTTER, M. MAUGHAN, B., MORTIMORE, P. and OUSTON, J. (1979) *Fifteen Thousand Hours*, London, Open Books.

19 See, for example, the critical symposium in the *British Journal of the Sociology of Education*, Vol. 1 No. 2, 1980.

20 CF. the following comments from WILLIS P. (*op. cit.*, p. 3);
> The qualitative methods, and Participant Observation used in the research and the ethnographic form of the presentation were dictated by the nature of my interest in 'the cultural'. These techniques . . . have a sensitivity to meanings and values . . . In particular, the ethnographic account, without always knowing how, can allow a degree of the activity, creativity and human agency within the object of study to come through into the analysis and the reader's experience.

21 Though it may be formulated in different ways, this has been a recurrent problem in educational research. Since both 'structure' and 'culture' are terms whose meaning has varied in different contexts within sociology, it is particularly important to clarify the terms of the debate within the sociology of education. As a theoretical problem of the relation between different perspectives, it formed an important theme of the first conference on the Sociology of Education at Westhill College, Birmingham, in 1978; see BARTON, L. and MEIGHAN, R. (1978) *Sociological Interpretations of Schooling and Classrooms*, Driffield, Nafferton Books.

22 Reprinted as chapter 9 in BERNSTEIN, B. (1971) *Class, Codes and Control Vol. 1*, London, Routledge and Kegan Paul.

23 COOPER, B. (1976) *Bernstein's Codes: A Classroom Study*, Education Area Occasional Paper, No. 6, University of Sussex.

24 BERNSTEIN, B. 'On the Classification and Framing of Educational Knowledge' in YOUNG, M.F.D. (Ed.) *op. cit.*, p. 50.

25 For example, BARNES, D., BRITTON, J. and ROSEN, H. (1971) *Language, the Learner and the School*, Harmondsworth, Penguin; BARNES, D. (1976) *From Communication to Curriculum*, Harmondsworth, Penguin. There are of course clear parallels between Barnes' concepts of the Transmission and Interpretation views of teaching and learning, and Freire's distinction between education as 'banking' and 'problem-posing education'. See FREIRE, P. (1972) *Pedagogy of the Oppressed*, Harmondsworth, Penguin. Freire presents a theory of liberatory education which places a prime importance on the relation between teacher and taught, and the form of communication;
> Liberation is a praxis: the action and reflection of men upon their world in order to transform it . . . Liberating education consists in acts of cognition, not transferrals of information . . . the practice of problem-solving education first of all demands a resolution of the teacher-student contradiction.

26 MARTIN, N., D'ARCY, P., NEWTON, B. and PARKER, R. (1976) Schools Council Writing across the Curriculum 11–16 Project Publications, London, Ward Lock. Particularly useful is the pamphlet, *From Information to Understanding*.

27 See, for example, CHANAN, G. and DELAMONT, S. (Eds.) (1975) *Frontiers of Classroom Research*, Slough, N.F.E.R; STUBBS, M. and DELAMONT, S. (Eds.) (1976) *Explorations in Classroom Observation*, Chichester, Wiley.

28 Cases which have received national publicity would include several of the 'Free' schools, Risinghill and Tyndale, and Countesthorpe, in England at least.

29 The most widely known are probably HARGREAVES, D. (1967) *Social Relations in a Secondary School*, London, Routledge and Kegan Paul; and KEDDIE, N. (1971) 'Classrooms Knowledge', in YOUNG, M.F.D. (Ed.) *op. cit.*

30 Other aspects I attempted to gather information on included the policy concerning external examination entry and pattern of entry and results; teachers' views on specific aspects of disciplinary policy (for example, on supervision at breaks and detentions, on pregnancies of pupils, on the wearing of prohibited clothing); pupils' assessments of trustworthy and sympathetic teachers in comparison with the formal pastoral organisation; attendance.

31 My method of gathering information from pupils was to take out groups of three of four from lessons which I had been observing, and tape a loosely-structured conversation with them which lasted approximately twenty minutes, though this depended very much on the pupils. I began with questions

about choice of subjects, how and why they had been chosen and whether the pupil was satisfied with the process. This moved on to a discussion of the characteristics of teachers they 'got on with' and more general opinions of the school, including what they knew of their parents' views. The aim was always to provoke a discussion among the pupils, stimulated by occasional questions from me, rather than eliciting answers to a series of questions. I therefore chose as far as possible (from my own observations or sometimes from the teacher's advice) groups of friends (or at least acquaintances – more difficult than it may sound in the Upper School of a comprehensive where hardly any two pupils share the same timetable) who seemed accustomed to talking with each other.

32 The impossibility of a systematic check on teachers' views throughout the three schools should give rise to serious reservations about this apparent congruence. This was an occasion where a questionnaire or circular to all staff with the single request for their view of the school's task in relation to its clientele might have been appropriate; however at least one head would not have permitted such an action (an initial approach met with the response that it was unnecessary to ask teachers such questions since they would reply according to the school's policy set out in its prospectus).

33 Nigel Wright, writing of the problems of Rank and File, comments wryly on the ambivalence of socialist teachers about educational practices; see WRIGHT, N. 'Teacher Politics and Educational Change' in WHITTY, G. and YOUNG, M. (Eds.) (1976) *Explorations in the Politics of School Knowledge* Driffield, Nafferton Books.

Teacher Ideologies and Pupil Disaffection

Rosemary Chessum, Brunel University.

Research base

This paper is largely an attempt to interpret some recent fieldwork observations of secondary school teachers' reactions to disaffection among their pupils.[1] The data were collected as part of a research project on pupil disaffection and the schools' responses to it. Four researchers used various qualitative methods to investigate these processes in six Outer London comprehensive schools. The term 'disaffection' was used to elicit from teachers a description of the full range of pupil problems which caused them concern in school. The intention was to avoid using traditional categories like 'disruptive', 'truant', 'underachiever' and to encourage teachers to be more explicit about the problems which certain pupils, or pupil behaviour, posed for them. Disaffection was loosely defined as apparent unwillingness or inability on the part of pupils to take advantage of the education being offered to them in school, whatever the manifestation or the cause. The teacher- interview material was supplemented by interviews with identified pupils, and direct observation of various facets of school life. This paper will take data primarily from two of the six schools, although it is informed by some knowledge of the others.

Aims of the paper

It is proposed to concentrate on a discussion of the sorts of ideas which prevailed amongst teaching staff when they talked about their difficult pupils. The paper is about the theories and perspectives adopted by teachers in their day-to-day practice, rather than about teacher ideologies in a broad, societal sense. Schools can be located structurally as part of the political and ideological apparatus of the state; as part of the process of 'bidding for the consent of the governed', which occurs in the 'developed forms of the democratic State'.[2] They are, therefore, not autonomous institutions and the teachers within them are partially constrained in what they do by political and economic forces beyond their control. They are also strongly influenced in their thinking about their work by ideological currents which are widespread and dominant in this society. Nevertheless, they have a degree of professional autonomy of thought and action. Ideas and cultural meanings are developed and generated at the level of practice. In English comprehensive schools, teachers' theoretical perspectives are not uniformly set out for them by some kind of state manifesto, issued as compulsory reading to all teachers. Equally, they are not merely the spontaneous, idiosyncratic creation of individuals. They arise from the teachers' active blending of available ideas with their relevant experience. This paper will not attempt a structural analysis either of the economic and political constraints on schools, or of specific ideologies. Many writers have addressed themselves to these complex questions.[3] Instead, it will outline some of the ideas which teachers within the schools found useful and meaningful when they confronted problems of pupil disaffection. An attempt will be made to show some links between the institutional context of the teachers' work and their espousal of certain kinds of theories and prescriptions. To some extent, the paper will adopt Sharp and Green's question, and ask, 'to what problems are these [teacher perspectives] viable solutions for the teacher?'.[4] It is suggested that certain theories and explanations are more attractive and helpful than others, because they appear to 'work'. That is, they navigate an acceptable way through the issues which are thrown up by pupil disaffection and are compatible with those remedies or responses which are available to the teacher.

The importance of ideology for teachers

Grace[5] has shown that, historically, the nature and strength of teachers' personal philosophies *vis à vis* working class pupils may have been crucial in enabling them to tread the fine line between their sensitive, civilising, professional role on the one hand, and personal or political over-identification with their charges on the other. Teachers in the late nineteenth-century, as part of their job, had to communicate and sympathise with their pupils, whilst distancing themselves from the alleged 'ignorance' and 'immorality'[6] of the populace whose children were their pupils. Teachers needed to feel personally committed to the active ideals of improvement and rescue which the job implied, yet it was important to the existing moral and political order that they did not become over-critical of the *status quo*, or their own or their pupils' position in it. Moreover, the Victorian middle class ideas about working class education embodied a complex blend of expectations:

> The basic imperative to control coexisted with a genuine humanitarian and Christian impulse to help, a radical interest in equipping the people for political membership, a capitalist interest in rendering them competent and efficient as workers, a religious interest in making them 'good', and a liberal/cultural interest in 'elevating' and 'refining' them to an appreciation of a higher order of culture.[7]

Teachers had to respond not only to this wide range of middle class expectations, but also to the realities of working class life, as they encountered them, through their pupils:

The teacher was at the focal point of class antagonisms which he was expected to ameliorate and contain. He faced the concrete manifestations of poverty, misery and exploitation and its associated bitterness and 'lawlessness'.[8]

He was therefore dependent to survive on personal resilience and management strategies, and also on 'the sustaining effects of a Christian or missionary ideology'.[9]

During the twentieth-century, there have been important social and educational changes. Nevertheless, it is arguable that teachers continue to be faced with a complex and confusing set of expectations about their task. There are, for instance, obvious potential conflicts between the expectation that schools will maximise their pupils' examination success whilst creating a supportive learning environment for the many children who, for various reasons, are unlikely to obtain any qualifications. Equally, there is considerable potential difficulty reconciling idealistic notions of child-centred, individually tailored education with the expectation that schools will teach children discipline and conformity to external rules. It is arguable too that schools remain 'at the focal point of class antagonisms'. 'Secondary education for all',[10] the great expansion of state resources for education, the erosion of the institutional separation of secondary modern from grammar school pupils, better welfare provision for poor families, and the accompanying egalitarian ideologies, might have been expected to diminish class antagonisms, to harmonise relations in school, by meeting the needs of all pupils equally and fairly, and to solve many of the earlier problems which may have impeded pupil learning and compliance. In fact, sociological literature points to continued inequality of educational opportunity,[11] to persistent problems of truancy, indiscipline and underachievement,[12] and to some fundamental political conflicts between the aims of schooling and the interests of working class pupils.[13] This poses the educator with the problem of explaining why, despite widely accepted social democratic reforms, many of these difficulties remain unresolved, or even intensified.[14]

Against this background, it is the teacher's lot to make sense, in terms of her daily work, of the various expectations which educationalists, administrators, politicians, parents and pupils have of schools and to operationalise them. She must also solve, at school level, the problems of pupil failure and pupil resistance, as they appear in a concrete form, or she must explain her inability to do so. It is not necessarily sufficient for her to understand that, sociologically speaking, these problems may originate, beyond her control, in the economic and political structure. Her personal and professional integrity, and her motivation to continue in her teaching role, are dependent on her concept of herself as an effective actor, within certain institutional limits. She therefore needs to develop a perspective which takes account of these wider issues but which is relevant to her social encounters in school and which can be useful in informing her actions at work.

The ideological challenge of disaffection

For various reasons, disaffection among the pupils is a particularly troublesome area to explain and handle. Firstly, it emphasises some of the contentious moral and political issues which underlie formal education, and which might lie dormant if all pupils placidly accepted the behavioural limits and mental attitudes prescribed by the school. When a child appears to reject important aspects of schooling, questions arise about the reasons and about what is to be done. Decisions have to be made about the extent to which the pupil's rejection is legitimate, in the sense of implying criticism of the school or its societal context.[15] Even if staff regard the pupil's behaviour as at least partially justified, decisions about what must be done involve a difficult process of balancing conflicting interests; the individual claims of that pupil, for instance, against the legal framework of schooling or against the organisational and curricular imperatives which make it necessary to impose a degree of conformity. Staff may agree that a pupil's individual interests, and those of his fellow pupils, are best served by allowing him a certain level of absenteeism but to condone it raises wider questions of whether it is right, and politically wise, to ignore breaches of the law. Similarly, staff may consider that, because of his personal circumstances, a particular pupil needs to be excused from some of the normal curricular and administrative requirements. They must then contend with the issues which this raises; is it fair on other pupils to grant privileges to the few? Is it right to appear to 'reward' misbehaviour by granting concessions to those who do not conform? Should the moral order be uniformly upheld and deviants punished or should the individual characteristics of the pupil affect the teachers' response to his behaviour?[16] The assessment of disaffected pupils is not an objective professional matter. In deciding what is to be done about a pupil who does not learn or behave as required, a teacher not only brings her teaching skills and professional insights to bear but also makes judgments of an unavoidably moral and political nature; she adopts, albeit implicitly, an ideological stance which informs her understanding of the problems and justifies her response.

A second problem is that disaffection among pupils is not easily understood by appealing to official ideological sources.[17] Education is generally assumed to be beneficial. The Newsom Report, in advocating an extension of compulsory schooling, invoked notions of 'human justice', and the 'economic self-interest' of the country as a whole.[18] Education is about enabling 'our children' to realise their 'potential abilities'.

> Again and again, teachers confirm that the pupils . . . stand to gain a great deal in terms of personal development, as well as in the consolidating of attainments from a longer period of full-time education . . .[19]

Newsom simultaneously recognised some of the less palatable aspects of classroom life:

> Too many [pupils] at present seem to sit through lessons with information and exhortation washing over them and leaving very little deposit. Too many appear bored and apathetic to school, as some will be in their jobs also. Others are openly impatient. They don't see the point of what they are asked to do, and they are conscious of making little progress.[20]

Certainly, in the schools studied, teachers repeatedly expressed dismay about their pupils' low levels of 'motivation', 'effort' and aspiration. The teachers largely believed in the inherent value of the education which they offered their pupils and, in their experience, many pupils derived considerable benefit from it. There was no obvious way of understanding why so many pupils virtually had to be wooed or threatened into taking advantage of their opportunities. Yet if, according to official social democratic ideologies, education is a civil right and a route to self-advancement, its rejection requires explanation.

A third factor making disaffection a difficult ideological problem is that dealing with it, or its manifestations, may be defined by many teachers as being beyond their professional brief. The imparting of knowledge and skills may be seen as the essence of the teacher's task and the management of deviance as peripheral. One teacher, for instance, talked of pupils' trips to the school counsellor as diversionary, in educational terms:

> They [the pupils] turn round and say, I'm going [to see the counsellor] and it's almost getting out of a lesson. What are we here for really? If you think we're here to teach, to educate the children, then perhaps we're failing to some extent. But if we're here to ... [be] social workers or whatever you like to call it – perhaps we are succeeding. It's how you define the job of teaching, isn't it?[21]

Some teachers willingly concern themselves with their pupils' moral attitudes and emotional stability, even if to do so extends their involvement beyond the boundaries of the classroom. Others take the view that pupils who cannot conform should be taken out of mainstream schooling until their behaviour has been modified. Many hold views somewhere in between, but for all of them, pupils who resist schooling, whether by extreme forms of disobedience or passively by the evasion of school rules and work, represent a challenge to their professional aims and competence. Whether or not they define it as part of their job, the associated behaviour requires management in practice. Therefore, teachers must find ways of conceptualising the problems and solutions. They need an 'operational philosophy'[22] which copes with disaffection and its manifestations because it exists as a feature of school life and because to respond to it inevitably draws them into the moral and political arena.

It is suggested here that each teacher has to work out her own philosophy in response to her daily work experience. She undoubtedly draws on her knowledge of wider ideological debates in society, on her own political and moral convictions and on her understanding of professional values. These are important resources for her. Equally, she must take account of the more localised policies affecting her particular school and the realities of classroom life as she finds it. The complexity and variability of these factors are likely to require not so much a resort to ready-made ideologies but a blending together of available ideas with a selection of practical observations. The resulting perspectives can then be used and developed in a flexible way to inform teachers' reactions to unpredictable and troublesome events as they arise.

The schools studied

The two schools on which this paper is primarily based must be mentioned briefly as they form the social context in which the discussion must be set. Both schools were fairly ordinary neighbourhood comprehensive schools in working class areas in Outer London. Both were handicapped by inadequacies in their facilities but neither was glaringly underresourced by local standards. Both schools had to deal with a fairly typical array of educational, social and emotional problems among their pupils but neither was exceptionally deprived, in terms of the economic and social background of its pupils, nor exceptionally rough, in terms of the relationships amongst pupils and teachers. Both schools claimed to have a strong pastoral ethos. Individual teachers were encouraged, in principle at least, to develop the pastoral aspects of their role. Both schools had defined pastoral structures and specified pastoral care staff, including a trained counsellor.[23] The overall dominant ideology was liberal, with the officially favoured response to pupil-based problems being tolerance and selectively administered socialization or therapy rather than a more undifferentiated or punitive approach. It could be located broadly as a positivist rather than a classical or radical view of deviance.[24] This does not imply ideological homogeneity. A great variety of perspectives were represented amongst individual teachers and issues of welfare and punishment were a continual source of debate.

Teachers' descriptions of disaffection

Teachers' readiness to name difficult pupils, to put forward explanations and to advocate or criticise certain kinds of institutional response testified to the relevance of these questions to staff at all organisational levels. Teachers were asked both to discuss disaffection in school, in general terms, and to identify and describe individual disaffected pupils. The resulting interview data indicated that there was a distinction between the nature of the explanations which the teachers were likely to advance when discussing disaffection from school in an overall organisational or reflective sense and those they advanced when describing particular crises with which they had to deal. Three broad categories were apparent. They could loosely be called the reflective, the operational and the specialist. When speaking *reflectively*, teachers fairly frequently raised wider sociological and institutional issues. They might draw attention to cultural differences affecting a child's educational and employment aspirations or to social and environmental factors affecting children's life chances. They sometimes recognised that formal education in school might not be as universally relevant and beneficial as pupils are led to believe. The following paraphrased quotation is an illustration:

> School is career-orientated. Children do not study because of their intrinsic interest in the subject matter. Instead, they ask what will be the use of the subject when they leave school. School tells children that certain subjects

and exam successes will assist them in their careers, yet, in fact, most subjects are only marginally relevant to specific jobs. Furthermore, CSE passes below Grade One are of dubious career value. The careers carrot is an easy one for teachers to hold up, but it is a con, and quite often, when a child sees through the con, he opts out of the education system altogether.[25]

At this reflective level, teachers were even more likely to highlight deficiencies in the organisation and management of their schools. They did not confine their comments to the pastoral and disciplinary processes but made links between pupils' reactions to schooling and matters such as the curriculum, teaching styles, available resources and so on. This is not to say that teachers denied more individualistic interpretations. There was often room for both but teachers seemed more inclined to make a point of raising broader issues in this type of discussion than if they were discussing individual events.

When teachers described their attempts to understand particular difficult pupils or handle particular crises in an *operational* sense, they referred to wider issues, but the emphasis shifted towards psychological and the moral explanations. Deviance was more likely to be depoliticised.[26] Teachers could list personal characteristics which singled out non-conformist children from the others. Sociological insights might be reduced to personal attributes. For instance, in one pupil's school records his home circumstances were described as a 'high-rise family', as if this form of housing environment infects its inhabitants with a particular social disease which others, reading the records, will recognise. Equally, a more reflective view of the local neighbourhood in terms of structural inequalities easily became collapsed into the personal attributes of the 'culturally deprived child'.

A third category of explanation took the process further and often involved assessment by other professionals. This was when *specialist* semi-technical definitions such as 'maladjusted', 'school phobic', or 'disturbed' were applied. Formal psychological assessments were not, however, performed on most children. Most pupils, disaffected or otherwise, were assessed and managed as a routine part of the ordinary teacher's job and this paper is therefore primarily concerned with their non-specialist perspectives.

Teachers' descriptions of and responses to the disaffected pupils they identified

When teachers identified particular pupils who seemed to be disaffected, they primarily discussed them in terms of those observable aspects of their behaviour and attitudes which caused trouble or concern in school. Ostensibly, they were describing pupils' personal habits such as irregular attendance, lateness, delinquency, disobedience; or personal characteristics, like forgetfulness, aggressiveness, poor concentration, lack of social skills. Such factors were the 'symptoms' of disaffection, in that they appeared to signify a lack of commitment to schooling or a lack of integration into the institutional community. It was, however, possible to reinterpret these 'symptoms' so as to link the sorts of observations which teachers made about the pupils not only with the pupils' behaviour, as such, but also with the teachers' professional and organisational interests, and to show how they embodied teachers' reflective ideas and their immediate operational concerns.

There were certain kinds of pupil behaviour which clearly had to be countered directly in order to safeguard the school as an organisation and the personal integrity of the staff. When teachers described public challenges to teacher authority, it was apparent that they were obliged to act, pragmatically, to reinforce that authority, regardless of their individual perspectives on the pupils' predicaments. One senior teacher, who strongly disliked resorting to drastic disciplinary measures, spelt out the necessity of doing so in these extreme circumstances:

> I make no bones about it ... we *do* it. If staff feel they've been put on the spot and they're in a very difficult situation with children, and they're outraged to the extent that their personal dignity has been affronted in some particularly objectionable way, then we have to [take drastic measures].[27]

Faced with such a crisis, the teacher sometimes had to sacrifice certain reflective interpretations and ideals to the operational realities. For some teachers, who held certain kinds of beliefs about discipline and punishment, there would be no need to justify a punitive reaction. For a teacher who doubted that punishment was a helpful or morally acceptable response to pupils' difficult behaviour, it might be necessary to work out reasons and justifications which enabled punitive measures to be accommodated within a strongly anti-punitive perspective. One senior teacher, for instance, found it acceptable to place the problem in the context of the welfare of the 'community', rather than appeal to notions of law and order.

> ... We're dealing with the formation of young lives; ... we've got to be tolerant and understanding ... I believe that's the way we ought to do it. But also, it's a community, and we've got to have rules, and you can't have this difficult minority kicking the thing over. So when we've *got* to be tough, we *are* tough.[28]

Another senior teacher reconciled the institutional requirement to control pupils' behaviour with the individual interests of the child by explaining that disciplining a pupil is a desirable contribution to building his character:

> ... you *could* say there is the negative side of discipline ... [but] ... disciplining a child must be ... part of the pastoral system. It would only be used [in this school] ... as a way of enabling a child to develop his character, and his academic [potential] ... in a much more positive way.

Discipline, it was further argued, is beneficial because it helps the child to adapt himself to the expectations of the world at large.

> The child has to know that, if he has done something that breaks the

law, then justice has to be seen to be done, not only in the eyes of the establishment, but also in the eyes of the rest of the population.[29]

In such circumstances, where there might have been a clash between the teachers' professional aspirations or the perceived interests of the child, and the institutional imperatives to contain a direct challenge, teachers developed their ideas to enable them to deal with the immediate crises without necessarily repudiating their basic principles.

Some of the symptoms of disaffection identified by teachers related directly to behaviour which threatened authority and control but teachers by no means confined their concern to such matters. Other observations seemed to derive from different sources, and they illustrated other aspects of teachers' thinking. The tremendous range of pupil problems which they described, echoed the variety of reflective perceptions which teachers voiced about pupil disaffection in general, even though the emphasis was on locating problems within families and on making individualised responses. They drew attention to pupils' impoverished family circumstances or their onerous domestic responsibilities; they referred to pupils' involvement with delinquent groups outside school and to cultural differences; they spoke of emotional insecurity and personality difficulties; they described the problems they, as teachers encountered when they tried to communicate or develop relationships with some pupils; and they indicated the apparent incompatibility of some pupils' life-styles with school work and school-approved attitudes.

Because of the variety of teachers' insights, tensions were apparent between teachers' professional and personal ideals in relation to their pupils, and what could be done in the school context. Teachers frequently expressed concern about pupils who did not apply themselves to school; those who conformed well enough to keep out of trouble and 'get by' but did not 'stretch themselves' and who appeared to be wasting much of their talent. Similarly, teachers worried about children with whom it was difficult to communicate, the pupils who were 'hard to get through to'.[30] These were frustrating and demoralising problems for the teacher because they represented important obstacles to her work in the classroom and also because they implied that the process of schooling might be failing to establish the necessary kinds of relationship between teacher and taught or to win the commitment of pupils to official educational goals. In some respects, such passive resistance was harder to explain than more extreme forms of misbehaviour, because it was more widespread and less easily relegated to the sphere of personal abnormality. On the other hand, it was easier to evade the associated issues because discontent or disinterest which did not impinge forcibly on routine organisational functioning, was a less urgent matter in practice. One class teacher, who was very committed to the pastoral care of her pupils, was asked whether she would tackle some of her charges about staff complaints that, although they were 'no trouble', they were 'a bit lazy'.

> Well, I'd have a chat with them, you know, but you see, it's terrible, but [sounding apologetic] it's really something you forget about because you don't really get a constant moan [from other staff] . . .[31]

Teachers, then, often recognised that many of their pupils were not being fully catered for in school; many believed that it was part of their job to remedy such problems as low levels of motivation and inadequate communication between teacher and taught. The more pressing priorities of school life and the causational complexity underlying pupils' attitudes to school appeared to place severe limits on the teachers' effectiveness, regardless of their concepts of what their work ought to encompass. Teachers therefore needed not only to explain the actions they took in respect of pupils' problems, but also their inability or failure to affect other worrying aspects of pupils' reactions.

Many of the 'symptoms' of disaffection identified by teachers can be seen in this light. That is, they had an explanatory and justificatory, rather than a purely descriptive, role. Teachers repeatedly drew attention, for example, to the 'home background' of pupils. Features such as marital breakdown, difficult family relationships, parental attitudes would typically be listed alongside references to the pupil's behaviour in school. Teachers' knowledge of these aspects of their pupils' lives was relatively small in most cases. It was not a primary source of teachers' impressions of pupils. Home background factors were usually investigated *after* a pupil had become a source of concern, as part of the search for explanations and prescriptions. Teacher-defined 'symptoms' of disaffection, then, illustrated a number of influences on teachers' thinking:

1. the institutional requirements which obliged them to condemn in principle, and counter in practice, certain kinds of pupil reaction;
2. the variety of the insights which teachers had into their pupils' circumstances, and the resulting problems of reconciling their professional tasks, in relation to pupils' un-met needs, with the operational realities in school;
3. teachers' use of certain observable or assumed aspects of pupils' lives and behaviour as resources to inform and explain the perspectives they adopted.

It may be useful to discuss two overall perspectives on disaffection which were prominent in the schools, and consider their relevance to the problems confronting teachers in these schools. These two perspectives could be described as a personal and family pathology theory of disaffection, and a 'hard core' theory of deviance. It was possible to list six ways in which these perspectives seemed to be particularly helpful ones for teachers to use:

1. they were readily available perspectives;
2. they were relatively uncontentious;
3. they made problems of pupil disaffection accessible to teacher influence;
4. they provided scope for professional and personal idealism;
5. they were compatible with the perspectives adopted by allied professionals;
6. they made allowance for acceptable teacher failure.

Personal and family pathology theories of disaffection

The salience in the schools of family pathology or 'home background' theories as explanations of pupil disaffection in all its manifestations suggested that they were extremely helpful to teachers. There is plenty of psychological and socio-logical literature to support the view that certain kinds of home-based factors, such as family relationship abnormalities or particular styles of child-rearing, are associated with emotional difficulties and intellectual handicaps among children.[32] The teachers dealt daily with problems in school which appeared to be a direct overspill of disturbances and deficiences at home. There is, conversely, literature which suggests that some forms of deviance, in school and elsewhere, may represent a rational and legitimate response to an oppressive environment.[33] Teachers' own contact with pupils, and their wider reflections on society and school, yielded insights into likely alternative sources of pupils' frustrations. Nevertheless, in individual cases of pupil disaffection, they almost invariably invoked notions of family pathology as the primary explanation.[34] Indeed, the overall theoretical perspective was tenaciously preserved despite teachers' contradictory experiences. Some teachers expressed astonishment that certain pupils were exceptionally resis-tant to teacher influence despite an apparently supportive home background. They were equally surprised if model pupils were inadvertently revealed to live under adverse home circumstances. Faced with a rebellious or unco-operative pupil, teachers were often prepared to assume that there must be something wrong at home, even if no evidence was immediately available.[35] Although the evidence generally supporting such theories is impressive, questions arise as to why they seemed to be so dominant that their explanatory value usually went unchallenged and contradictory evidence often went unexplained. What problems might this sort of perspective solve for the teacher? What follows is some speculation on this theme.

A disruptive or unwilling pupil was sometimes effectively ignored or left out of mainstream teaching processes. Many such pupils, however, had to be managed, in practice, and many staff wanted to understand the pupils' resistance in conceptual terms and to find ways of helping both teachers and pupils. They had limited time and energy at their disposal for this area of their work and had to make rapid use of available explanatory resources. Ideas about pupils' home circumstances as determinants of their response to school were readily *available* resources. They were well-documented and were reinforced by their central place in social demo-cratic ideologies and state welfare activities generally.[36] Their credibility could be largely assumed, despite any gaps or contradictions in the information to hand, because the ideological work of establishing the theories had been done elsewhere. They appeared *uncontentious* and universal and difficult to challenge, even if anyone wanted to do so. In the context of these schools, this type of explanation was virtually a fact of life, rather than a theoretical perspective, and seemed to act as a partial constraint on alternative ways of thinking about the issues.

Even so, it seems unlikely that these ideas, however available and uncunten-tious, would have remained dominant if they had not offered teachers useful approaches to operational difficulties. Crucially, they rendered pupils' problems *accessible* to teacher influence. This was important for reasons of institutional necessity and professional satisfaction. It has already been shown that certain types of pupil reaction to school had to be countered urgently and that, in addition, teachers worried about a wide range of other manifestations of pupil discontent or withdrawal. By developing an understanding of these problems in terms of inter-personal or intrapersonal difficulties, teachers could go on to devise solutions in terms of individually administered training, counselling or therapy. An alternative conceptualisation of the problems which, for example, located the problems and solutions in the political sphere or implied profound changes in the structure of schooling might find sympathy among some teachers, as they reflected on educational matters, but would not easily offer courses of action which met their existing operational requirements as they tried to cater for their pupils in the given institutional context.[37] Nor would such interpretations necessarily fulfil teachers' professional aspirations to be an effective influence on pupils' development and progress, rather than a helpless observer of social events. Indeed, family pathology and deprivation theories offered important opportunities for teachers who wished to extend their role and effectiveness in pupils' lives. Such a perspective enabled a teacher to take account of social and economic inequalities, as mediated through home circumstances, whilst still seeing ways to ameliorate the effects at a personal level. It was often because teachers had considerable insights, through their contacts with the pupils, into the class realities affecting pupils' lives that they were drawn towards a theoretical framework which suggested scope for rehabilitation and rescue[38] rather than repression or resignation. For some teachers, increasingly sophisticated forms of pastoral care were a logical development, drawing on these sorts of explanation, appealing to their *personal and professional ideals*, and compatible with the basic organisational constraints on school functioning.

The schools did not work in isolation but formed part of a network of *state agencies and professionals* who took responsibility for selected aspects of the welfare and control of the pupils in and out of school. The schools were expected to co-operate with these other bodies and often needed to draw on their services. Psychologists, social workers, child psychiatrists, staff of special schools and education welfare officers were examples. These were the schools' sources of help when staff felt unable to deal adequately with pupils' problems and they strongly reinforced an individualised, family-based perspective on pupils' adverse reactions to school. It was part of the task of staff who liaised with other professionals, and won acceptance from them, to share this sort of paradigm. Most ordinary classroom teachers did not have direct contact with outside professionals but their diagnostic interpretations filtered through the school and represented a powerful reinforcement, particularly as access to special facilities outside school depended on their recommendations.

A major source of frustration and disillusionment for teachers who applied themselves to the problem of pupil disaffection was that none of the available solutions seemed to be entirely successful. Disciplinarians attributed pupil disobedience to a relaxation of rules and punishments. Pastorally-minded teachers pointed out that direct disciplinary measures had often failed in the past and concluded that alternative approaches were tactically necessary as well as ethically desirable. Yet, when more liberal, therapeutic methods failed, they, in turn, often had to resort to a firm disciplinary stand. Theories of personal and family pathology had a major explanatory, even consolatory, role to play in that, whilst giving scope for teacher intervention, they also provided an ultimate justification if all the interventions failed. A teacher who sought actively to help, and not just contain a difficult pupil, needed an acceptable way to understand the *failure* and rejection which she met in respect of some of her efforts. Teachers' ideas about the intractability of certain adverse home factors enabled them to explain why their extensive efforts sometimes came to nothing and protected them from total demoralisation.

The 'Hard Core' theory of deviance

It was possible, then, to identify some of the factors which made personal and family pathology theories extraordinarily relevant and powerful inside the schools but they did not explain all aspects of disaffection to the teachers' satisfaction. Teachers also found it necessary to discuss the problems which pupils presented collectively. They drew attention to the ease with which a disruptive pupil could recruit the allegiance of a whole group of otherwise compliant pupils. One teacher, talking of a difficult girl, said of her class:

> [it] has been so much better since she's been gone, because her influence! – the fact that she used to get away with more than anybody else was the downfall of a few of the other girls, who saw her misbehaving. They thought, 'Right! If she gets away with it, why shouldn't we?'.[39]

Teachers recognised that many pupils were not sufficiently well motivated, for whatever reason, to resist the opportunity, if it arose, to enjoy disruptive antics or to wriggle out of work requirements. Whilst it made sense to invoke theories of personal and family pathology to explain the more overt and extreme forms of disaffection, it was less helpful to do so to explain the stance of the relatively large body of more typical pupils who, according to teacher accounts, were neither notoriously difficult or hostile nor exceptionally enthusiastic about school. They were the pupils in between who accepted that school had certain benefits but were not wholeheartedly committed to it. These pupils were potential recruits to the ranks either of the conscious rejectors or of the committed conformists. Teachers were engaged in an active struggle to maximise the number of pupils who adopted the educational goals and behavioural standards of the school; to impress on sceptical pupils that school was important to their future lives.[40] It was arguable that those pupils who were blatantly unco-operative in such matters as work, behaviour and attendance were little more than a symbol of a more fundamental malaise located either in the school's internal functioning or in the education system generally. Teachers were much more likely, however, when faced with particular incidents, to attempt to locate what might be described as a 'hard core' of offenders as the real source of the problem. As in the case of the personal and family pathology theories, the 'hard core' theory was espoused despite flaws in the analysis and the existence of counter-arguments. Teachers were often reluctant, on a practical level, to describe particular pupils as members of the 'hard core'. Their understanding of the complexity of pupils' motivation made it easier to portray individuals as being under the influence of ill-intentioned characters rather than as being such themselves. Moreover, teachers could not always agree on which pupils comprised the essential hard core. It seemed to vary significantly over time and amongst teachers.[41]

Despite these discrepancies, the 'hard core' type theory clearly had explanatory relevance. It complemented and was supported by personal and family pathology theories, in that both rested on a view of deviance prominent in the literature which suggests that deviants can be categorised as a separate minority. It was readily *available* and relatively *uncontentious*. It rendered the problem *accessible* to teacher intervention; they could split up undesirable groupings and distinguish named pupils who could be dealt with through the established pastoral or disciplinary measures. Ultimately, it linked easily with the work of *other relevant professionals* who, virtually by definition, dealt with an identifiable difficult minority of clients or patients.

The 'hard core' type of theory could be seen to serve an important symbolic function within the school. The stigmatisation of undesirable attitudes and behaviour, as embodied in publicly identified individuals, played its part in establishing what the school's standards were, in drawing the line between deviance and conformity[42] which was a necessary process for the maintenance of order and control. Other pupils[43] understood this process and could often be recruited to the conformist majority by learning to disassociate themselves from selected peers. Moreover, this apparently negative process gave scope for teachers' *personal and professional aspirations*. It won support from teachers who regarded the 'hard core' as primarily in need of punishment or removal from the classroom; it also provided teachers, whose orientation was therapeutic, with justifiable scope to individualise their assessment and treatment of a few children to an extent which would not have been possible for large numbers. Some teachers invested a great deal of time and energy in guiding and counselling a few individuals outside the mainstream activities, partly as a necessary containment strategy but, also, because they saw this as an opportunity to achieve high professional ideals. If teachers' efforts *failed*, the 'hard core' theory might ultimately be used to explain this in terms of 'hopeless cases', and teachers often seemed to feel, in the light of this, that it was acceptable to resort to policies of non-confrontation or avoidance of the problem; to resort to the view that many of the problems and conflicts in school were beyond the teachers' sphere of influence and had simply to be lived with.

Both of these perspectives provided an explanatory framework within which teachers could locate the array of problems which pupils presented to them. Both tended to individualise disaffection, or define it in terms of particular families or particular minorities. They ultimately implied a denial that resistance to schooling might be rational and legitimate, not because teachers lacked insight into societal and institutional factors which might cause pupils problems but because, in order to carry out their tasks and implement their teaching ideals, it was necessary for them to defend the organisation and their professional role within it against attack. These schools were not under severe physical attack, although the potential for disorder was inherently present, but like all schools, they were vulnerable to ideological attacks. Pupil resistance, in any form, coupled with wider societal questioning of the role and content of schooling, had considerable potential for undermining teachers' confidence and professional convictions. These perspectives, amongst others, enabled teachers to take account of the existence and apparent inevitability of some conflict and failure in schools without abandoning their commitment to the schooling process or their aspirations to improve life for their pupils as a whole.

Conclusion

This paper is not arguing that the predominance of one set of ideas over another was either inevitable or intractable. Numerous ideological currents existed in the schools and notions of family pathology or deviant minorities could be developed to justify a number of different responses to pupil disaffection. The liberal therapeutic approach was officially advocated in both schools but there were always teachers ready to argue that, on available evidence, alternative approaches – for example, a more punitive one – would 'work' better or describe the problems more accurately.

The schools differed significantly in the strength and coherence of their overall official perspective. In one school, senior and other staff persistently articulated liberal, therapeutic interpretations and demonstrated their explanatory relevance. What is more, there was a set of workable and relatively satisfactory procedures for dealing with problem pupils which backed up the liberal, therapeutic perspective. In that context, teachers with opposing views found themselves fairly isolated. In the other school, where there was less concerted effort by influential staff to apply officially approved ideas and where the associated pastoral system worked less smoothly, the liberal, therapeutic perspective had far less credibility and the way was more open for competing perspectives. In that sense, the work of establishing and sustaining coherent explanatory and prescriptive frameworks was done by the teachers themselves and it seemed that individual teachers were more likely to support a particular ideological stance if it could be shown to lead to effective strategies for action.

Notes and References

1 'Disaffected Pupils' Project, Educational Studies Unit, Brunel University, 1977/80.
2 FINN, D. GRANT, N. and JOHNSON, R. (1975) 'Social Democracy, Education and the Crisis', in CENTER FOR CONTEMPORARY CULTURAL STUDIES (University of Birmingham) *On Ideology*, London, Hutchinson, p. 145.
3 For example, see YOUNG, M. and WHITTY, G. (Eds.) (1977) *Society, State and Schooling*, Ringmer, Falmer Press, and YOUNG, M. (Ed.) (1971) *Knowledge and Control*, London, Collier-Macmillan.
4 SHARP, R. and GREEN, A. (1975) *Education and Social Control*, London, Routledge and Kegan Paul, p. 13.
5 GRACE, G. (1978) *Teachers, Ideology and Control*, London, Routledge and Kegan Paul.
6 *Ibid.*, p. 12 (quoting).
7 *Ibid.*, p. 10.
8 *Ibid.*, p. 31.
9 *Ibid.*, p. 31.
10 See FINN *et. al., op. cit.*
11 See, for example, DOUGLAS, J.W.B. (1964) *The Home and the School*, London, MacGibbon and Kee; DOUGLAS, J.W.B., ROSS, J.M. and SIMPSON, H.R. (1968) *All our Future*, London, Peter Davies; HALSEY, A.H. (Ed.) (1972) *Educational Priority: Vol. 1: E.P.A. problems and policies*, London, HMSO.
12 See, for example, Report of the Central Advisory Council for Education (England) (1963) *Half our Future*, London, HMSO (*The Newsom Report*); TYERMAN, M.J. (1968) *Truancy*, London, University of London Press; RUTTER, M. (1975) *Helping Troubled Children*, London, Penguin Books; LAWRENCE, J. STEED, D. YOUNG, P. (1977) *Disruptive Behaviour in Secondary School*, London, University of London, Goldsmiths College; RAYNOR, J. and HARRIS, E. (Eds.) (1977) *Schooling in the City*, London, Ward Lock Educational in association with Open University Press.
13 See, for example, WILLIS, P. (1977) *Learning to Labour*, Farnborough, Saxon House.
14 See GRACE, *op. cit.* Also HOLLY, D. (1977) 'Education and the Social Relations of a Capitalist Society', in YOUNG and WHITTY (Eds.), *op. cit.*, p. 185. Both suggest that certain kinds of conflict and uncertainty in schools have intensified in the latter half of this century.
15 See HAYWOOD METZ, M. (1978) *Classrooms and Corridors*, Berkeley, University of California Press. She discusses student rebellion in two American schools and describes how certain forms of it, for example, truanting in order to attend demonstrations against the Vietnam War, might be regarded as legitimate by some teachers, because of the political climate of the time.
16 These issues are well documented in criminological literature. See TAYLOR, I., WALTON, P. and YOUNG, J. (1973) *The New Criminology*, London, Routledge and Kegan Paul.
17 SHARP and GREEN, *op. cit.*, p. 69, contrast teachers with the psychiatrists studied by Strauss in STRAUSS, A. *et. al.*, (1964) *Psychiatric Ideologies and Institutions*, London, Collier-Macmillan. The psychiatrists were able to draw on well established schools of thought to inform and defend their practice.
18 *Newsom Report, op. cit.* Para 9.
19 *Ibid.*, para 20.
20 *Ibid.*, para 47.
21 Teacher interviewed in 1979.
22 Strauss, *op. cit.*
23 This broadly pastoral ethos was a feature of all six schools in the research project, although the detailed structures and procedures were different in each case. It seems likely that in schools without such strong pastoral ideas, teachers' perspectives would be different.
24 This terminology is drawn from TAYLOR, WALTON and YOUNG, *op. cit.*
25 Teacher interviewed in 1977.
26 This concept is drawn from TAYLOR, WALTON and YOUNG, *op. cit.*
27 Teacher interviewed in 1979.
28 *Ibid.*
29 Teacher interviewed in 1979.
30 These are typical phrases, quoted from various teacher interviews.
31 Teacher interviewed in 1979.
32 See, for example. DOUGLAS, ROSS and SIMPSON, *op. cit.*; BANKS, O. and FINLAYSON, D. (1973) *Success and Failure in the Secondary School*, London, Methuen; RUTTER, M. and MADGE, N. (1976) *Cycles of Disadvantage*, London, Heinemann Educational; WILSON, H. and HERBERT, G.W. (1978) *Parents and Children in the Inner City*, London, Routledge and Kegan Paul. (These authors do not confine their discussions to family-based factors, but deal extensively with them.
33 For example. WILLIS, *op. cit.* See also PEARSON, G. (1975) *The Deviant Imagination*, London, Macmillan

for a review of relevant literature on the sociology of deviance.

34 There is evidence from other data derived from the project that teachers may tend to shift their explanatory emphasis when pupils reach the fifth year and disaffection becomes more widespread. It may then be interpreted more in terms of pupils' impatience to transfer to paid employment.

35 See HARGREAVES, D. HESTOR, S. and MELLOR, F. (1975) *Deviance in Classrooms*, London, Routledge and Kegan Paul p. 193. They also noted that teachers made selective use of information on pupils' home backgrounds.

36 See FINN *et. al., op. cit.*, for a detailed analysis of the relationship between social democratic ideologies, educational policies and the development of professionalism among teachers.

37 None of the teachers interviewed in the six schools advanced views which implied a revolutionary transformation of their given institutional context.

38 See CLARK, J. 'The Three Rs – Repression, Rescue and Rehabilitation: Ideologies for control for working class youth'. Stencilled Occasional Paper. Sub and Popular Culture Series: S.P. No. 41. (Centre for Contemporary Cultural Studies, University of Birmingham.)

39 Teacher interviewed in 1979.

40 The daily battle between teachers and pupils over homework provided a good example of the difficulties which teachers met when they tried to impress on pupils the degree of priority which should be given to school work.

41 See BIRD, C. (1980) 'Deviant Labelling in School: the pupils' perspective', in WOODS, P. (Ed.) *Pupil Strategies*, Croom Helm, for a discussion of the contextual variation within schools affecting teachers' perceptions of individual pupils.

42 See COHEN, S. (1971) introduction to COHEN, S. and TAYLOR, L. (Eds.), *Images of Deviance*, Harmondsworth, Penguin Books.

43 There is evidence of this in the project data, from teacher and pupil interviews.

Locations of Learning and Ideologies of Education: some issues raised by a study of Education Otherwise.

Roland Meighan, University of Birmingham,
Christine Brown, Wolverhampton Polytechnic.

Introduction

In response to an invitation made by the *Observer* in 1967, one twelve year old described the school that he would like:[1]

> The school I'd like is what I have: my mother teaches my brother and me at home. We study maths, English, science, history, geography, French and scripture.
>
> This system has many advantages. The most important is that we can learn at our own speed; thus I have recently started A-level maths but am still struggling with O English, while my brother, who is three and a half years younger, is advanced in English but only average at arithmetic. Another advantage is that we have much more free time than other children; we don't waste time travelling to and fro and, as we have individual work, the education officer agreed to shorten lesson times for us. I spend a lot of my leisure time reading, bird watching, stamp and coin collecting, doing jigsaws, carpentry, painting, listening to radio, watching T.V., swimming, playing chess, draughts, tennis and table tennis. Another advantage is that we are not hedged in by a lot of silly rules and regulations. We are also free from bullying big boys and from pressure to start bad habits like smoking and drug taking. We dress in comfortable, sensible clothes and do not have to wear some ridiculous uniform, nor do we have to play compulsory games. Again, we have home cooking all the time.
>
> When my mother started, a lot of people told her she was foolish because we would never learn to mix. I don't think this is true because, although I've always liked some time by myself, my brother likes and has lots of friends with whom he goes to play and who come and play with him ... It was also said that we would grow up selfish: I hope we're not. About once a fortnight we have a stall in our front garden to aid Oxfam

and have collected £4 2s 3d so far this year. We also do a few odd jobs around the house. People also said Mother would find it too much. I know we get her down at times, but she survives and looks, so people say, much younger than she is. . . .

There have been many individual initiatives of this home-based educational kind in the past, but in 1977 the organisation *Education Otherwise* was established to give support to parents and children involved in such ventures. The purpose of this paper is to report a study of *Education Otherwise* that is based on the notion of ideologies of education. The study attempts to establish the complex of ideologies of education that exist within the organisation and gives an account of the various components that make up such ideologies. A little recognised component, a theory of locations of learning, will be discussed and proposed as the major linking feature of the various families involved, in their attempts to develop an alternative to mass schooling. In conclusion, the possibility of the location of learning figuring more centrally in education systems of the future will be developed.

Education Otherwise

The name of the organisation is derived from section 36 of the 1944 Education Act (England and Wales) which states that:

> It shall be the duty of the parent of every child of compulsory school age to cause him to receive efficient full-time education suitable to his age, aptitude and ability, either by regular attendance at school *or otherwise*.

In the United Kingdom education is legally compulsory; schooling is not. The law is clear on this point. Parents are accorded the primary responsibility for their children's education and, while they commonly delegate this to schools, they need not do so. Members of the Royal Family frequently have periods of education at home and other people who have had home-based learning include John Stuart Mill and Margaret Mead.

Education Otherwise consists primarily of families who have decided that in present circumstances the only way to ensure that the children's education is satisfactory, as they see it, is to take upon themselves full responsibility for their education rather than delegate it to the schools. The literature of the organisation states that these families and their supporters believe that children have the right to relationships of concerned equality in which they can mature; that they should have considerable freedom of thought, decision and action; and that their value as people should not be related to their performance on narrow academic criteria. They also state that children have a right to a wider community than the home itself. It is on this basis that they claim that 'education otherwise' should be conducted, and the group exists to support any families practising or seeking to practise education of these principles. The group was formed in 1977, and its formation was encountered by Roland Meighan who was assembling information about educating his own child at home. He developed a personal involvement as well as a research interest in the organisation. The group's immediate objectives are stated to be as follows:

1. To strengthen the links between members by a newsletter, by helping in the formation of local groups, by arranging meetings, etc.
2. To disseminate through the newsletter, handouts and otherwise information about (a) people's experiences, (b) available resources, (c) exchanges of skills and facilities.
3. To support people with general advice and where needed with specific help on (a) legal aspects, (b) presenting their case to the authorities, (c) for those educating children over 16, problems of tax, social security, etc.
4. To provide advice about devising programme of activities and educational method and materials.

Recently, interest has been stimulated by several television programme including ATV's 'Parents Day' and 'Format V', ITV's 'World in Action' and BBC's 'Open Door' showing various families and their educational activities. Nationally, there appear to be between 100 and 200 families; precise figures being difficult to establish, not least because some families feel it necessary to operate in a clandestine manner.

It is necessary to stress that the families in *Education Otherwise* are educating their children as a positive alternative to, rather than simply refusing to send them to, school and are attempting to cooperate with the Local Education Authority. *Education Otherwise* provides support and various kinds of advice to such families. Some families opt into the system again at various stages. Some organise the Primary phase at home and opt in at the Secondary phase; others reverse this. Others opt out for a year or two only whilst some opt in at the Further Education stage.

Some LEAs are helpful and sympathetic, indeed some have such a well-established procedure that a form exists for parents to fill in describing their programme. Other LEAs are suspicious, even hostile, and court cases sometimes result. So far, most cases appear to have gone against LEAs because they have been unable to prove beyond reasonable doubt that what local schools provide is superior to the efforts of a concerned and energetic family. (Since many of the families have started their programme *in desperation* because the children were so unhappy at school, this is perhaps not all that surprising).

LEAs vary considerably as to what they define as an acceptable educational programme. This may often turn on the particular vision of education adopted by the LEA officers. Some have a Protestant/Puritan outlook and have informed parents that their children were far too happy being educated at home and that school was necessary to teach them to cope with an unhappy world. Others have expressed the longing for the courage to adopt something similar for their own children who are alienated from their particular schools. Many parents report that they are treated from the start as deviants, rather than people who care enough about their children to devote extra time, energy and financial resources on them, and that they are held to be guilty unless they prove their educational innocence.

A similar organisation to *Education Otherwise* exists in the USA and it is called *Growing Without Schooling* and one well known person behind it is John Holt, author of *How Children Fail*. Two quotations from the GWS newsletter No. 3 indicate some parallel experiences to those of British parents:

> In its short life to date, GWS has already changed its character somewhat. It is turning out to be less about teaching than I thought it would be, and more about law, less about what your children can do once you get them out of school, and more about what you may have to do to get them out. I rather regret this. I am much more interested in helping children to explore the world and to find out and do interesting and worthwhile things in it, than I am in arguing about and fighting with schools. But it begins to look as if, like Moses in Egypt, we may have to find ways to make things a bit hot for the school Pharaohs, if only so that they will let our people go.
>
> The dozen or so letters and phone calls I have had about this during recent months don't add up to much of a sample, perhaps not even a representative one. They suggest, though, that many people who ask their local schools to approve some kind of home study program are going to meet, not sympathy and support, not even intelligent questions, but threats – 'we'll take you to court! We'll put you in jail! We'll take your kids away from you!'.

The second quotation discusses the irony of caring parents being treated as deviant whilst those who do not care are 'normal'.

> The Boston *Globe* of 2 February, 1978, in a story about school attendance, says, 'On a typical day, about 70 per cent of the school system's 65,000 youngsters attend classes'. They say nothing about the missing 30 per cent. Who are they? Why do they stay away? What do the schools do about them? The answers are, probably, that most of them are poor; that they stay away because they hate school and can see, even if they haven't got any-thing much else to do with their time, that the school is wasting it; and that the schools do almost nothing to get them back.
>
> There is irony here. As I said in an earlier GWS, compulsory school attendance laws were invented by rich people and aimed at poor kids. These rich people said in effect, 'We educated people are perfectly capable of teaching our own children, but the poor don't give a damn about their kids and wouldn't know enough to teach them anything even if they wanted to. So, unless we lock up those kinds in school all day long they are just going to run around the streets, cause trouble, get in bad habits, become drunks and criminals. We've got to put them in school to make them into good, obedient, hard-working factory hands.'
>
> The irony is that if you are in fact the kind of kid that compulsory

attendance laws were first aimed at, you can skip school all year long and nobody will pay any attention. The streets are full of the kinds of kids that schools were designed to keep off the streets. But if you are one of those now rare people who really care about the growth of your children and are willing to take the responsibility for helping that growth, and you try to take them out of schools where they are not growing but shrinking, the schools are likely to begin shouting about courts and jails. Strange.

The Concept of Ideology

Ideology is a highly ambiguous concept and it is necessary to give some discussion to the competing uses, at the outset. An early usage of ideology was as a philosophical concept to distinguish a science of ideas from an ancient metaphysics. The use of ideology in this sense is now rare. Another usage of ideology as a concept, traced to Napoleon Bonaparte, was that of revolutionary thinking; this revolutionary thinking being interpreted as an undesirable set of ideas. Ideology thus threatened 'sound and sensible' thinking about a vision for a society. From this developed the notion of ideology as fanatical or impractical theories about society, and it was largely a term of abuse.

One use of ideology by Marx and Engels in *The German Ideology* (1845–7) is related to the earlier view of undesirable sets of ideas. Engels, in a letter to Mehring in 1893, interprets ideology as abstract thought false in its assumptions about human society:

> Ideology is a process accomplished by the so-called thinker consciously indeed, but with a false consciousness. The real motives impelling him remain unknown to him, otherwise it would not be an ideological process at all. Hence he imagines false or apparent motives.

The true consciousness is sometimes referred to as 'science' setting up a distinction between Marxism, as science and other social thought, as ideology. This notion of ideology as illusion has become a common view:

> Meanwhile, in popular argument, ideology is still mainly used in the sense given by Napoleon. Sensible people rely on *experience*, or have a *philosophy*; silly people rely on ideology. In this sense, ideology, now as in Napoleon, is mainly a term of abuse ...[2]

Elsewhere Marx uses ideology in a more neutral sense where he refers to the legal, political, religious, aesthetic or philosophic as ideological forms in which men become conscious of conflict arising from conditions and changes in economic production. Ideology is not seen as false consciousness here.[3]

This second use of ideology by Marx is close to a more sociological use of the concept where it refers to a group philosophy. *Ideology is defined as a broad interlocked set of ideas and beliefs about the world held by a group of people that they demonstrate in both behaviour and conversation to various audiences.* These systems of belief are usually seen as 'the way things really are' by the groups holding them and they become the taken for granted way of making sense of the world.

It is this last use of ideology, as competing belief systems, that is employed in the analyses of ideologies of education that follow, since this makes the concept capable of being used as an analytical tool to demonstrate alternative patterns of ideas that coexist and compete for acceptance.

Individuals and Ideology

A psychological view of ideology begins with the attitudes and opinions of individuals and sees these as structured in an hierarchical manner. One attempt is that of Eysenck:[4]

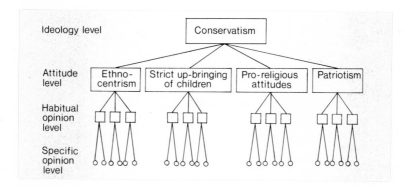

Specific opinions uttered on one occasion (such as 'what a naughty child that was in the supermarket') may give rise to habitual opinions uttered on several occasions (such as 'children should be seen and not heard'). A large number of habitual opinions about one central issue (for example, the place and behaviour of children in society) is defined as an attitude. When groups of attitudes are related, this is referred to as an ideology.

This raises a difficult issue, that of the relationship between an individual's consciousness and the social world. The psychological analysis above tends to a *psychological reductionist* approach: the ideology is constructed out of the opinions of individuals. An alternative possibility is that the individuals' attitudes and opinions are fashioned out of the ideologies available in an inherited language, inherited institutions and the situations that present themselves over which individuals have limited control, a *cultural formation* approach. It is not necessary to decide for or against either of these positions if they are both seen as partial explanations: both can be seen as having some credibility as well as there being an interaction between the two sets of influences.

However, for the purpose of some sociological analysis, it is useful to operate on the distinction that individuals have beliefs and opinions, whereas organised groups of people have ideologies. The point is argued in this passage:

> But ideology is not opinion; is it then perhaps the sum total of the relevant opinions and beliefs of those who participate in the given social group? For example, is it correct to say that ideology of grammar school teachers is what you get if you add up all the opinions and beliefs of grammar school teachers about grammar schools, or about education in general? Unless they all share exactly the same opinions about these subjects, we could not describe their ideology in that way, unless we assumed that you can add opinions up like apples. But if you 'add' one opinion to another, you get not only two opinions, but an argument, a debate, a belief and one of its presuppositions, a qualified agreement, an exemplification of a general idea in a particular situation, and so on. Since relations between ideas can assume different forms, and since ideas must be understood in terms of their relations to other ideas, we must be prepared to find an ideology containing more than all the relevant opinions and beliefs of those who adhere to it.[5]

Availability and Non-availability

Systems of belief may have several states of existence. They may exist *in theory only* since they have not yet been adopted or recognised except perhaps in science fiction writing or futuristic novels. Ideologies may exist but be *non-available* because the sponsoring group lacks the means of transmitting the beliefs widely or chooses to remain small and exclusive. It has been argued by Allen[6] that the term ideology is best reserved for those systems of belief that are *available* in that the sponsoring group has a means of transmitting the ideas widely and takes the necessary action to achieve this. For the purpose of the analysis to follow, ideology will be taken to be any system of beliefs – whether available or not, whether theoretical or in practice – to allow the discussion to be as wide-ranging as possible.

A philosophical approach to ideology would be interested in the question of true and false ideologies. For the purpose of sociological analysis, this question is often suspended and the definition of knowledge is taken to be what the participants define as true information, beliefs, ideas and attitudes. This allows any ideology to be investigated in terms of how far it functions to advance or defend the interests of a particular group, and also in terms of the consequences of actions derived from that ideology. Nothing about the truth or falsity of an ideology is indicated by this kind of analysis.

Ideologies in Competition

The idea of competition introduces an analogy with possible distorting effects, for example, ideologies can coexist in a state of mutual tolerance with no competition. However, where the ideologies conflict and compete, several outcomes are possible.

Domination

One ideology may achieve a position of dominance over the others. One way that this may be done is through cultural domination. Gramsci calls this *cultural hegemony* where a dominant culture represents itself as the natural, obvious or mainstream culture and attempts to contain all others within it. Such a dominant culture becomes the basis of a dominant ideology.

Incorporation

One ideology may absorb, take over or combine with another in a variety of ways and, if this is successful, it is referred to as incorporation. One example is the proposition of the incorporation of radical educational ideas about equality in educational provision into the traditional educational ideology by the offer of equality of *opportunity* in the form of an apparent equal start in the race to become unequal. This preserves the traditional idea of an élite but appears to shift the means of recruitment from aristocratic inheritance and patronage to merit. The incorporation is completed, the explanation runs, by ensuring that the competition is of such a nature that similar people enter the élite under the merit system as would have under the inheritance/patronage system.

Legitimation

One ideology, to become dominant, has to achieve acceptance of its beliefs. One form of this is direct repression through armies, police, secret police and prisons:

> Of course, in many societies where the dominant group is insecure legitimation occurs through the methods of overt repression. Armies, secret police, machineries of summary imprisonment, torture and execution have been, and continue to be, used by rulers and their socially-powerful supporters to enforce their view of social order. Whether we talk about the Inquisition during the sixteenth-century, or Stalinist Russia in the 1930s, or the student uprisings of 1968, we have to take account of the 'legalised' use of force which is always available to the controlling groups in a society. Easy though it is to overlook the existence of these powers in contemporary Britain, it is important to remember that, even in their mere availability, they exert a powerful level of secondary reinforcement if the first line of legitimation gives way. Furthermore, most advanced societies have perfected numerous techniques of counter-intelligence and covert surveillance of likely centres of dissent, so that any major attack on the social order is likely to be anticipated.[7]

A softer form of legitimation is in the use of major institutions such as education, mass media, religion, law and the economy to put over a 'consensus', 'common sense' or 'sensible person's' point of view as against the 'lunatic fringe' view which turns out to be almost any view inconvenient to the group with the dominant ideology. Control of the mass media and education may be one way of preventing an alternative ideology from becoming available; for example, the British television companies and the schools combine to give special privileges to one form of the Christian viewpoint and to deny similar access by either other religions or non-religious life stances.[8]

The Multiplicity of Ideologies

The concept of ideology is ambiguous not only because of competing definitions but also because it is used to describe sets of ideas operating at various levels in society and in various contexts. A ruling class may be said to have an ideology, or a middle class or a working class. Banks, retail organisations and trade unions may also be said to have them. So may the professions, education, the mass media and the nation. Pressure groups of various kinds whether for car owners, pedestrians, for motorways or against motorways may be said to have ideologies. It helps to try and specify the level or context of the ideologies in question, and when this shifts but this is not always easy. In the analysis that follows, ideologies of education operate at various levels: nationally, in the Education Acts; regionally, in Local Education Authority policies; locally, in a particular school and, internally, between rival groups in a school. Furthermore, ideologies of education are linked with other ideologies; ideologies of politics, of the economy, of social classes. Failure to grapple with this has created considerable confusion in educational writings, as we shall see.

Ideologies of Education

An ideology of education may be defined as the *set of ideas and beliefs held by a group of people about the formal arrangements for education, specifically schooling* and, often by extension or by implication, to informal aspects of education, for example learning at home, as well.

Dichotomous approaches

There have been a number of attempts to describe alternative ideologies of education. Some of these have been theoretical and others have been based on empirical studies. A common approach has been to contrast two polarised types, a dichotomous approach:

Teacher centreed	v	child centreed[9]
Open teaching	v	closed teaching[10]

Meaning receiving	v	meaning making[11]
Authoritarian	v	democratic[12]
Traditional	v	progressive[13]
Transmission	v	interpretation[14]
Open schools	v	closed schools[15]
Dependent study	v	autonomous study[16]

The limitations of the approach based on dichotomies emerge if an attempt is made to link the ones listed above. There is some similarity in the ideas of teacher-centered, closed, meaning receiving, authoritarian, traditional, transmission, closed schools and dependent study but, nevertheless, considerable variety of emphasis. But the other partners of the pairs have little in common other than being contrasted with a similar alternative. Child-centered, open teaching, meaning making, democratic, progressive, interpretation, open schools, and autonomous study vary considerably and can be seen as alternatives to each other. This becomes clear if we consider just one aspect, the activity of the learner. In the child-centred approach, the learners choose from a range of activities provided by the teacher, in open teaching the learners make decisions about how learning is best undertaken. In meaning making the activity of learners is somewhat similar. In the misleadingly-named democratic system, learners respond to a pleasant authoritarian teacher who allows learners some privileges in a contrived pleasant working atmosphere. Progressive teaching is seen as something similar. In interpretation teaching, a negotiation takes place and a dialogue emerges at the initiative of the teacher. The learners in open schools are also involved in negotiations and dialogues. In autonomous study, the learners gradually take on all the decision making about what to learn and how to learn until they are able to control all aspects of learning themselves.

The activity of teachers varies also. In some cases they make all of the decisions but implement them in a pleasant 'nice strict' fashion, in others they negotiate, in others they facilitate the decisions of the learners, in others they initiate a dialogue, in others they gradually hand over decision-making to the learners in a systematic way.

The conclusion is that these pairs of ideologies are operating at different conceptual levels and also contrasting pairs from a wider range of alternatives. The latter point is clear from the analysis above. The former point is clear if we note that some of these pairs are describing classroom teaching ideologies, others ideologies of the whole education system and others ideologies of whole schools.

Attempts to Identify more than Two Ideologies of Education

A number of attempts go beyond dichotomies. One well known attempt is that of Raynor.[17] He outlines four ideologies of education, aristocratic, bourgeois, democratic and proletarian. Another attempt is that of Cosin.[18] He distinguishes between elitest/conservative; rationalising/technocratic; romantic/individualist and egalitarian/democratic. Davies[19] distinguishes between four ideologies of education, conservative, revisionist, romantic and democratic. These approaches have several features in common. They all attempt to go beyond dichotomous models to more complex versions but the problems associated with the former remain:

(a) They appear to be selecting out from a wider range of alternatives since the attempts do not match up well,

(b) They are operating at different conceptual levels; some at the level of classrooms, some at the level of comparing educational systems across states and nations.

It is tempting to try and resolve the second problem by categorising into *levels* of operation. This would allow a comparison between ideologies of whole education systems, competing ideologies within a national system, ideologies within schools, and ideologies of classroom practice. However level is an analogy with the built-in assumption of an hierarchy of power or influence of significance and it, therefore, prejudges the relationships between these levels. One attempt to avoid this has been the distinction between ideologies of legitimation and ideologies of implementation. The first addresses the question of why, the second the problem of how. Legitimation refers to the goals, values and *ends* an education system should foster whereas implementation refers to organisational alternatives, methods of attempting to achieve the legitimated goals and, in general, the *means*. A limitation of this approach is that most ideologies of education contain ideas about both ends and means.

A further possibility is to regard the ideologies as networked. The ideologies of education systems and of classrooms have some links, though they are not seen as tightly and completely linked. The ideologies of education in the classroom may have some links with other parts of the network but also have logics of their own at the same time, according some autonomy of action. An example from Religious Education teaching shows the possibilities of this pattern. Religious Education teaching is compulsory by law so secondary schools have appointed staff for the subject and allocated time on the timetable for an Agreed Syllabus to be taught. Many teachers find this unteachable either for their own personal reasons or because of the reaction of pupils, or both, and spend the time teaching and learning about issues like morals and decision making in personal relationships often without a specifically religious interpretation being dominant. The national ideology here has consequences for the school ideology but does not determine it. Put another way, the notion of a network of ideologies allows contradictions to emerge which might be hidden in a view of levels or a view of legitimation distinct from implementation.

Analytical models based on criteria

An alternative approach to describing ideologies of education is to establish criteria of the major features of such ideologies and then to plot all the combinations that are possible. Some will exist in practice and others may not.

One attempt to identify national ideologies of education in this way is that of

Smith[20] and another is that of Hopper.[21] A model that concentrates on the ideologies within and amongst schools is that of Hammersley.[22] He develops five groups of criteria: teacher's role; pupil action; view of knowledge; view of learning and teaching technique. An attempt (which includes features from the approaches of both Smith and Hammersley) to give a model that might serve to analyse particular classrooms, schools or systems is that of Meighan.[23] Here an ideology of education is taken to have various component 'theories'. Theory here is used in its colloquial sense of a view about something rather than its scientific usage. These components are as follows: (the order is not significant).

(a) a theory of knowledge, its content and structure,
(b) a theory of learning and the learner's role,
(c) a theory of teaching and the teacher's role,
(d) a theory of resources appropriate for learning,
(e) a theory of organisation of learning situations,
(f) a theory of assessment that learning has taken place,
(g) a theory of aims, objectives and outcomes,

The research study, outlined later, on children educated at home suggested an additional feature,

(h) a theory of the location of learning.

Other components that might well be added include a theory of language and its educational use. Each of these component theories can be analysed in detail by being broken down into sub-divisions. The following discussion gives some examples of such sub-divisions.

a) *Theory of Knowledge; its content and structure*

(i) Knowledge may be interpreted as predominantly past-orientated, present-orientated or future-orientated. Past-orientated approaches will rely heavily on existing subject divisions on the grounds that the knowledge gathered in the past is comprehensive and reliable. Present-orientated knowledge approaches will stress integration on the grounds that current problems like terrorism, pollution, computer technology and mass media are both cross disciplinary and in need of new knowledge to cope with them. Future-orientated knowledge approaches will stress the rate of change and the rate of production of new knowledge and the consequent need for learners to acquire skills of learning, relearning and of both developing and adjusting to this 'knowledge explosion'. It follows that a past-orientated view would favour Latin, a future-orientated view Esperanto as an attempted international language.

(ii) School knowledge may be interpreted as distinct from pupils' everyday knowledge. The teaching task will vary, in consequence, from replacing the false or inadequate knowledge, to establishing a dialogue, to grounding learning in the existing knowledge of the learners.

(iii) School knowledge may be seen as hierarchically structured in terms of perceived difficulty and status of subjects, or of equal availability and similar status, or not seen as subjects at all. In the first case, high status subjects (for example, mathematics) may be contrasted with low status (for example, domestic science) so that GCE. 'A' level in the latter will only be interpreted as equivalent to an 'O' level for the purposes of university entrance. This also illustrates a contrast between views that knowledge is sex typed, with some more appropriate for females or males, and views that all knowledge is equally suitable for both sexes.

(iv) A view of knowledge that holds that only a limited number of subjects or studies are appropriate for schools may be contrasted with the view that a wide range should be included with few exceptions, and a further view that there should be no exceptions. In the case of foreign languages, the first view might imply that one stipulated foreign language should be offered, the second view that a range of Western European languages should be available, the third that any language including attempts at international languages like Esperanto should be available. (Currently, few schools teach Esperanto and they cannot get it established as an examination subject.)

b) *A Theory of Learning and the Learner's Role*

(i) One view of learning is that it is predominantly a collective activity best organised in groups, another that it is predominantly an individual activity. The contrast between a conventional university with students in lectures and seminars and the Open University with students at home with units and broadcasts shows how the difference in emphasis leads to different organisational solutions.

(ii) A view of learning as competitive against others may be contrasted with a view that it is competitive against criteria of achievement. A further view is that it is a co-operative venture.

(iii) In one view, learners learn to avoid disagreeable consequences like low marks, censure, non-promotion and punishment, in another view they learn to increase desired personal competence, in another intellectual curiosity is a feature of human consciousness unless it is discouraged.

(iv) Learning is related to ability manifested in the successful performance of the increasingly complex tasks provided in schools, in one view. In an alternative view, learning is related to the skill with which the learning situation has been devised: you do not kick the piano for playing the wrong notes, the argument runs.

(v) Learning is best undertaken by listening, alternatively by seeing, alternatively by doing.

(vi) The learner's role is to receive decisions made by the teachers without question, or to engage in consultations and negotiations of the teachers' initiatives, or to make decisions for themselves.

(vii) The learner's role is to reproduce what the teacher knows, or to produce a personal synthesis from the resources available, or to produce new insights and knowledge. Learners are trainees, or scholars, or explorers.

c) *A Theory of Teaching and the Teacher's Role*

(i) The expertise claimed for the teacher's role can be of various kinds. It can be based on the knowledge to be acquired where teachers are single subject teachers or multiple subject class teachers. Alternatively the claim can be based on methods for achieving learning in learners, an educational technology or learning systems expertise. A third possibility is that of facilitator and consultant where the teacher responds to the initiatives of the learners for instruction, learning systems advice, or whatever counselling is appropriate. The teacher gets very close to a real *in loco parentis* situation in this last option.

(ii) The teaching role links closely with the claim for expertise. Teachers may predominately be instructors, learning systems designers and administrators, or learning counsellors.

(iii) Teaching may stress product or process. If the stress is on product, then the task is to get learners to give correct answers. Where the stress is on process, the task is to achieve thinking; for example, thinking historically, thinking scientifically or thinking critically. The latter view is not entirely specifiable or simple to assess, and requires some notion of 'constructive doubt' rather than the comfort of certainty.

(iv) Teaching may imply coercion, negotiation or control by democratic principles with pupils' responses tending to compliance, bargaining and participant decision making. The various forms of authoritarian teaching, where learners remain dependent on teachers and non-authoritarian teaching, where learners either have, or eventually gain, independence, are discussed in detail in the next chapter.

d) *A Theory of Resources Appropriate for Learning*

(i) Resources may be first hand, second hand, or third hand experiences. First hand experiences are research studies, simulations, or making your own text or reading books. Second hand experiences are accounts of first hand experiences given in books, films or visiting speakers. Third hand experiences are contained in items like textbooks which give summaries of what people other than the writer experienced. Schools differ in the emphasis they place on these kinds of resources.

(ii) Resources may be books, multi-media materials or first hand experiences. In the first case the prime resources for learning will be a school library, a class library and subject book storerooms. In the second, the outcome may often be a multi-media school resources centre. In the third case, the whole environment of the learners, in and out of school, is defined as the prime resource.

(iii) Resources may be available to learners with varying degrees of access. Access may be very limited and resources only available through a teacher. Resources may be limited to one sex (for example, domestic science facilities) or access to a resources centre open to teachers and sixth formers only. Alternatively access may be licensed to insiders only: community schools operate on a different assumption, that insiders and outsiders may have access to some resources. Open access to resources is another possibility.

e) *A Theory of Organisation of Learning Situations*

(i) The general organisation of a school may be seen as an individual's responsibility – the headteacher, or senior staff concern, or a whole staff concern, or whole staff with senior pupils, or the concern of the whole learning community including service personnel such as caretakers and cleaners.

(ii) Grouping of learners may be organised on the basis of age, sex, achievement, or some combination of these, or none of these.

(iii) Timetables may be decided well in advance of the arrival of the learners, predicting their activities or as a result of learners, options or negotiated with learners as a first activity of a new school year.

(iv) Teachers may be organised as subject teachers, as class teachers teaching a range of topics, or as a team of teachers working with a large group.

(v) Other details of school organisation may be expressed in various ways:

Resources: there may be a resources centre or not, with various kinds of access.

Records: there may be open record systems or secret record systems with reporting systems of various kinds.

Rewards and Punishments: may range from individual incentives to team incentives, physical punishment to loss of privileges to restitutionary activities, decided in authoritarian or non-authoritarian ways.

School Uniforms: may be present, absent or voluntary, styles imposed or negotiated, decisions imposed or arrived at democratically.

House Systems: or other sub groupings of a school may exist for various purposes, pastoral, sporting, or social.

Extra Curricular activities: may range from school choirs, orchestras, plays, clubs and societies, to none at all as in the case of many European countries where schooling is limited to classroom learning.

f) *A Theory of Assessment that Learning has taken place*
(i) The view of who is best able to assess learning ranges from the external examiners of an examination board to the teachers of the learners to the learners themselves.

(ii) The notion of what should be assessed varies across the courses for their efficiency in achieving learning, the teachers for their results, and the pupils for their achievement in learning.

(iii) The purposes of assessment may be diagnostic to direct further learning, or for selection of some kind.

(iv) The method employed may vary from criterion referencing performance against known criteria, to norm referencing to produce an agreed proportion of successes and failures.

(v) The assessment may focus on the processes of learning, adapting, revising and thinking, or an end product of written right answers.

(vi) Assessment may refer to written performances, non-written performances, institutional adjustment or personal character.

(vii) The form of assessment may vary from references to reports, to profiles, to certificates, to self-report profiles.

g) *A Theory of Aims, Objectives and Outcomes* It is in the theories of outcomes and objectives that ideologies of legitimation link with ideologies of implementation since the legitimation refers to the goals and ends of education whereas the other theories of learning (assessment, organisation and the like) refer more to the means of implementing such aims.

(i) The society for which education prepares pupils may be envisaged in various ways. It may be seen as a society of rigid inequality where pupils are allocated to roles of rulers and ruled by birth or limited patronage and sponsorship. It may be envisaged as a state of fluid inequality with mobility for some based on merit or some other principle of selection. Some visions stress some version of equality. Others stress a pluralistic society with conflicts of interests resolved in a social democracy. Another alternative is an individualistic society with a high dispersal of, or access to, political power. The ideologies outlined by Raynor, Cosin and Davies, indicated earlier in this chapter, give names to these visions, aristocratic, élitist, egalitarian, democratic and romantic.

(ii) A well known attempt to classify theories of outcomes is that of Williams,[24] conveniently summarised by Young[25] as follows:

Ideology	Social Position	Educational Policies
1. Liberal/ conservative	Aristocracy/ gentry	Non-vocational – 'the educated man', an emphasis on character.
2. Bourgeois	Merchant and professional classes	Higher vocational and professional courses. Education as access to desired positions.
3. Democratic	Radical reformers	Expansionist – 'education for all'.
4. Populist/ proletariat	Working classes/ subordinate groups	Student relevance, choice participation.

h) *A Theory of the Location of Learning* Learning may best be undertaken in a special building, a school, college, or university, or university, or in a locality operating from an organisational base as the case of 'anywhere', 'everywhere', 'street' schools (for example, the Philadephia Parkway Project) or using home as a base as in the case of the Open University and the *Education Otherwise* families educating children at home.

Summary

These are examples of how the theories can be analysed further by proposing subdivisions and they do not exhaust the possibilities. Future work will no doubt extend the list but enough has been achieved here, it is claimed, to demonstrate that, although the concept of ideologies of education is highly ambiguous, it is capable of being used as an analytical tool.

The attempts confined to dichotomies, it has been suggested, have severe limitations; first of all because they select out two from a range of possible alternatives and, frequently, a different pairing each time. Second, they operate at various conceptual levels ranging from national systems to individual schools without always specifying the level in question. Attempts to establish more complex typo-logies of four or more ideologies of education have pointed the way to a more systematic attempt based on criteria.·

The attempt to establish an analytical model based on criteria discussed here has centreed on the establishment of various component theories that make up an ideology of education. These theories can be looked at in detail by outlining sub-divisions within these theories. A previous attempt along these lines,[26] suggested that these sub-divisions were dichotomous but the attempt above has demonstrated that there are frequently three or more alternatives that can be discerned.

Such an approach does not resolve all the difficulties associated with the concept of ideology. The analytical approach based on components can have hidden values. One taken-for-granted assumption may be that there are no proposals for education currently on offer that are convincing, so that tolerating several alternatives is the only feasible course of action. Therefore the characteristics of the alternatives need to be described in order to see what it is that is being tolerated. This view is close to the notion of an open, pluralistic society based on an uncertainty principle and held in the spirit of 'the open society is the worst kind of society – except for the alternatives'.

Related to this possible hidden assumption is the difficulty that any grounds for exclusion are not stated: all alternative ideologies of education may not be tolerable but how the identification of those to be excluded is undertaken is left unresolved. The components approach may also demonstrate a range of contradictions within and amongst ideologies with no apparent means of resolving them apart from a hidden assumption of coexistence.

Other problems can be cited including the limitations of an analogy like com-ponents, which has an assumption of a rational, logical construction like a Meccano set, when applied to a human activity like education forged in an historical and political context.

Ideologies of Education and Education Otherwise

The official position of *Education Otherwise*, as outlined in the publicity and informa-tional material, is that of a non-authoritarian ideology. However the analysis by Christine Brown established a wide variety of ideologies of education within the organisation. This analysis was based on the written material of the organisation including its newsletter, interviews with members in their homes, correspondence, and interviews at a national conference.

Theory of Knowledge, its contents and structure

Officially *Education Otherwise* was fairly compatible with non-authoritarian alter-natives. Traditional subject divisions were treated as arbitrary if not discarded. Knowledge was seen as acquired through individual and subjective experience. Among the members, however, there was a large section who accepted traditional subject divisions as the basis of their programme. Many found this forced on them by the LEAs. Others opted for the security of creating a miniature formal school at home, at least as a starting point.

Theory of learning and the learner's role

Officially *Education Otherwise* was compatible with non-authoritarian alternatives. The learner was seen to develop his own pattern of learning through direct experience within his environment – 'learning by doing' stimulated by learner curiosity: autonomous learning was envisaged. Among members, however, there was a large proportion where learning was traditionally teacher/parent directed in prescribed areas. The attitude of some LEA officers was that unstructured and spontaneous approaches were unacceptable: Rousseau's Emile and A.S. Neill's vision of education were rejected outright with the sure certainty of the bigot.

Teaching and the teacher's role

Officially *Education Otherwise* was compatible with non-authoritarian alternatives; authoritarian roles were avoided and guidance, where guidance was accepted, was in Russell's 'spirit of freedom', i.e. as a *temporary* necessity not as a permanent state. The concept of specialist educational expertise exclusive to a profession was rejected. But among members there were those who assumed an authoritarian role in the teaching of their children: for example, one parent supervised set lessons; others employed tutorial help from qualified teachers; and others used correspondence courses.

Resources appropriate for learning

Officially *Education Otherwise* was compatible with non-authoritarian alternatives – all resources were regarded as appropriate for learning and special emphasis was placed on the use of the public media. The relationship between the learner and the resource was viewed as direct rather than filtered through a teacher. Many members however still concentrated on school text-books in specialist subject areas, or used specialist media transmissions, or correspondence texts.

Theory of assessment

Officially *Education Otherwise* was critical of competitive examinations and of assessment for and by professional 'experts'. Self assessment by the learner seemed integral to the process of learning. But many members substituted the assessment of prescribed behaviors by the professional teacher for the assessment of prescribed behaviours by themselves and many adopted procedures compatible with the state school in preparing for public examinations. In these cases the parent took on the role of the traditional teacher for some of the time.

Organisation of learning situations

Again *Education Otherwise* was officially compatible with non-authoritarian alternatives in that it advocated learner-directed organisation; unstructured and free-ranging. Many members however presented very highly structured programmes with set time-tables for considerable periods of the week.

Aims and objectives

Officially *Education Otherwise* was compatible with non-authoritarian alternatives in that it emphasised the free growth of the individual towards self-directed goals; like the free schools it attempted to promote individualism and criticised the mass conformity of authoritarian settings in the state school. To resist the power of professional conglomerates was a specially stated aim. In practice, however, many members were expressing dissatisfaction with the state school system not over the aims themselves but over their inefficiency in carrying out those aims. Their objectives were similarly prescribed and monitored but were, in their opinion, being executed more efficiently.

Ideologically, therefore, *Education Otherwise* emerges as a very complex organisation; its official line and the attitudes of some of its members is well within the context of non-authoritarian alternatives – varying from free school and libertarian approaches pursued in the home setting to community oriented learning networks. Among its members, however, were many with ideologies highly compatible with the state school norms and having the location of education and, to a much lesser extent, the practical rejection of state-directed professionals, as their *only* radical features.

A Further Component of an Ideology of Education – A Theory of Locations of Learning

Non-authoritarian ideologies of education can provide alternative views of the location of learning to that in current use which confines it to the school building and to the relatively total institution of the school. Contemporary free schools move towards smaller units, less isolated from the rest of the community and community-based, providing much opportunity for outside exploration and lacking in the authoritarian or bureaucratic control of the large state school. But they are still schools – located in special and separate premises, often organised by professionally trained teachers, requiring at least a minimum of bureaucratic management. Deschoolers question the school – any form of school – as the locus for learning and begin to think in terms of learning without any kind of closed institutional arrangement – learning networks, for example. *Education Otherwise* has proffered the home setting as an alternative base.

Conclusion

The one single aspect where *Education Otherwise* was consistent throughout was that the school as a locus for education was replaced by the home. Some, although not all, entertained concepts of learning networks compatible with de-schooling theory, but all questioned the locus of the school.

One of the most taken-for-granted aspects of education has been location in a special building, that is, the school. Education systems of the future may develop a variety of locations, and *Education Otherwise* poses the possibility of this becoming an important component of ideologies of education. The Open University has already opened up similar issues with regard to higher education where learning takes place at home, at a study centre, on a summer school, in a self help group or by a telephone link up. The Parkway program in Philadelphia raises similar issues since the school exists without a special building by holding classes and other learning experiences anywhere in the city (for example, museums, church halls, libraries).

The current situation between LEAs and *Education Otherwise* families tends to be polarised in two ways. Firstly education is either located at school or at home. It is possible to envisage a range of possible arrangements between schools and homes in between these two poles, with programmes of study agreed between parents, pupils and teachers for half the time in school and half at home, or a quarter of the time in one and three quarters in the other. The Open University alternation of summer school, study centre and home points the way here. Secondly, the situation is polarised in terms of ideologies of education. In a recent court case, LEA Hereford and Worcester opposed a particular family because its approach to education was other than a transmission style organised with a set timetable and employing direct instruction. The family were operating an autonomous study system of the kind encountered in some private schools but rarely available in state schools. LEAs tend to approve transmission types of home education and oppose any other approach, even when it is legitimated in the private sector, thus sustaining a dogmatic 'one right way' view of education.

The feasibility of managing a more flexible home/school relationship presents one practical problem which seems to freeze the imagination of the current genre of educational administrators. However, the administrative skills, systems and procedures already exist. The organisation of the Open University, the administration of Evening Institutes in a multitude of study situations, the operation of correspondence colleges and of Technical Colleges with large part-time populations of students, are all working models that can be adopted, to say nothing of resource facilities like BBC and ITV schools broadcasting. Using such systems, a prospectus of possibilities for learning, where schools are in an *active* partnership with families, becomes feasible. Visions of how a Learning Society and *'Education Permanante'* might work, emerge from such considerations. The role of school teachers might become closer to that of their higher status cousins, university teachers, using a similar range of tutorial, instructional, consultancy and research skills. For politicians and civil servants, there is the additional possibility of such a system being considerably cheaper than the present one: both the Parkway Program and the Open University have proved to be cost-effective alternatives to traditional systems. We have been given alternative visions of the future in recent years.

These range from nuclear holocaust, through economic stagnation with lower standards of living or the self-sufficiency society (as scarce resources and energy supplies run out) to the leisure future brought about by the micro-processor revolution. It is interesting to speculate how the school/home partnership might serve several of these better than the present system by being cheaper, encouraging self sufficiency, or solving the 'problem' of increased leisure by providing families that wanted it with more involvement in the educational process.

Notes and References

1 BLISHEN, E. (1967) *The School That I'd Like*, Harmondsworth, Penguin.
2 See WILLIAMS, R. (1977) *Ideology* in Open University E202, Unit 20, Bletchley, Open University Press.
3 MARX, K. (1859) *Contribution to the Critique of Political Philosophy*, reprinted (1971).
4 EYSENCK, H. (1957) *Sense and Nonsense in Psychology*, Harmondsworth, London, Lawrence Wishart, Penguin.
5 COSIN, B. (1972) *Ideology*, Open University E282, Unit 13, Bletchley, Open University Press.
6 ALLEN, V. (1975) *Social Analysis*, London.
7 ESLAND, G. (1977) *Legitimacy and Control*, Open University E202, Unit 4, Bletchley, Open University Press.
8 Each year, the BBC is approached by the British Humanist Association on behalf of the majority of the population, that is, the unbelievers and non-church attenders, to allow time for the discussion of non-religious moralities and life stances on a similar basis to that of Christians on Sundays. An arrangement of this kind operates on Dutch television. Each year the application is refused.
9 DEPARTMENT OF EDUCATION AND SCIENCE (1967) *Plowden Report, Children and their Primary Schools*, London, HMSO.
10 KOHL, H. (1969) *The Open Classroom*, London, Methuen.
11 POSTMAN, N. and WEINGARTNER, C. (1969) *Teaching as a Subversive Activity*, Harmondsworth, Penguin.
12 LIPPITT, R. and WHITE, R.K. (1958) An Experimental Study of Leadership and Group Life, in MACCOBY, E.E. *et. al.*, *Readings in Social Psychology*, New York, Holt Rinehart Winston.
13 BENNETT, S.N. (1976) *Teaching Styles and Pupil Progress*, London, Open Books.
14 BARNES, D. and SHEMILT, D. (1974) Transmission and Interpretation, *Educational Review* 26, 3.
15 BERNSTEIN, B. (1967) 'Open School, Open Society', *New Society*, September 14th.
16 HUSEN, T. (1974) *The Learning Society*, London, Methuen.
17 RAYNOR, J. (1972) *The Curriculum in England*, Open University E282, Unit 2, Bletchley, Open University Press.
18 COSIN, B. (1972) *Ideology*, Open University E282, Unit 13, Bletchley, Open University Press.
19 DAVIES, I. (1969) Education and Social Science, *New Society*, May 8th.
20 SMITH, D. (1973) *Distribution Processes and Power Relations in Educational Systems*, Open University, E352, Unit 1, Bletchley, Open University Press.
21 HOPPER, E. (1971) 'A Typology for the Classification of Educational Systems', in HOPPER, E. (Ed.), *Readings in the Theory of Educational Systems*, London, Hutchinson.
22 HAMMERSLEY, M. (1977) *Teacher Perspectives*, Open University E202, Unit 9, Bletchley, Open University Press.
23 MEIGHAN, R. and ROBERTS, M. (1979) Autonomous Study and Educational Ideologies, in *Journal of Curriculum Studies*, 11, 1.
24 WILLIAMS, R. (1961) *The Long Revolution,* Harmondsworth, Penguin.
25 YOUNG, M.F.D. (Ed.) (1971) *Knowledge and Control*, London, Collier Macmillan.
26 HAMMERSLEY, M., see Note 22.
27 HUSEN, T., *op. cit.* (Note 16).

Curricula are Social Processes[1]

Gary Easthope
University of Tasmania

During the 1960s a number of curriculum innovations were presented to schools: French for primary schools; Nuffield science; Mathematics for the Majority; the Humanities Curriculum Project and Man, a Course of Study (MACOS). Those who were given, or took upon themselves, the task of disseminating these innovations soon became aware that curriculum content was inextricably linked to the social processes of interaction between teachers and between teachers and pupils. The implementation of a new curriculum subject implied more than merely a change in what was taught, it also implied a change in social relationships. Hamilton[2] expressed it in these terms:

> the introduction of integrated studies is not merely equivalent to intro-
> ducing a new syllabus but implies a radical change of emphasis in the
> organisational context and thinking of secondary education ... simple
> questions of content cannot be separated from complex questions of
> grouping children by ability, from questions of 'responsibility' and
> authority, or, even from questions of school democracy.

And yet that awareness – that social relationships are as much a part of the curriculum as its content – appears to have faded into the background once again. Debates about the common core curriculum seem to treat the social relationships of teaching as non-problematic. The purpose of this article is to re-assert that simple sociological insight – gained with so much effort by educationalists in the 1960s and now largely ignored – that curricula are social processes. They are not just collections of facts but complex social creations. Social creations in which what is to be transmitted is linked to how it is transmitted. The article therefore says nothing new. It just re-asserts the sociological insight on the curriculum that argues that it is a social process. What is new is the way of expressing that insight and the hope is that a new presentation may help readers to understand more fully what is implied by asserting that curricula are social processes.

Three ideal types of education will be delineated. I am using education to mean socialization carried out with deliberate and planned intent.[3] My concern is with the manifest intentions of those involved in creating socialisation settings although, later, the unintended consequences of one of the settings, schooling, will be explored. The term socialization setting is taken from Wheeler[4] who describes them as

> settings where some people are formally charged with the task of influencing others so that the others will leave the setting with different skills, attitudes, values or other qualities from those with which they entered.

The three ideal typical socialization settings are:

1. Communal resocializing agencies. These are those settings which seek to remake the individual completely. They include a wide variety of institutions: asylums, struggle groups to re-educate small petty capitalists in China, army induction camps, rehabilitation units for drug addicts and public schools[5]
2. Apprenticeship
3. Schooling

An examination of each of these settings has much to offer to an understanding of curricula as social process. By anticipating later arguments a little, this point can be illustrated. If we examine how each of these settings would deal with guns, we can begin to see the interest of them for this argument. Learning about guns in that communal resocializing agency, the army, would involve learning how to use them in the company of fellow recruits under the command of an NCO. All would be taught together and learning about guns would be only part of learning to be a soldier. Learning about guns as an apprentice would involve the apprentice in aiding an experienced user of guns (or a gunsmith if the apprentice was learning how to make them). Initially he might just carry the gun and only be allowed to use it when both he and the experienced man felt he could use it safely and with ease. Finally learning about guns in school would involve learning as a group, as in the army, but it is unlikely that actual guns would be used and the process would involve learning about types of guns and their historical and strategic importance.

Now there is a simplification here but that is deliberate. Obviously there are parts of army training where soldiers are taught in schoolrooms the strategic and military importance of guns and there may even be a few schools where pupils are taught how to handle a gun. However by setting up the three modes of socialization as distinct types – as ideal types – we gain more than we lose. We gain an understanding of the unique characteristics of each particular socialization setting although we lose the complexity of any actual socialization process which may well involve elements of communal resocialization, apprenticeship and the schoolroom.[6] As the purpose of the article is to use an examination of these settings to illuminate the social relationships involved in any curriculum rather than to describe an actual curriculum, the gain outweighs the loss.

Let us start this examination by describing the processes involved in a communal resocializing agency. These processes are ordered but the ordering is oriented toward not the skills or knowledge to be learnt but the individual to be transformed.

It is, thus, the processes of social interaction that are ordered not the skills or knowledge. This ordering is not immutable, however, but is dependant on the individual undergoing the process. Thus, in the sense that movement within the process of social interaction is inextricably linked to transformation of self, if the individual does not transform himself then his movement within the ordering ceases until that transformation is achieved.[7]

Three elements in the process can be distinguished analytically:

(i)   the stripping of the old self
(ii) the denial of an active self
(iii) the provision of a new self

It is important to remember that these are analytic categories and although I will illustrate them as a temporal sequence this is a heuristic device. There is empirical variation in how far they do form a temporal sequence – the provision of a new self may have its origins before the individual enters a community (if entry is voluntary) or shortly after entry and may only be recognised at a much later date when the individual suddenly comprehends his new identity in a flash of insight.[8] To illustrate this process, I am going to use an example of drug rehabilitation because I have an account of such a process written for me by a Canadian student who underwent the experience. (For obvious reasons I cannot reveal the name of the student). The example should not divert us from the fact that similar processes occur in all communal resocialising agencies.[9]

The stripping of the old identity is achieved by removing all those things by which we express ourselves – clothes, jewellery and hair. In addition any documents that locate your old identity are taken away and often even your name is taken from you to be replaced by a number. You are also, of course, taken away from all the old social ties that sustained your old identity:

> From the beginning I was isolated; isolated from old friends, old routines, old securities . . . the hair is cut and the clothes are changed. The impact this has on people is phenomenal. Boys that were 'tough' and 'cool' become meeker. Girls that were 'hip' and 'with it' become ordinary. Their own opinion of themselves changes – they actually feel 'un-cool' . . . You are not allowed to see old friends, they cannot visit you nor write to you. Within a very short period of time you are out of touch with what's going on.

The denial of an active self takes several forms. First of all there is almost invariably a degradation ceremony;[10] a debasement procedure whereby the individual is humbled:

> For seventy-two hours you are talked to intensely. They confront you with who you are. You are told what kind of liar drugs have made out of you; what kind of thief, what kind of degraded character you have changed into . . . You're told what kind of bum you've become – out of school and out of work. You're told what kind of scum you've become.

This degradation may be repeated at any time if an individual shows signs of not committing themselves to their new identity:

> One such technique was 'the chair'. It was a chair like any other chair yet what is stood for is almost too hard to explain. It was the most dreaded 'Activity' in the house, brought on yourself, by things such as breaking house rules, not getting involved in work, not doing the program, not talking. It was called 'your own private therapy' and it began at 11 p.m. when everyone else went to bed. You got a chair and placing it in front of two or three people you sat on it. You stayed there without being allowed to go to the bathroom, smoke, move about or sleep. You were there to save your own life and you were expected to talk. Talk about you, your past and how you felt about the people you lived with and how you felt about the things you did every day ... I guess it was close to 4 a.m. before I exploded! I screamed and yelled about how stupid everything was and how much I hated most of the people I was with ... Contrary to what I had expected I was not praised for my verbal outburst. I was confronted with the knowledge that I didn't have the *right* to hate any other human being ... I was told what an arrogant, selfish, empty person I was ...

Secondly, the denial of an active self is achieved by denying the individual control over his own actions:

> I had nothing to think about or worry about. I was told when to go to bed, when to get up, when to eat, when to work, when to play; even what times I could use the bathroom. Every minute of my day was organised for me.

Even control over thoughts is attempted:

> At no time was I alone. Regardless of where I went, even to the bathroom, someone else came along. It was explained to me if I was alone I could think. Think things that might cause me to run from the house, run from facing the truth about me.

The provision of a new self begins at entry to the institution and is achieved by that most efficient socializing agent, the human group. Individuals entering these institutions are quickly taught by existing inmates who are little different in rank from them and by their fellow sufferers:

> Left foundering in this sea of 'newness' and 'strangeness' it is only natural to turn to those around you ... you try to seek out new friends from those you are amongst and what they have to say is a far cry from what your old friends said.

and

> These people said they were like me and had changed. I wanted to. Their

admission of being like I was, strengthened the ties between us ... To belong to this group I had to change. I had to mould myself after these people who had started to change.

It is important to realise that a new self is not just provided for the individual. They have to actively seek to be a new person:

> My next three months I was expected to start practising the things I had learned ... to start 'living' my program – my new beliefs and not merely talking about them ... I was expected to realise those things in me that needed changing. How? By looking at others. The things I saw in other people that I didn't like I had to change in myself ... our preamble stated clearly that everyone around us was a mirror of ourself, consequently what we saw in others was ourselves. Talking about the things I was going to change fell on unlistening ears. I was confronted with the slogan 'show me, don't tell me.' I was to become a living example of the things I believed in.

The impact of a successful communal resocializing agency is immense. It literally remakes an individual into a new person:

> We, the over 6 months, became responsible to lead therapies, to get others talking. We became the example ... During the days we were expected to watch the others. To see if they were thinking or not getting involved with whatever they were doing or not putting their words into action ....

The impact of a successful communal resocialising agency is immense. It literally remakes an individual into a new person:

> The impact this experience had on me still affects me today. I am still 'in-tune' with myself. I still watch for defects in my character. It has been two and a half years since I was part of this program and yet the guidelines for a good way of life, something my program taught me, still motivates a lot of my actions ... To be honest, it is difficult for me to state how much of what I do now is a by-product of my program. My program became my way of life and even today I cannot differentiate what was 'learned' and what wasn't.

Now what stands out from this account is that such processes achieve their effect by utilising the power of social pressure. The individual is separated from one set of social forces that provide him with an identity and placed in a situation where there are other social forces providing a different identity. It is also apparent there is no set curriculum that can be mastered. What is required is a change of orientation, a new way of looking at the world. There may be skills to be mastered but these are not important in themselves but only as an index of change in identity. It is also apparent that such an educative process never ends, nor is it expected to end. The individual continues to view the world using the guidelines of his education.

If we turn now to the second example of a socialization setting, that of apprenticeship, we can first note that apprenticeship was, in origin, a form of domestic education. The apprentice lived with his master and his family. Even when this was no longer true there still remains in the notion of apprenticeship a concern with the individual as well as a concern with the technical skill of a craft:

> Originally the term 'apprenticeship' was employed to signify not merely the practical training in the mysteries of the trade, but also that wider training of character and intelligence on which depends the real efficiency of the craftsman. Apprenticeship was regarded as a preparation for the workshop.[11]

The central element in the ideal type of apprenticeship is a close interpersonal relationship between a master craftsman and an apprentice, or apprentices, which endures over a long period of time and during which the master and apprentice come to know each other as people, as individuals as well as teacher and pupil, and which raises all the difficulties and complexities of such a close personal relationship. It is no accident that many a doctoral student marries her supervisor nor is it unusual for many such relationships to be terminated in bitter arguments in which accusations of incompetence in the craft are entangled with judgments of moral worth, that is, judgments of them as a total human being. The type of words that are used in such judgments are the words that purport to describe character, for example, 'feckless', 'lazy', 'inconsiderate' on the one hand and 'diligent', 'mature', 'warm', on the other. The point about such judgments is that they are applied not just to the work task but are seen as immutable characteristics of the individual to which they are applied, in all aspects of his life. The ideal type focusses on a hierarchical relationship which, over time, becomes also a personal relationship. In terms of the common dichotomy between personal and positional relationships expressed in sociological writing,[12] it is both: both personal and positional and therein lies its interest.[13]

It might be useful at this point to contrast apprenticeship with communal resocializing agencies. In communal resocializing agencies the primary aim is to transform the identity of the individual. Any skills learnt are secondary and merely indicators of success in that aim. The skills themselves need not have any use although this does not imply that all such skills are useless. Calligraphy, as the mark of a mandarin, or Latin, as the mark of a gentleman, may have little utility but engineering, as the mark of a graduate of *École Polytechnique* in France, or mathematics, as the mark of a graduate of West Point, do have clear utility. What is important is not their utility, however, but their function as a status indicator.[14] In apprenticeship by contrast, the skills are of great importance. However, the difference between apprenticeship and communal resocialising agencies is a matter of emphasis rather than an absolute divide. The skills learnt in apprenticeship are not learned in an emotional vacuum. The successful mastery of the skills implies more than technical competence. It implies a change in identity, a change in the way one looks at the world. As well as a differential emphasis on skills or identity change there are also different methods of achieving the identity change. The successful transformation of the individual in communal resocializing agencies is largely achieved by the actions of social equals or near equals – thus the fagging and prefect system of the English public school, the cadets and upper classmen of West Point and the six and nine monthers of Synanon's drug rehabilitation programme.[15] The agents and the models for change are those who are just slightly further forward in the process. They are not much different from the neophyte so it is conceivable that he, too, can be like them. In apprenticeship, by contrast, the major method of identity transformation is by interaction between master and apprentice – a strong hierarchical relationship. However, as was pointed out earlier, this relationship is not only hierarchical it is also personal. This has important consequences for the apprentice becoming, in turn, a master – for seeing the master as a person shows him as fallible and, hence, it is conceivable that the apprentice, too, can become a master. I shall return to this point again.

Let us turn now to look at the processes involved in apprenticeship. The major processes are those of personal interaction. The apprentice has to interact with the master as a person not just as a technician. Judgment in apprenticeship is not just of technical skill but of moral worth. This moral worth is tested in several ways. First there is the fact that the new apprentice may spend much of his time in boring routine tasks. This is not because such tasks have to be done but because, through undertaking such tasks (cleaning boots for the football apprentice for example), the apprentice demonstrates his commitment. The 'good' apprentice will persist in spite of such routine. At the same time, such tasks have to be done well. This signals to the apprentice that high standards are required at all times, even in mundane matters; that standards of performance do matter and slipshod workmanship is unacceptable. The tasks themselves often form an implicit unspoken hierarchy. The very new apprentice is given the task of keeping the workplace clean and tidy. He is asked, in fact, to demonstrate respect for the place of work. In time, he may be given responsibility for maintaining the tools of the craft, keeping them tidy and clean (as in the football apprentice example).[16] He is asked to demonstrate respect for the instruments of the craft. When he has demonstrated commitment and respect in this manner, then he is finally allowed to help in the work task itself. It is important to realise that I am not arguing that the apprentice has to show efficiency and skill in these mundane matters. The result has to be good but the method of achieving it, hard work – 'elbow grease' – is more important than any technical competence. In fact any apprentice who, for example, developed a machine for cleaning football boots would be missing the point of the exercise. It is not his efficiency and skill that is being judged; it is his attitudes. It is a moral judgment that is being made, not a technical judgment, although one of the features of an apprenticeship is that the two types of judgment are not discrete. As well as in the performance of routine tasks, moral worth is also tested in the social interaction that takes place in the workplace. The apprentice has to learn to 'take a joke' and endure insults in the correct fashion. Such 'hazing' may be undertaken by fellow apprentices rather than the master. If this is the case, then the process is akin to that in the communal resocializing agencies described earlier. Being sent for a sky-hook or green oil for the starboard light fulfils several purposes. It demonstrates to the apprentice that he is still a learner, at the bottom of the heap, and must continue to appreciate this fact. It thus re-asserts hierarchy. Equally important, the way the apprentice reacts to the joke played on him is an indicator of his personality, his moral worth. The routine tasks and the sky hooks are the equivalent to the puberty tests of small scale societies.[17] In some apprenticeships the parallel may be even stronger. Haas,[18] for example, talks of steel erectors expecting apprentices to walk on the high beam and cadets to the Navy were once expected to climb the rigging. These tasks not only test the courage of the novitiate, they are also requirements of the craft. A steel erector must be able to walk without flinching many storeys high and anyone who cannot do this may as well leave the job immediately. Similarly, until recently, it was the practice of many colleges of education to put the new student into the classroom in the first term of their college course. If they can't survive such an experience it is better to find out earlier than later. A parallel with puberty rites may also be drawn with respect to the rituals associated with completing an apprenticeship. Such rites involve a large element of trust. The novitiate has to give himself over completely to his future colleagues and trust their judgment in what appear to be threatening situations.[19] A final test of his moral worth.

So far the description has been largely about the apprentice and the judgment of his moral worth. It is important to remember that the master, too, is being judged. In a master/apprentice relationship those that can, do, and *also* teach. The master is on continuous display to his apprentices and has to demonstrate his technical skill and moral worth, just as the apprentice has to demonstrate his technical skill and moral worth, and he has to do this in close personal interaction day after day for years. This has important consequences for the process. It means first of all that the master has to be master of his trade. He has to demonstrate he can do the task and he has to demonstrate it in the ordinary workplace not as an infrequent special display. Second, it means the apprentice is observing the full complexity of the task from the beginning of his apprenticeship. The meaning of the skills he is learning are apparent to him, the skills are never irrelevant. Also he can decide for himself when he wants to try out his skills subject to the master's approval. The pace and content of his learning is to some extent under his control. Finally, because he gets to know the master so well, he gets to know him 'warts and all'. This is vitally important for the learning involved. A realisation that the master is fallible makes it conceivable to the apprentice that he, too, might be able to do as well or even better than the master.

Master/apprentice relationships, thus, have this peculiarity of extreme hierarchy coupled with respect for the master as a moral being *and* an awareness of his failings.[20] Such relationships have these characteristics because the process of apprenticeship is one of close personal interaction in which personal judgments of moral worth inevitably enter, coupled with a situation where the teacher is also a practitioner. Such a type of close personal interaction has the effect of moulding the personalities that undergo it so that the term 'craftsman'. or 'master of his trade' implies more than technician. It implies not only technical skill but a particular type of person who will exercise probity and care in his task.

Let us now turn to look at the third ideal type: schooling.[21] There are two features that characterize schooling:

1. a separation of education from work
2. an ordering of the education process

When we examine the first feature – the separation of education from work – several implications emerge. The separation implies, first a physical separation of the school from the workplace.[22] In elementary education this happened very early in the development of mass education but more recent examples can be found, both in the training of teachers and in the training of nurses. In teacher training, my impression is that less and less time is being spent in the classroom[23] and in nurse training less and less time is being spent on the ward. It is not just a physical separation that is implied, however. There is also a separation of 'education' and 'training' with training being granted a lower status.

The separation of training and education inevitably implies also a distinction between 'theory' and 'practice'. Once again examples from nursing and teaching are particularly apposite. Practice in both implies and involves social interaction. Theory, on the other hand, is separate from social interaction.[24] It is an abstract set of ideas. In colleges of education the growth of the academic study of education divorced from teaching practice is a good example of this abstract theory. Then there is the separation of the teacher from the practice of the craft he is teaching so that the gibe 'those than can do, those that can't, teach' strikes home. The teacher becomes separate from the craftsman, (including under the heading of craft, the craft of scholarship). A teacher, unlike a master craftsman, does not have to demonstrate he can do a task, merely that he knows it Academic knowledge, 'book-learning' becomes more important than experience at performing a task, experiential knowledge. One of the consequences of the dominance of academic knowledge over experiential knowledge is that age is not a criterion for selecting teachers. Once again, colleges of education provide a good example of this with their recruitment in the expansion of the 1960s of academically qualified but younger staff to teach their increasingly academic curriculum

The fact that the teacher is separated from his craft also has consequences for the pupils. They cannot see the teacher practising his craft and so they are not able to judge his competence as a craftsman although they are often able to judge his competence as a teacher. At the same time, however, the teacher, like the master craftsman, remains the expert because he has control over the knowledge or skills to be transmitted (unless the teacher opens up alternative knowledge sources for pupils by which his own sources can be judged). The hierarchy is strong. Pupils thus find themselves confronted with an expert whose expertise is not open to scrutiny. There is no way in which the pupils can aspire to be a craftsman like the teacher for the craft of the teacher, if he has one, is not visible to them.[25] They can aspire to be teachers but not practitioners of a craft.

The second feature of schooling is the ordering of the educational process. This ordering consists first of an ordering of the content of the knowledge to be transmitted. A set of ideas or skills are usually written down and oriented around a conceptual theme. In short, school subjects – whether these be mathematics or a primary school project on water. Second, it consists of the ordering of these ideas of skills in terms of an ordering of pupils and time. These ordered ideas may be ranked in terms of a progression that links certain ideas or skills to certain pupil ages, sexes, social classes or races. A simple example can clarify the point – we expect all eight year olds to be able to read. As Aries[26] has demonstrated, such ordering is not an immutable feature of human nature. Initially the ordering can be vague, as Aries demonstrates by looking at the age range of pupils in school classes in the early modern period (ranges of 8–18 years of age are given by Aries) but in time they acquire definition so that people come to expect a seven year old to do this, an eleven year old to do that, and a fifteen year old to do something else. It is when they acquire this degree of objectivity, this degree of hardening of definition that they begin to dictate interaction.

The separation of theory from practice, so that education becomes the transmission of abstract knowledge, and the ordering of that knowledge, in terms of pupils and time, opens the way to the application of rationality to the educational process. Given a concept of education as a way of getting ideas across to people in a limited time span, then a technology of syllabus construction can be developed, with its rhetoric of aims and objectives.[27]

The interesting feature of schooling in comparison to communal resocializing agencies and apprenticeship is that social interaction becomes a secondary rather than a primary feature of the process. This is in spite of many teachers' wishes to stress their contacts with their pupils. More extremely, for some theorists and practitioners, social interaction is not even considered to be a necessary part of a learning process. With the microchip we are promised computers for teachers, television for lectures and data retrieval for books. We do not have to wait for the microchip, however, to see a schooling process that makes social interaction secondary. We have only to look at modular systems of schooling.[28] In such systems, where pupils collect units of knowledge, there is little possibility of sustained interaction between teacher and pupil who meet infrequently for short periods of time. Not only does the student lack a sustained personal relationship with his teacher, he also lacks such a relationship with his fellow students. He lacks this relationship with his peers because modular systems celebrate the freedom of the student to collect his own modules and thus each module may consist in the class-room of a new collection of students each time. The student in such a system is presented with a disconnected series of experts who, because he never gets to know them personally, remain remote and hierarchical. A brilliant if polemical description of the possible consequences of such a system is given by Jerry Farber[29] describing students at California State University:

> They haven't gone through twelve years of public [state] school for nothing. They've learned one thing and perhaps only one thing during those twelve years. They've grown to fear and resent literature. They write like they've been lobotomized. But, Jesus, can they follow orders ... Students don't ask orders that make sense ... Things are true because the teacher says they're true ... Outside of class, things are true to your tongue, your fingers, your stomach, your heart. Inside class things are true by reason of authority.

Miss Wiedemeyer tells you a noun is a person, place or thing. So let it be. You don't give a rat's ass; she doesn't give a rat's ass.

This is the irony of schooling. Communal resocializing agencies and apprentice-ship *seek* to change the individual. They are concerned with the individual as an individual, as a person, and they are organised to mould people, to get people to see the world in a new way. Skills and knowledge form part of the curriculum but that part is entangled with the moulding process. To achieve their aims both types of curricula have clear and strong hierarchies and present a superficial picture of autocracy. In fact, because they are processes that involve intimate and sustained personal interaction those subject to them, in time, learn to master them and act independently – albeit with a style that derives from the experience they have undergone; as Bourdieu[30] elegantly put it:

> schools of thought may, more often than is immediately apparent, represent the union of thinkers similarly schooled.

By contrast, schooling,[31] especially the modular version, does not claim to mould the individual. Skills and expertise are separated from judgments of moral worth. The individual is free to use his knowledge and skills in his own way. It thus presents a picture of liberal freedom. In fact, because they are not processes that involve sustained and intimate interaction in which the teacher demonstrates his skill in a craft, the pupil has no standard by which to judge his teacher who remains always the expert. The pronouncements of the teacher have to be taken on trust because he or she is not observed practising his craft. There is no way for the student to get to grips with the teacher – the flow is all one way and the teaching machine is the ultimate embodiment of such a system.[32]

In addition, the rational organisation of the curriculum that is a feature of developed schooling – in the form of modular or course units – stands over and above the pupil and the teacher. The syllabus may, in these circumstances, come to be confused with the curriculum and the syllabus become the controller of human action rather than human action controlling the curriculum as process. It is little wonder that such a situation has been seen as an example of alienation by Marxist writers.[33]

Conclusion

What are the implications of these ideal types; to what use can they be put? Most importantly they can stand as a corrective to views of curriculum which see it as only a question of content. The debate about the common core curriculum is, viewed from the perspective of this argument, a misplaced debate. The advocates of a common core curriculum are not advocating anything as radical or reactionary as they seem to think. What they are suggesting is merely a change in the content of modules and their frequency. There will be no change in the process of education.

The 'curriculum' that is effective at the present is the 'hidden curriculum' of schooling that teaches pupils they are inadequate and ignorant because they do not know while their teachers do know. Some accept this judgment on themselves and give up in despair. Others exploit the system to get the GCEs, CSEs and degrees needed to get good jobs while treating the knowledge transmitted as interchangeable counters with no real meaning.[34] Some reject the whole business and seek a new and valued identity from their peers.[35] A few, a very few, struggle through to become scholars engaged in a meaningful attempt to be craftsmen of knowledge.

This article has set out two ways, other than schooling, of changing people so that they leave with 'different skills, attitudes and values with which they entered'.[36] These ways are themselves not free of difficulties. The unintended consequences of schooling have been explored here but no attempt has been made to look at the unintended consequence of communal resocializing agencies[37] or apprenticeship. Even in looking at their intended consequences problems arise. Communal resocializing agencies when they are effective are terrifying. As long as we agree with their aims they seem to be a good alternative to schooling but it must be remembered that they can be used to produce Hitler Youth as well as public school boys. Apprenticeship, too, has its problems. It is extremely expensive in manpower, requiring a small master/apprentice ratio. More importantly, it is basically a conservative system with a built-in inertia in which old skills are maintained for generation after generation.

Nevertheless both communal resocializing agencies and apprenticeship are concerned with producing more than an individual with a particular set of skills. They are concerned with producing the 'good citizen' or the 'good craftsman' where good means more than efficient, that is, they are concerned with the moral worth of the individuals they produce. Once upon a time – and I use the phrase deliberately – this was also true of schooling. The concern was to produce an 'educated man' where educated meant more than someone who had the skills of literacy. However to defend this aim of schooling is becoming more and more difficult. On one side governments judge by utility and have no time for woolly-minded ideas of education which have no clear pay-off. As Eric Ashby[38] suggested about universities:

> Under the patronage of princes or bishops they were cultivated as garden flowers of no more significance to the state's economy than the court musician. Under the patronage of modern governments they are cultivated as intensive crops, heavily manured, and expected to give a high yield essential for the nourishment of the state.

Hence, the Association of University Teachers felt forced to respond to cuts in university income by a demonstration of their utility in pounds and pence. If governments attack the notion of the educated man by conceptions of utility so, too, do radical critics of society pressing from the other direction. There are strong intellectual arguments which suggest that the notion of the educated man is merely a rhetoric to disguise a coterie of privileged individuals who use their education as a status badge.[39]

However, as this article has attempted to demonstrate, to abandon the notion plunges us into a sterile world where there are no ideas of moral worth and the academic process becomes a mere game. There is no simple solution to this problem. I do not believe, as T.S. Eliot did, that we should reserve the creation of educated men to a small privileged élite but to open it to more than a few would require profound changes in schools, colleges and universities. The elements in such a change, that are important, can be derived from the ideal types. First, personal relationships. By that is not meant intimate relationships but relationships that are concerned with more of a person than their prescribed essay. Second, a concern to avoid the separation of theory and practice, that is so iniquitous and ubiquitous a feature of many educational processes, by an expectation that a teacher will practise his craft before his pupils. Finally and crucially, a commitment to produce a person of moral worth at the end of the educational process. Without *some* notion of moral worth education becomes a sterile game. Precisely *what* notion is open to debate but it should be debated not ignored.

Notes and References.

1 This article owes much to the helpful criticisms of many colleagues. I am especially grateful for the help given by the members of the graduate seminar held at our house and one member of that seminar in particular, Adrian Bell, who initiated my thought on this subject by his stimulating doctoral thesis on colleges of education. BELL, A. (1979) 'A Study of Social Structure, Interaction and Commitment in Teacher Training Institutions', University of East Anglia. I am also very grateful to the student who allowed her experience of drug rehabilitation to be reproduced.

2 HAMILTON, D. (1973) 'The Integration of Knowledge: practice and problems', *Journal of Curriculum Studies*, 5. 2, p. 154.

3 For my reasons for this usage see EASTHOPE, G. (1976) 'Comparative Education – a theoretical problem', in *Research Intelligence* 2, 1.

4 WHEELER, S. (1966) 'The Structure of Formally Organised Socialisation Settings', in BRIM, O.G. and WHEELER, S. (Eds.), *Socialisation after Childhood*, New York, Wiley, p. 54.

5 For a wide bibliography of such settings see, JONES, R.K. (1978) 'Paradigm Shifts and Identity Theory', in MOL, H. (Ed.), *Identity and Religion*, London, Sage. For asylums see, GOFFMAN, E. (1968) *Asylums*, Harmondsworth, Penguin. For struggle groups see, LIFTON, R.J. (1963) *Thought Reform and the Psychology of Totalism*, Norton, New York. For army induction camps see, LAWRENCE, T.E. (1955) *The Mint*, London, Cape; and ELLIS, J. and MOORE, R. (1974) *School for Soldiers*, New York, Oxford University Press. For drug rehabilitation see, SUGARMAN, B. (1974) *Daytop Village: A Therapeutic Community*, New York, Holt, Rinehart and Winston. And for public schools see, WAKEFORD, J. (1969) *The Cloistered Elite*, London, Collier-Macmillan.

6 Thus actual apprenticeship, as distinct from the ideal type, can include communal resocialisation (see BROWN, R. and BRANNEN, P. (1970) 'Social Relations and Social Perspectives amongst Shipbuilding Workers – a Preliminary Statement – Parts I and II', *Sociology* 4) and Schooling (see LEE D.J. (1966) 'Industrial Training and Social Class', *Sociological Review* 14) as well as the ideal typical apprenticeship described later in this article.

7 Although the concept of self and individual are extremely complex and important to the argument of this article, a full exposition of my conception of self would require several papers. It is sufficient for the argument here that self is used primarily with the meaning of a passive social creation although I believe that a fuller understanding of the processes I have described can only be achieved by having in addition an active concept of self as a meaning creator as I suggest later.

8 Strauss calls this 'the turning point' STRAUSS, A. (1962) 'Transformations of Identity', in ROSE, R. (Ed.), *Human Behaviour and Social Process*, Boston, Houghton-Mifflin, and it parallels accounts of conversions, see HEIRICH, M. (1977) 'Change of Heart: A Test of Some Widely Held Theories about Religious Conversion', *American Journal of Sociology*, 83, 3.

9 Though not all are as equally effective see MOUZELIS, N.P. 'Critical Notes on Total Institutions' in *Sociology*, 5, 1971. A particularly good account of identity stripping is given in ELLIS and MOORE,

op. cit., and LAWRENCE, *op. cit.*, provides a good description of the denial of the active self.

10 The concept is taken from GARFINKEL, H. (1956) 'Conditions of Successful Degradation Ceremonies', *American Journal of Sociology*, 61.

11 BRAY, R.A. (1911) *Boy Labour and Apprenticeship*, London, Constable, p. 1.

12 See, for example, BERNSTEIN, B. (1971) 'Ritual in Education' in COSIN, B.R., DALE, R., ESLAND, G., MACKINNON, D. and SWIFT, D. (Eds.), *School and Society*, London, Routledge and Kegan Paul.

13 Most writings on this type of relationship have looked at patron-client relationships. Apprenticeship differs from that type of relationship in that the apprentice becomes a master but the client does not become a patron.

14 See COLLINS, R. (1977) 'Some Comparative Principles of Educational Stratification', *Harvard Educational Review* 47.

15 See Note 5.

16 The difficulties raised by using ideal types were brought home forcefully to me by Dr. Leslie Bell who was kind enough to point out to me, that football apprentices can move into and out of the first team, being master one week, apprentice the next and then once again master if they are selected. Not all actual apprenticeships have the clear temporal sequence of craft apprenticeship which is the basis of the ideal type utilised here.

17 A point developed in ONG, W.J. (1970) 'Latin Language Study as a Renaissance Puberty Rite' in MUSGRAVE, P.W. (Ed.), *Sociology, History and Education*, London, Methuen.

18 HAAS, J. (1972) 'Educational Control among High Steel Ironworkers', *American Behavioral Scientist*, 16, 1.

19 A good account of such a rite is given in EVANS, G.E. (1966) *The Pattern Under the Plough*, London, Faber and Faber.

20 Lancelot Spratt of Richard Gordon's 'Doctor ...' books provides a good example. Another good example is the medicine man invented by Castaneda in his works, for example, CASTENADA, C. (1970) *The Teachings of Don Juan*, Harmondsworth Penguin.

21 This ideal type draws heavily on the work of COLLINS, *op. cit.*, and WEBER, M. (1948) 'The Rationalisation of Education and Training' in GERTH, H. and MILLS, C.W. (Eds.), *From Max Weber: Essays on Sociology*, London, Routledge and Kegan Paul.

22 LEE, *op. cit.*, gives a good example of this in apprenticeship training in large firms.

23 A similar point is made in BARTHOLOMEW, J. (1976) 'Schooling teachers: the myth of the liberal college', in WHITTY, G. and YOUNG, M.F.D. (Eds.), *Explorations in the Politics of School Knowledge*, Driffield, Nafferton Books.

24 This is not always true. Microteaching, for example, seeks to bridge the theory/practice divide. See BROWN, G. (1975) *Microteaching*, Methuen. The efforts of the team at the Centre for Applied Research in Education (CARE) to stimulate teachers to be researchers also tries to cross this divide. (For a discussion of some of the problems and possibilities of creating a method of teacher training that is both theoretical and applied see McNAMARA, D. and DESFORGES, C. (1979) 'The social sciences, teacher education and the objectification of craft knowledge', in BENNETT, N. and McNAMARA, D. (Eds.), *Focus on Teaching*, London, Longman.

25 Interestingly craft teachers often do make their craft visible to their pupils by working on a 'piece' of their own in front of the pupils.

26 ARIES, P. (1979) *Centuries of Childhood*, Harmondsworth, Penguin.

27 A good example of this process, the Open University, is considered in HARRIS, D. and HOLMES, J. (1976) 'Open-ness and control in higher education: toward a critique of the Open University', in DALE, R., ESLAND, G. and MACDONALD, M. (Eds.), *Schooling and Capitalism*, London, Routledge and Kegan Paul.

28 A consideration of modular systems in colleges of education is given in BELL, A. 'The Moral Basis of the Modular B. (Ed.)', *Research Intelligence*, 3, 2, 1977.

29 FARBER, J. (1972) 'The Student as Nigger', in FARBER, J. *University of Tomorrowland*, New York, Pocket Books Inc., Simon Schuster.

30 BOURDIEU, P. (1971) 'Systems of Education and Systems of Thought', in YOUNG, M.F.D. (Ed.), *Knowledge and Control*, London, Collier-Macmillan.

31 To avoid confusion: schooling does *not* equal schools. Many schools, infant schools and public schools, for example, do seek to mould the individual. Schooling is an ideal type of which the closest empirical example can be found in aspects of the Open University, some University education and some aspects of secondary schools.

32 For discussion of some of these points see HOLT, J. (1969) *How Children Fail*, Harmondsworth, Pelican, who argues cogently against the notion of teaching and learning as reducible to teaching machines; HAMMERSLEY, M. (1974) 'The Organisation of Pupil Participation', *Sociological Review* 22, who spells

out in some detail the way pupils come to accept the teacher's pronouncements as gospel if they are to be successful in school; and YOUNG, M.F.D. (1976) 'The Schooling of Science', in *Explorations in the Politics of School Knowledge op. cit.*, who illustrates many of the features of schooling in his discussion of school science.

33 See, for example, HOLLY, D. (1974) *Education or Domination*, London, Arrow; and DALE, R. (1977) 'Implications of the rediscovery of the hidden curriculum', in GLEESON, D. *Identity and Structure*, Driffield, Nafferton Books.

34 The instrumental attitude of many pupils to schoolwork is documented in KING, R. (1969) *Values and Involvement in a Grammar School*, London, Routledge and Kegan Paul, and the possible consequences of paper chasing are examined in DORE, R. (1976) *The Diploma Disease*, London, George Allen and Unwin.

35 See, for example, WILLIS, P. (1979) *Learning to Labour*, Farnborough, Saxon House.

36 WHEELER, *op. cit.*, Note 4.

37 For example, the 'stiff upper lip' of the upper class English, it has been speculated, may be a product of their schooling: WEINBERG, I. (1969) *The English Public Schools: The Sociology of Elite Education*, New York, Atherton.

38 ASHBY, E. (1967) 'The Future of the Nineteenth Century Idea of the University', in *Minerva*, 6, p. 16.

39 The best examples of this literature are: BOURDIEU, P. and PASSERON, J.P. (1964) *Les Heritiers*, Paris, Educations Minuit; and COLLINS, R. (1971) 'Functional and Conflict Theories of Educational Stratification', *American Sociological Review* 36; COLLINS, R. *op. cit.*, (Note 14).

Towards a New Socialist Sociology of Education

David Reynolds and Michael Sullivan, University College, Cardiff

During the last decade, the British Sociology of Education, in the wake of its rejection of the positivist empiricist paradigm dominant during the 1960's, has wallowed in a slough of paradigmatic confusion. This paper examines the reasons for the break-up of the old paradigm, elucidates the influences on, and contributions of, the competing paradigms which have struggled for dominance within the discipline in recent years and proposes that a paradigm grounded in classical Marxist theory offers one (and we believe a correct) resolution to the contemporary paradigmatic conflict in the sociology of education.

The Old Sociology of Education

The 'old' sociology of education of the 1950s and 1960s was generally structural functionalist in its theoretical orientation. Within this perspective, society is usually viewed as an ordered, consensual whole with needs that have to be met to ensure the maintenance of the societal pattern. These needs, or 'functional pre-requisites' as they are called, are met by the activities of various inter-related parts of the social system, all of which perform functions for the totality. In most part determined by their functionalist perspective on the relationship between the sub-system or 'micro' system of education and the wider social system whose needs it was supposed to be meeting, the concern of the members of the old sociology of education was, firstly, whether the educational system met the changed needs of an expanding industrial society. Jean Floud expressed this concern by noting that 'we were fascinated by the spectacle of educational institutions struggling to respond to the new purposes of an advanced industrial economy'.[1] In an advanced industrial society, education was seen by adherents to this paradigm in Britain and the United States as offering the prospect of increased economic growth by its potential provision of increased numbers of trained personnel – particularly applied scientists and technologists – who would enable the economic system to generate more wealth.[2] Floud again in 1962 urged that 'a modern economy depends on maximisation of the output of every individual' and that 'in a modern economy, the quality and efficiency of the working population very largely depends on the educational system'.[3]

The second major concern of the old sociology of education was the distribution of academic credentials that the system accomplished. Acquisition of such credentials had been 'unjust' in the 1930s, since public schools unfairly sponsored their charges and since the secondary schools were fee paying and, therefore, largely closed to working class pupils. Whether the tri-partite system of education that the 1944 Education Act had permitted was any 'fairer' in its development of talent amongst different sections of the population became almost an obsession for adherents to the old paradigm.[4] Researchers documented the disproportionate numbers of working class pupils in secondary modern schools, the heavy middle class pro- ponderance of the grammar schools and the consequent substantial wastage of mostly working class ability that was shown by documents such as the *Crowther Report* of 1959.[5] In the tradition of the great social reformers, such as Booth and Rowntree, careful fact gathering was utilised to produce the truthful water of an empirical sociology which it was hoped would wear down the stone of ignorance and – in the longer term that all Fabians talk of – ensure social justice for working class children.

The sociology of education, then, married together these two concerns of social justice for the working class child and economic efficiency to generate more wealth for all and by the early 1960s increasing numbers within the discipline began to argue for reform of the system of secondary education on comprehensive lines.[6] The systems of early selection and subsequent resource distribution of tri-partite schooling 'reinforced', 'contributed to' or 'intensified' the disadvantages which working class pupils were seen as already possessing because of their position in the occupational structure. Although such factors as poor housing, low wages, parental values and (often ill-defined) social disadvantage were regarded as re- stricting the opportunities of working class children, intellectual talent (as the *Newsom Report* argued) 'is not a fixed quantity with which we have to work but a variable that can be modified by social policy and educational approaches'.[7]

There were, of course, very close links between the practitioners of the old sociology of education and the Labour Party. Many within the discipline were Labour Party members – most appear to have shared the Fabian, reformist ideology which looks for progress for the working class and other disadvantaged groups to be attained within a relatively free enterprise *capitalist* system rather than in a *socialist* economic and political system. There is also clear evidence that practitioners of the old sociology of education such as A.H. Halsey, Tyrrell Burgess, Michael Young, David Donnison and Maurice Kogan had an important influence in shaping Labour Party policy for the 1964 election – in which the party advocated for the first time the reform of secondary education on comprehensive lines – and in subsequently shaping policy when Anthony Crosland was Minister of Education from 1965 until 1967.[8]

Furthermore, the findings of the old sociology of education and the policy implications that were drawn from the work found a ready acceptability in the Labour Party leadership of the 1950s and 1960s. After its post Second World War flirtation with an 'institutional redistributive' model of the Welfare State – where these institutional arrangements were seen as an active engine of equality, humanitarianism and fellowship (the three socialist principles which are still reflected in the policies of the Labour left-wing today) – the Labour Party moved quite considerably towards an 'industrial achievement performance' model of State welfare provision.[9] Capitalism was no longer to be transformed by public ownership; it was simply to be managed more effectively both by ensuring that those of merit replaced those whose merit was social rather than intellectual and by ensuring that the State – through planning machinery such as the National Economic Development Council – took a more active role. The Welfare State was seen as an adjunct to the economy; its role was increasingly seen as the ensuring of equality of opportunity, rather than the generation of equality.[10]

In its proposals for the introduction of comprehensive secondary schooling that were debated and approved at Conference in 1963 and which were contained in the 1964 Election Manifesto, the Labour Party united the policy prescriptions of the two themes of the old sociology of education. Capitalism was to be better managed and made more productive by the existence of more talent and social justice, under capitalism, was to be maximised by the attempt to modify the structure of an existing system that was socially unjust for working class children. Crosland in 1966 could conclude – echoing the practitioners of the old sociology of education – that the existing system of education was 'educationally and socially unjust, inefficient, wasteful and divisive'.[11]

To summarise so far, the old sociology of education was therefore functionalist in orientation, empiricist in method and committed to the furtherance of the twin policy goals of an economic efficiency and a social justice that were in no sense seen as being mutually exclusive. In their political and social ideology, the members of the paradigm were generally social engineers, reformist and Fabian, and their ideas found a ready acceptability in the Labour Party of the early 1960s, being reflected in the policies of comprehensive reform proposed in Circular 10/65,[12] in the positive discrimination proposed by the *Plowden Report*,[13] in the proposed raising of the school leaving age and in the other policies that reflected a liberal commitment to achieving social change through the educational system. In general, the members of the paradigm held that the traditional curriculum was 'excellent' knowledge – educational policy was to open up access to it.

The New Sociology of Education

Since the end of the 1960s, both this dominant explanatory paradigm and the political and social ideologies associated with it have been radically challenged within the sociology of education in particular and within the wider discipline of sociology in general.[14] The factors that have brought about this challenge are clearly numerous but of primary importance has been the growing realisation of what Bernbaum labels the inefficacy of remedy.[15] Educational policies have simply failed to attain their goals. Greatly increased levels of educational expenditure have clearly not been associated with any noticeable reduction in inequalities between the members of social classes in their benefit from the system via their obtained qualifications. The proportion of students within the higher education sector from working class homes has, for example, remained at around 25–27 per cent, in spite of the large overall expansion in the total numbers obtaining higher education.[16] Although, overall, the educational system now generates more children with paper qualifications than ever before – over 80 per cent of school leavers have at least an 'O' level or a CSE pass at grade 1 – inequalities between social classes in the distribution of these credentials remain large.[17] Increased provision clearly does not, of itself, reduce differentials between social classes in the utilisation of that provision.

If increases in the overall quantity of resources have not brought social justice for disadvantaged groups, neither have they brought higher levels of economic growth to those societies where such expansionist educational policies have been followed. Furthermore, many specific programmes, concerned with changing the precise nature and organization of the education offered, have also failed to attain the social reformers' twin goals. Comprehensive education has appeared to have effects upon its pupils' academic, cognitive, occupational and social development that are little different from those of the old tri-partite system and may even – as Julienne Ford's research and other more impressionistic evidence suggests – have had adverse effects upon pupil outcomes of all kinds.[18] Specific programmes of compensatory education, both in the United States (such as the Operation Headstart that was launched as part of the War on Poverty) and in Britain (such as the Educational Priority Area interventions in the West Riding monitored by Halsey and his team), appear to have had little long term effect upon children's developmental progress or cognitive functioning, since many of the quite minor short term gains in pupil performance disappeared or 'washed out' as the children grew older.[19]

Specific innovations also have produced disappointing results in both the United States and in Britain. Performance contracting (through which the administration of local schools' systems is handed over to private enterprise contractors) and voucher systems of parental choice of school (as at Alum Rock in California) have had what are regarded as disappointing effects in the United States,[20] whilst specific programmes of planned curriculum change, innovations in the use of educational technology, and even change in the formal organisation of schooling to either a more 'open-plan' or 'progressive' structure, have had – in Britain – remarkably little effect upon any of the measures of outcome that have been used.[21] In spite of what the general public, the mass media and many Black Paper writers may have perceived and argued, liberal educational reforms appear to affect pupils to only a marginal degree. Further evidence from American researchers suggesting the relative unimportance of academic qualifications in determining precise position in the occupational structure and growing public disillusionment with the schools (reflected in some of the scandals of malfunctioning institutions), have merely compounded the liberals' demoralisation.[22]

At the same time as the policy prescriptions (the 'means') of the old sociology of education have, increasingly, been recognised as inappropriate for attaining the liberals' twin social goals, the theoretical and methodological orientation of the paradigm has come under threat from the major changes in the theoretical and methodological orientation of the parent discipline of sociology itself. Structural functionalism – which presupposes the existence of collective or shared norms which orientate actors towards fulfilling the needs of the society – appeared increasingly unable to explain the value dissonance, social conflict, ideological pluralism and social disturbance that characterised the early years of the decade. A variety of radical Marxist or 'neo-Marxist' conflict perspectives subsequently appeared, all viewing what functionalism took for granted (the nature of the existing social order) as constructed and maintained to serve powerful vested interests. Social order became increasingly viewed as the 'problem' to be explained by sociological meta-theory.[23]

At the same time as this group of sociologists moved towards mostly Marxist macro theories, others moved towards a closer examination of the micro world of face-to-face interaction in everyday life, believing that any search for the explanation of the nature of the social world must begin with the exploration of the subjective reality and subjective perceptions of societal actors. For most, if not all, ethnomethodologists and phenomenologists, *sociological* accounts were to be seen as subjective and context bound like all other member accounts. Although the number of sociologists actually undertaking work utilising this theoretical and methodological paradigm was very small, the influence of the new 'interpretive' paradigm in eroding confidence in the possibility of objectifying accounts of the social world through using the positivistic, empirical, quantitative paradigm that had been so popular in the 1960s, was substantial.

In the early years of the 1970s, therefore, the quantitative, positivistic methodology of the old sociology of education was increasingly being rejected, within sociology, in favour of the use of qualitative methods, its functionalist theoretical orientation was increasingly regarded as inadequate and its practitioners' social engineering policy perspective was increasingly seen as having failed to attain the societal goals of its proponents. The political and social orientation – the reformist, Fabian, 'Statism' – of the adherents to the old paradigm was also increasingly rejected by other members of the sociological community and by the intellectual middle class in general. Many flirted with anarchism (either of the violent, agitational Bakunin variety or with that of the active withdrawal, Illichian kind) and many others moved towards neo-Marxist perspectives. Liberalism and Fabianism – the British midway between the consequences of the illusory freedom of *laissez-faire* capitalism and the restriction of freedom that seems entailed by most Socialist or Communist States – attracted an ever smaller number of adherents.

In place of the old paradigm have arisen a number of new or, some may uncharitably argue, resurrected explanatory paradigms, the most important and influential of which has been the 'new' sociology of education associated in its early years with the writings of Michael F.D. Young. In works such as *Knowledge and Control*,[24] Young has drawn attention to purported deficiencies in the old sociology of education. Sociologists, it is argued, have taken for granted educators' problems and have attempted to individualise (as due to cultural pathology or material deprivation) problems which may have their cause in the organisation of schooling and in the ways in which the educational system defines certain kinds of knowledge and certain cultural styles as more valid, valued and worthwhile. It is argued that sociologists should treat as problematic the dominant legitimising categories of educators and view them as 'constructed realities' which are realised in particular institutional contexts. Young urges that 'existing categories that for parents, teachers, children and many researchers distinguish home from school, learning from play, academic from non-academic and able or bright from dull and stupid must be conceived of as socially constructed, with some in a position to impose their constructions or meanings on others'.[25] The task of the sociology of education is to explore both the reason why certain dominant categories persist and the nature of the relationship between these dominant categories and the wider economic, political and social structures outside the educational system. Crucially, at the same time as it encourages a certain cultural relativism (by its view of school knowledge as not necessarily more valid or accurate accounts of the world than any other possible or actual accounts but merely the ideology of a particular interest group with the power to posit such knowledge as valid and legitimate), the writings of Young appear to encourage the belief that the knowledge, truth and objectivity of sociologists, too, are human products and, therefore, not judgeable against some external reality. In the sociological community, as well as in the schools, Bernbaum notes that 'new knowledge, changed paradigms are not to be judged by their relevance to an external reality and their accuracy in facilitating a description and an understanding of that reality but in relation to the interests and power of those who create and use the knowledge'.[26]

The 'new' sociology of education marks, then, a clear break with the old paradigm – as Barton and Walker note,

> the approach, based upon a view of man as an active participant in the creation and construction of social reality, emphasises an investigation of the processes by which those involved in the educational enterprise construct, manage and define their everyday world. The nature of school knowledge, the organisation of the school, the ideologies of teachers, indeed any educational issue all become relative – and the central task for the sociology of education becomes to reveal what constitutes reality for the participants in a given situation, to explain how those participants came to view reality in this way and to determine what are the social consequences of their interaction.

Crucially, sociological knowledge is also relativised, since there is no external reality independent of human interpretation.[27]

The effects upon the discipline of the sociology of education of the propositions advanced by Young and popularised by himself and others can only be described as dramatic in that they have produced a multi-paradigmatic or pre-paradigmatic state of what can only be described as utter confusion. The discipline of the sociology of education appears divided into at least two groups, with a large number undertaking work at the micro societal level of the school or classroom and a rather smaller number undertaking work at the macro societal level, studying the relationship between the educational system and the societal superstructure. Description of micro level processes is conducted by phenomenologists and ethnomethodologists (usually explaining processes only in terms of social actors' accounts of cause), and by symbolic interactionists (who usually reserve the right to add a social scientists' analytic account different from that of societal members). Analysis in some cases explains educational phenomena as constructed by social actors' unconstrained micro level interaction, and in other cases as explicable by the operation of macro societal factors acting out their influence in the classroom or school interaction. Prescription of what ought to be is likewise varied – whilst nearly all accounts call themselves 'socialist' prescriptions, many wish for an anarchist or libertarian form of society and unstructured form of schooling where knowledge is discovered free from any State control or external imposition. The policy implications of these views are also varied – some Idealists see raising teacher consciousness as likely to change the nature of educational processes, other Materialists see such micro level change as only possible after forms of action to alter radically the nature of the capitalist State, economy and superstructure.

What is observable currently, then, is a discipline with a wide variety of methodologies, a wide variety of theoretical and analytical approaches to the problem of analysis and a bewildering variety of prescriptions of what should be the nature of the future educational system, the future British society and what are the nature of the means to reach those stated goals. What follows in this chapter is an attempt to suggest ways in which the pre-existing paradigmatic confusion can be reduced by the adoption of an approach derived from classical Marxism to the description, analysis, proscription and prescription of the nature of our discipline and our society.

Description

The first task of the sociology of education must clearly be the accurate description of the nature of educational processes and arrangements in our society, a description that it is necessary to undertake at both micro and macro societal levels. Work undertaken at these two levels has clearly increased considerably in recent years, with ethnography the usual method of study for most micro level work and a more conventional use of written materials, historical sources and documents usual for macro level work.

To take the micro level work as an example, although this varies in theoretical and methodological orientation from conventional symbolic interactionism to conventional ethnomethodology and to the recent situated or contextualised ethnography of Sharp and Green[28] and of Willis,[29] we now have an interesting body of material that closely focusses upon the processes of schooling, upon face-to-face interaction within classrooms, upon teacher decision making and upon the nature of the usually oppositional culture of the pupils. Much of this literature appears plausible, interesting in its implications and, in the view of its authors, eminently accurate and valid. What is not currently being done with this large amount of material, though, is the sifting out of inaccurate portrayals of member accounts from accurate, or the additional sifting out of accurate use of social scientists' analytical analysis from inaccurate use of such analysis. This is not being done because, quite simply, it is impossible to undertake. Few of the ethnographic studies conducted at the micro level give enough information about their methodology, about the way in which their data was collected and interpretations of that data reached, for any assessment of the validity of the portrayals of member accounts and the use of social scientists' analysis to be made.

All ethnographers are likely to be involved in the activities that characterised the positivistic research of the old sociology of education – the selection of which data to study out of the universe of data available within a school or within a classroom and the interpretation of those data once selected for study. Three types of checks would usually have existed within the positivist, quantitative framework that would have permitted an assessment of the validity of the research: these are checks upon internal validity (controlling for the influence of some variables to study the patterns of influence of others); external validity (are the results generalisable outside the social setting that generated them?); and construct validity (are the description and observation reliable in the sense of being reproducable by others?).

Although all ethnographers must, then, be using methods to select data and to interpret it and although many may well be doing quietly what positivists would have done loudly and proudly, it seems virtually an impossible task to assess the validity of more than a handful of the ethnographic accounts and studies of the last decade that have been undertaken at the micro level. In its enthusiasm to distance itself from some of the uses to which positivistic methods have been put, the new sociology of education has rejected rigour in favour of the sensitivity offered by more 'experiential' approaches to the study of schooling. In so doing, it has become difficult to assess the extent to which research findings reflect the reality of school life, the perceptions of school life by ethnographers, or an unknown combination of both factors. In the absence of such basic information about the validity of ethnographic accounts, it seems very unlikely to us that the sociology of education, which appears to be quite sensibly in a classificatory phase, will be able to produce a progressively more accurate account of the nature of educational processes. Development may be hindered by the blind alleys that invalid ethnography may lead to. Explanation of relationships and processes may be hindered by the need to explain invalid accounts. Replication, which is the one sure way of accumulating 'known to be valid' knowledge, will remain simply impossible and it will also remain impossible even to attempt to understand the extent to which research results reflect the influence of the researcher and of the research process. In the absence of any means of assessing the validity of ethnographic accounts, it seems likely that Halsey and Karabel's strictures that the new interpretive paradigm has produced 'many new departures but disturbingly few arrivals' and that 'proponents of the new sociology of education seem to have been more successful in criticising existing research than in producing their own body of substantive propositions' may remain all too true.[30]

Why have so few ethnographers taken the trouble to describe their methodology in the detail that any assessment of validity demands? The new sociology of education rejects this because it smacks of positivism, which is regarded as flawed and old fashioned. Positivism has been associated with much atheoretical number crunching, with the structuralist dictum to treat social facts as things and with the operationalisation of concepts that are favourable to the definitions of the situation of governments, of educational authorities and of the middle classes in general. At the same time as rejecting positivism, though, the new sociology of education appears to have rejected all conventional modes of academic rigour. Answers to questions are reported without the question, quotes are given that support authors' views without any indication of whether there were quotes that did not support those views; the influence of the ethnographer upon the research process is rarely discussed. Ideas are generated by – and then validated on – the same set of observations, data or impressions and are therefore invariably accurate.[31]

It is possible to argue – and many believe this currently – that any attempt to objectify accounts, analysis and description within the sociology of education is bound to be futile, given the relativity of all knowledge that is proclaimed by many adherents to the new sociology of education.[32] However, it is interesting that much of the discussion of these issues within British sociology, as Lawton notes, has neglected two thousand years of philosphical discussion in general and much discussion that has taken place on this precise subject within the humanities in particular.[33] The fact that individuals and cultures may differ in how they perceive social reality and in how they explain the existence of that reality is a well understood phenonemon, but to draw the further extreme relativist conclusion that it is not possible to say that certain views of social reality are more in accordance with the reality of human existence than others is simply an unwarranted extension. Pring has pointed out that the fact that we distinguish between a furry animal that miaows – a cat – and an animal less furry but which barks – a dog – may be due to certain cultural, social and linguistic conditions, but the fact that we can distinguish at all between something that is called a cat and something that is called a dog has something to do with the physical reality and characteristics of cats and dogs.[34]

The external world has a reality, then, that is independent of human perceptions of it. The most fundamental external reality of all – the fact that if human beings do not eat they soon die – is still a reality completely independent of whether people believe it to be true, want it to be true or would rather it were not true. Indeed, virtually the whole of Marxist thought is concerned with how human societies cope with the externally imposed need and reality of how to survive in an environment that is in reality hostile. There is, therefore, no reason why objectification of accounts should not be theoretically possible and most philosophical discussion of this issue would appear to have moved beyond the naïve extreme relativist position of those members of the new sociology of education who have apparently just discovered the existence of the philosophical doctrine of cultural relativism – Nyberg could speak for many philosophers of science (especially those in the American tradition) when he concludes that 'there are criteria for objectification and justification that we can and do agree on and consistency underlies them all'.[35]

Theoretically, to Marxist socialists, objectification is clearly not just possible but is also highly desirable. Marx was, as many neo-Marxists are anxious to point out, a relativist who believed that much of what passed for knowledge in a capitalist or pre-capitalist society at a given point in time was distorted by ruling class interests into simple ideology – to use his famous quote from *The German Ideology*, 'The ideas of the ruling class are, in every age, the ruling ideas; that is, the class which is the dominant material force in society is at the same time its dominant intellectual force'.[36] Yet Marx himself clearly believed that intellectuals such as himself could transcend the relativism that results from class position and generate accurate accounts of the social world and its nature. Marxist theoretical formulations were therefore presented in testable form together with the evidence that generated them, and – in their use of the hypothetico/deductive model, scientists' analytical constructs and collection of empirical evidence – they have much in common with the much derided positivistic methods that the old sociology of education used to employ. They have consequently very little in common with the unscientific lack of rigour that is evident in most of the studies that have been undertaken at both macro and micro levels over the last decade of the new sociology of education.

Analysis

The second task of the sociology of education – apart from the description of micro level educational processes and their relationship to macro societal, structural factors – must clearly be the explication and explanation of why those educational and societal arrangements exist in the form that they take and why the nature of schooling and of the educational system is patterned as it is. Within the sociology of education, currently, it is apparent that there are two major areas of dispute; first, about adequate methods for this task and, second, about an adequate mode of analysis for the task.

At the level of analytical methods, it is clear that much debate centres on the relative importance to be attached to social actors' analytical perspectives and to social scientists' analytical perspectives in the explanation of the nature of the social world. Much of the micro level material gathered by practitioners within the new sociology of education focussed – as is to be expected from those influenced by phenomenology and ethnomethodology – on the sense-making practices that actors use to construct their social worlds. Many others working within the interpretive paradigm rely heavily upon actors' perspectives as their explanations.

It is important to remember, though, that a Marxist socialist approach would retain a role for the intellectual – who in some cases may be a sociologist! – who could interpret actions and social phenomena as caused by factors of which social actors may have no idea. Intellectuals have a role for Marxists in pointing out that many individuals' common sense understandings or constructions of reality are invalid, erroneous beliefs that are especially damaging if they prevent people from seeing, through false consciousness, the nature and causes of the social reality around them. The primacy and importance that is given to actors' explanations within the new sociology of education is, then, a thoroughly unsocialist method of analysis.

Turning to the current disputes about which mode of analysis is appropriate, a debate which is of course related to the debate about appropriate methods of study for that mode, much of the new sociology of education has been Idealist in its analysis.[37] It has emphasised both the ways in which the micro systems of education, classrooms and schools are independent of the constraints of wider societal forces and the ways in which social reality is actively constructed by social members. Situation more than background is emphasised as a determinant of human action and the processes of bargaining, truce making, rule formation and impression management are all viewed – sometimes implicitly, sometimes explicitly – as, to a great extent, independent of extra-human constraints. As Young and Whitty aptly summarise it, the new paradigm

> ... has tended to focus ... upon the ways in which teachers and pupils make sense of their everyday experiences and on how educational reality is continuously reconstructed in the interaction of individuals, rather than imposed upon them by mysterious external forces ... what secretly keeps society going is crucially the practices of individual teachers and pupils and the assumptions about knowledge, ability, teaching and learning which are embedded in them.[38]

However, by focussing such attention on the micro level and on the processes of interaction within schools and classrooms there has been a clear tendency for macro societal influences to be under-recognised. As Sharp and Green (and Willis from a more materialist perspective), emphasise '... it would seem that a view of man which emphasises his ability to transcend his environment and a view of society which sees it as nothing but the emanation of intersubjective processes has lost sight of the sociological phenomenon of externality and constraint'.[39] Young himself, in some of his more recent work, has acknowledged some of these deficiencies within the new sociology of education that he himself encouraged and now argues, with Whitty, that 'many of these studies about the minutiae of classroom interaction, or analyses of assumptions underlying prevailing definitions of curricular knowledge, seem to present education as being carried on in a social vacuum ...'.[40]

As a reaction to the Idealism (in a classic Hegelian sense) of the sociology of education of the early 1970s though, the emergent neo-Marxist – or one might argue vulgar Marxist – perspectives of the last few years show an equally un-Marxist Materialist determinism. One of this genre, Louis Althusser, has argued that schooling in a capitalist society is a means whereby the existing class relations of the society are perpetuated.[41] Education reproduces the social relations of production by instilling in the young a set of attitudes that will ensure the continued patterning of exploitative class relations. There is, through education, a 'reproduction of a submission to the ruling ideology for the workers and a reproduction of the ability to manipulate the ruling ideology correctly for the agents of exploitation and repression'.[42] Bowles and Gintis also assert unequivocally that there is a direct correspondence between the social relations of production and the system of schooling.[43] In their words, 'there is a structural correspondence between its social relations and those of production' and 'by attuning young people to a set of social relationships similar to those of the work place, schooling attempts to gear the development of personal needs to its requirements'.[44]

It is important for so called neo-Marxist socialists to realise, though, that the relationship between the structure of a society, its educational system and its material base that is portrayed in these and related accounts appears to neglect many of the writings of classical Marxism. Gramsci, who attacked the ideas of those like Bukharin who saw the whole realm of ideas as conditioned by the means of production, himself wanted to leave room in Marxist analysis for the influence of ideas and of individual men upon the course and process of history.[45] Gramsci relied heavily on certain texts of Marx and Engels which he believed to have been subsequently neglected and notes that Marx, in the Introduction to the *Critique of Political Economy*, argues that in considering the possibility of revolutionary change '. . . a distinction should always be made between the material transformation of the economic conditions of production which can be determined with the precision of natural science, and the legal, political, religious, aesthetic and philosophic – in short, ideological – forms in which men become conscious of this conflict and fight it out'.[46] Gramsci was aware that Engels too had written of the ways in which 'the reflections of . . . struggles in the minds of the participants . . . also exercise their influence upon the course of the historical struggles and in many cases preponderate in determining their form'.[47]

To pretend, as many neo-Marxists do now, that the appropriate mode of analysis for sociological work is a materialist form of analysis is not only profoundly un-Gramscian but, in its neglect of 'the necessary reciprocity between structure and superstructure, a reciprocity which is nothing other than the real dialectical process',[48] it is profoundly un-Marxist. A Marxist socialist sociology of education would see schools and the educational system as both dependent upon, and independent of, wider societal constraints, much on the lines of the relative autonomy theses of Bernstein[49] and Bourdieu,[50] both of whose formulations grant the sphere of the 'cultural' a partial independence from the economic relations of production. Recent ethnographic work by Willis appears to give support to this thesis and he notes that the educational system may itself generate a 'culture of opposition' from amongst the lads which is not a direct outcome of class membership.[51] Our own work in South Wales suggests also that individual schools have considerable freedom in their choice of means although, of course, being tightly constrained in their goals by the demands of the macro societal systems. Specifically, these Welsh schools can utilise strategies of incorporation or coercion as mechanisms of social control. Such choice of strategies will have implications both for the nature of the pupil output from the schools and for the nature of pupil and teacher experience within the schools. Micro level strategies will have, in our view, implications for macro societal factors.[52]

The adoption of a Marxist socialist perspective, then, would suggest an urgent need for rapprochement between uncontextualised micro level accounts that neglect to focus on societal constraints and rather abstract, mostly neo-Marxist macro level accounts that grant human consciousness and action little independence from the societal material base. Man can, and classical Marxists are quite clear on this point, affect his development and his surroundings as well as being affected by them.[53]

Prescription

To sum up our discussion so far, we have argued that the old paradigm within the sociology of education was initially replaced by that of the new sociology of education. This new paradigm focusses upon the processes of the school and the classroom in the explanation of why some pupils fail and others succeed. It treats as problematic the knowledge that the educational system wishes to distribute, regarding it as not necessarily any more valid, accurate or worthwhile than any other form of knowledge but simply the ideology of certain particular interest groups. The possibility of the academic community arriving at the objective 'truth' within the sociology of education is also cast doubt on by what can only be called this extreme relativist position. This new Idealist paradigm, and the structuralist or Materialist reactions to it, have created a paradigmatic confusion that clearly needs some form of resolution if the discipline is to make progress.

First, we have looked at attempts within the sociology of education to describe the nature of educational processes and found them to be of doubtful value, since no attempt is made to 'objectify' the knowledge obtained. There is no reason why this is not possible, although, of course, there may be many reasons why it is difficult, and Marx himself, and classical Marxists subsequently, have attempted such objectification of knowledge.

Second, we have looked at the dominant modes of explanatory analysis within the sociology of education and found that they are either naively Idealist or unjustifiability Materialist in orientation. A classical Marxist mode of analysis would view the educational system as both constrained and the participants within the system as in part free of constraints. Such an approach would serve partially to reconcile the 'macro' and 'micro' divisions within the discipline that are so visible, and so destructive, at the time of writing.

Lastly, we wish to look at some of the prescriptions that are current in the new sociology of education for the sort of society that some of our visionary writers wish for and for the educational system that hopefully will exist in the future prescribed societies. In essence, there seems to exist within the sociology of education a form of 'New Radicalism' which we – Marxist socialists – find profoundly disturbing in many ways. It is disturbing that it is hard to find examples of the new radicalism clearly spelt out in the detail that is necessary for any valid assessment of worth. Many prescriptions are vague, many reflect authors' clear tendencies to dislike capitalist educational systems and to be at the same time rather unsure of what possible alternatives there are or what alternatives there could be. Many accounts are called 'socialist' or 'radical socialist' or 'neo-Marxist' which are, in essence, basically libertarian, anarchist or merely trivial transcendentalism.

From recent reviews of the variety of prescriptions that exist, though, it seems that the new radicalism has been moulded by three major influences – by the deschooling perspective of anarchists like Ivan Illich,[54] by the progressive tradition both of the old and reformed varieties and,[55] lastly, by cultural relativist notions originally encouraged by the new sociology of education and latterly flirted with even by some self-styled Marxists.[56] We will describe these three influences in turn.

To take the deschoolers first, their attack upon compulsory schooling usually reflects their concern with the quality of life in high technology advanced industrial societies. Illich, for example, believes that

> A desirable future depends upon our deliberately choosing a life of action over a life of consumption, on our engendering a life style which will enable us to be spontaneous, independent, yet related to each other, rather than maintaining a life style which only allows us to make and un-make, produce and consume.[57]

The capitalist state, in association with high technology manufacturing industry, encourages a 'commodity fetishism', which is the belief that individual wants and needs of many kinds can best be satisfied by the acquisition of material goods.[58] Schools function to encourage this belief and also function to make individuals dependent upon the State for their learning, a dependence which disables them from learning themselves and which brings them under a State control which lowers the quality of their lives.[59] Furthermore, schools, according to Illich, widen inequality between rich and poor countries and between rich and poor individuals within any country.[60] They devalue other types of useful knowledge that exist outside their walls and in the community at large, and are also social control against children – 'the great lock up' as Illich labels them.[61] Heavily influenced by Illich, Reimer,[62] Freire,[63] and their distinction between education which is 'good' and schooling which is by definition 'bad', the new radicalism increasingly doubts the usefulness of the compulsory education system in generating their future 'socialist' society or in attaining their socialist educational goals. Young and Whitty, for example, claim that 'many of those who consider themselves to be on the Left in politics have begun to take seriously ... the suggestion that compulsory schooling for all may be counter-productive for the realisation of their political ideals'.[64] Similar references to the undesirability of compulsory education and the undesirability of the system in general are to be found in many radical educational prescriptions of the last ten years.[65]

The second set of influences upon the new radicalism of the sociology of education is the progressive tradition in general and what Hargreaves[66] labels as the 'New Romantics' in particular. This latter group, like Holt,[67] Goodman,[68] Kozol[69] and many others,[70] wants to reformulate the content of the curriculum and the nature of pedagogy but do not seek to change the basic institutional structure of schooling. They believe learners to be naturally motivated to learn and quite capable of exercising choice in the determination of what is to be learned. The curriculum in many of these formulations is to be 'a collaborative adventure' between teacher and learner. Learners in schools should therefore be given much greater freedom to define both their own goals and the means to realise those goals. This group of writers often draw on the Freudian psychology of Eric Fromm[71] and share his concern about the adverse psychic effects of repression under capitalism, and draw also from Carl Rogers'[72] emphasis upon the importance of self-actualisation and of developing ego strength for healthy psychological adjustment and development.

The third influence upon the new radicalism has been the doctrines of cultural relativism espoused by the new sociology of education in its early years. Increasing numbers of writers have wanted the disestablishment of the so called middle class culture of the school curriculum and its substitution by so called working class culture. Whereas early socialists such as Jackson and Marsden[73] and, later, Jackson[74] himself wanted the school system to recognise working class *values* such as co-operation, friendliness and a sense of community and would have retained the *curriculum* apparently intact (with the addition of some courses on pigeon breeding or brass band playing in the case of Jackson's later writing), the new radicalism wants to change the curriculum wholesale and apparently does not recognise the middle class culture and curriculum of the schools as in any way superior to any other culture. Such a view is alluded to in Holly's[75] prescriptions that 'not only the general economic character of a neighbourhood but its specific regional, national and religious culture should be consulted in making the school open to a two way educative current' and it is alluded to in Eric Midwinter's[76] ideal of a community school whose curriculum reflects the 'culture' of its catchment area. It is alluded to by Keddie in the much quoted book *Tinker, Tailor: The Myth of Cultural Deprivation,*[77] where she states that 'this individualisation of failure ... rests on a perception of mainstream culture that is by definition ... a minority culture: the culture of the middle class which is then said to stand for 'society at large'. It is not a question of whether the middle class culture (whatever that vague term means) is desirable or not, nor which of its values deserve to be transmitted to the next generation, but, rather, the recognition that mainstream and middle class values are one and the same thing and that neutrality in the construction of indices is impossible'.[78] Keddie views working class culture as 'adequate' in its own right (although adequacy for *what* is left unsaid) and it is apparently as worth-while as the middle class culture that the school transmits through its curriculum.[79]

The new radicalism is, therefore, as we have noted above, increasingly opposed to compulsory schooling, advocates more individualistic forms of pupil experience and comes close to a view which sees the school curriculum as reflecting a middle class body of knowledge that is not in any way superior to, or more valid than, other forms of knowledge. It is important to point out, though, that few prescriptions that have appeared within the sociology of education of the last decade have necessarily embraced all three of these tenets of the new radicalism. Many of the new romantics, for example, wish for individualised learning within an ongoing educational system and also wish for the culture of that system to be a balance between what has accumulated as 'excellent' and what the child can discover. De-schoolers like Illich could easily embrace all the three parts of the new radicalism, and Young and Whitty[80] appear to flirt rather outrageously with all three positions, but most prescriptions are dissimilar to these latter formulations.

However, although widespread adoption of all the planks of the new radicalism appears not to have occurred so far, very recent prescriptions suggest that these views may not be far from becoming the new policy orthodoxy of the sociology of education. The recent contribution of Kevin Harris, in *Education and Knowledge*,[81] manages to embrace within, in the author's words, a 'materialist that is, Marxist framework'[82] a desire for the existence of 'anti-education', which would consist of people in community, disinterestedly trying to learn what they need to know, in contrast to people having to accept as knowledge a distorted and misrepresentative picture of the world'.[83] Anti-education would have nothing to do with schools, would put a high value on 'informal talk and discussion ... on self discovery, or on activities that don't have an immediate pay off (*sic*.)',[84] and would clearly embrace a belief in cultural relativism. The dust jacket says it all – '... in capitalist liberal democracies formal education functions essentially not to reveal reality but rather to transmit to each new generation a structured misrepresentation of reality'. In defence of this controversial and thought provoking view, he argues that all knowledge of the world is theory laden and a neutral detached view of the world is impossible. That Harris calls his prescription socialist serves as ample evidence for the recent debasement of that term within the field of sociology of education.

Prescriptions and Proscriptions – A Marxist Perspective of Education in Pre-Socialist Society

Viewed from a classical Marxist perspective, the practical implications of the policy prescriptions associated with the new radicalism appear to be profoundly conservative and inhibiting for socialist social and political change. Writers within the classical Marxist tradition have argued, and continue to argue as we shall see below, that a crucial predeterminant of the transformation from capitalism to socialism is the universalisation of access to a national education *system* which retains in its curricular content and pedagogy much that is presently associated with the educational processes of capitalist schooling.

The necessity of a schooled society as both a protection against greater social, political and economic inequality within a capitalist society and as a predeterminant of the transition to a socialist society is, for classical Marxists, quite clear.[85] If compulsory education for all in a capitalist society were disestablished and replaced by a voluntaristic approach to education, the result would be an increase in inequality (social, political and economic) between individuals and between social classes. Individual intellectual development would depend almost exclusively on chance reaction to the stimuli of the particular environment in which individuals were located. Since such social environments vary more than do schools and since social environment has a demonstrable association with levels of intellectual (and in our society social and economic) achievement,[86] then a de-schooling policy is likely to retard rather than advance the progress of the working class. It is a realisation of the crucial importance of an openly accessible national compulsory education system in equalising life chances that has led most British Marxists, like the great majority of the progressive and labour movement, to promote the need for such things as genuinely non-selective comprehensive secondary schooling for all children.[87]

A classical Marxist perspective also, in our opinion, eschews the idea that one of the functions of education in pre-socialist society should be to facilitate the individual learner's freedom to define his own goals and the means to attain those goals. For Marx, the concept of individual goal definition is incompatible with the achievement of goals which are universally beneficial, except in the ultimate communist society in which genuine and free individual development takes place within the context of societal solidarity.[88] In capitalist society, the organisation of which promotes individualistic achievement, such freedom to define educational goals and means would act to impede further the growth of that collective political action which is one of the predeterminants (though not the sole predeterminant) of the social and political change from capitalist to socialist society. It is interesting to note that the classical Marxist objection to this particular educational prescription is argued in terms which echo Durkheim's anxiety that the separation of the individual from collective social life facilitates merely the growth of a pathological form of egoism.[89] It is because of these fundamental convictions, that the transformation of socialist society depends on the united political action of the working class *and* that the growth of anti-collectivist, individualistic values are likely to be facilitated by an educational experience which emphasises the importance of individual goal definition, that most writers who work within the theoretical framework of classical Marxism reject this particular educational prescription of the new radicals.

A classical Marxist educational perspective prescribes as necessary both the maintenance of an education *system* and the promotion within that system of *collectively* (rather than individually) defined educational goals. It rejects the deschooling perspective on the grounds that a deschooled society would be characterised by greater inequality rather than greater equality. It rejects the notion of education as a process of facilitating individually defined goals on the grounds that such a process in a capitalist society would be likely to lead to the generation of social, educational and political goals inimical to the development of collective social and political action. Whilst such a classical Marxist perspective prescribes changes in the organisation of capitalist schooling (such as the universalisation of access to high status education and the transmission of socialist, co-operative values rather than capitalist, individualistic values), it holds no truck with the disestablishment of the school system or the abolition of its function as an instrument of socialization into the values of the adult society.

We have noted before that the new radical perspective in the sociology of education also appears to have embraced the theoretical concept of cultural relativism. Those who write from within this perspective appear to be prescribing the replacement of the traditional curriculum, which is seen as a cultural artefact of the bourgeois class, by a curriculum rooted in the pupils' experience of working class culture. Once again, both this prescription and the theoretical constructs which have given birth to it have been argued to be profoundly conservative by writers and thinkers within classical Marxism. Our rejection of the new radicalism's theory and policy prescriptions is based on Marx's own analysis of the role of education and of ideas in the movement to socialism and is echoed in the work of both Lenin and Gramsci. This rejection carries with it (sometimes implicitly, sometimes explicitly) a prescription of its own which is for the retention of what is argued to be the rational empiricism of the 'bourgeois' mode of thought and also for the retention of the knowledge base of 'bourgeois culture' as useful for facilitating working class advancement.

To understand the rejection, by Marxists, of the cultural relativist perspective of the new radicalism it is necessary to understand Marx's own conceptions of the role of ideas and theory in effecting the transformation from capitalism to socialism. This transition is dependent, according to Marx, on two factors:

1. The degeneration of the capitalist mode of production to the point where it is continually in economic crisis.[90]
2. The development of political action by the working class which is informed by a theoretical awareness of the nature of the old society together with an understanding that the crises and alienating economic relationships of capitalism cannot be solved by capitalism itself but only by a radically different societal organisation based on a radically different world view.[91]

According to Marx, however, it is not inevitable that either the experience of capitalism in crisis or the alienating social and economic relations of capitalism will thrust upon the working class a profound understanding of the nature of the old society and an intellectual conviction that the anomalies of capitalism can be resolved.[92]

This theoretical awareness of the reasons why things are as they are develops, according to the Marxist hypothesis, only as the result of a scientific analysis of an empirical situation. This critical awareness – or *socialist consciousness* – which transforms the proletariat from a defensive class 'in itself', perplexed by the effects of the capitalist crisis and politically reactive, into a revolutionary class 'for itself',[93] politically active to effect social change, is developed only on the basis of what Lenin calls 'a profound scientific knowledge'.[94] Such transformation of a defensive working class into a revolutionary class can only take place on the basis of the development of a revolutionary theory which aids in Marx's words, 'the logical and relentless criticism of the old world'. For Marx, then, the crisis and contradictions of capitalism are not, in themselves, sufficient to evoke in the working class a transition from a defensive, albeit militant, class into a purposive revolutionary class. Only when to the irrationalities of the capitalist mode of production is added a critical awareness of the cause and solution of these irrationalities is the transition of an expoited class into a revolutionary class possible. It is also clear from Marx's writing that he regarded this philosophy of practice as essentially *rational* and *empirical* – *rational* because of the possibility of social change when the practice of the revolutionary class is 'comprehended practice' and *empirical* because the realisation of change is based, in part, on a scientific enquiry of what the capitalist class does and why it does it.

Later Marxists have argued that the modes of thought and knowledge base necessary for such an enquiry are those which are labelled as useful or superior by the capitalist educational system, rather than those which would result from an educational process located in the defensive reactions of a non-revolutionary working class. Lenin, addressing himself to the growth of the 'proletcult' in post-revolutionary Russia, argued strongly that the 'only adequate cultural resource for the development of revolutionary practice was what had served as the content of the traditional humanistic curriculum.' In contrast to those Soviet thinkers who promoted the idea of the development of a socialist culture bereft of the thought paradigms and knowledge base of bourgeois society, Lenin defined as 'theoretically wrong and practically harmful all attempts to invent a special culture'.[95] In a speech to the Soviet Young Communist League in 1920, Lenin stressed that the education of socialist youth should incorporate the curriculum and the intellectual mode of bourgeois society:

> The tuition, training and education of the youth must be based on the material that was bequeathed to us by the old society. We can build communism only on the sum of knowledge, organisation and institutions, only on the stock of human forces and means left to us by the old society.[96]

Lenin's strictures were, of course, addressed to a *post-revolutionary* situation. Antonio Gramsci echoes Lenin's warning that the attempt to create a special working class culture is 'theoretically wrong and practically harmful' in *pre-socialist*, Fascist Italy. He argues that a working class denied access to the humanistic rationality of the traditional scholastic mode itself reinforces the ideological and political hegemony of the ruling class by its incapacity to perceive that the social and economic relations of capitalism can be transcended.[97] In Gramsci's view, Marxism aims 'to raise new strata of the proletariat to a higher cultural life and political understanding'.[98] in order that they should become capable of this perception'. For him, the education necessary for the proletariat in a pre-socialist society was one which developed 'the love of free discussion; the desire to search for truth rationally and intelligently'.[99]

It is clear, then, that a classical Marxist perspective rejects the idea that the disestablishment of the bourgeois intellectual mode and the knowledge base of bourgeois culture is in any way socialist. Education in pre-socialist capitalist society should, according to this Marxist prescription, incorporate the rational empiricism of bourgeois culture because such rational empiricism is a prerequisite of a critical awareness of the nature of capitalist society and the subsequent development of a revolutionary theory of practice. It should, in our view, adopt the knowledge base of the capitalist curriculum (although the Marxist prescription is less explicit here) because possession of that knowledge base is a prerequisite of administering and controlling the organisations and institutions of a complex industrial and technological society.[100]

A classical Marxist educational perspective rejects the practical implications and policy prescriptions associated with the new radical perspective as conservative and inhibiting for socialist social and political change. It rejects the disestablishment of the education system because the disestablishment of a system of schooling would lead to greater rather than lesser inequality. It rejects the idea of the education process as a facilitator of individual goals because such goals are likely to be inimical to the generation of collective political action. It rejects the disestablishment of bourgeois culture because such disestablishment would preclude the development of any revolutionary theory, itself necessary to make the collective political practice of the working class purposive and comprehended practice. Such a Marxist perspective prescribes instead an education system organisationally transformed to offer genuine access to high status education for all children; the promotion of socialistic and co-operative values rather than capitalistic and individualistic values by that system and the adoption and utilisation of the bourgeois intellectual mode and knowledge base of capitalist education in the service of the generation of a critical revolutionary theory of practice.

Traditional Schooling in a Socialist Society

We have outlined above what we believe to be a classical Marxist view of the structure, role and function of the educational system in the transformation of a capitalist society into a socialist society. In this section we wish to suggest also that the education system of an emergent socialist society would of necessity bear more resemblance to the educational system as we now know it than to the educational visions of the new radicalism. The following section presents an analysis of the functions which it would be necessary for the educational system to perform in a socialist society if that society is to be transformed into the ultimate *communist* society of Marx.[101]

As we have already noted, classical Marxist theory suggests that the struggle of the revolutionary class based on a revolutionary theory will lead to the transformation of the nature of the capitalist state and to the transition from capitalism to socialism. Marx clearly saw that the State would continue to exist at the time of the intermediate stage of socialism but conceived of its transformation, during the revolutionary process, from an institution which acted in the interests of the bourgeois class into one through which the majority class carried out rational and democratic planning for a communist society.[102] He believed that this control of the State apparatus by the majority class, entailing the democratic control of the executive, State functionaries and the judiciary, was a necessary precursor to the classless equality of communism and a necessary precaution against the reassertion of capitalism by the erstwhile ruling class. Whereas, under capitalism, the ruling class use the State to regulate and control society in the interests of the maximisation of profits for one class at the expense of the continued exploitation of another,[103] the State would be used in socialist society by the majority class to control and regulate society in order to effect the gradual socialization of the means of production, the end of exploitation, and the ultimate achievement of social, political and economic equality.[104]

However, it must be remembered that Marx also saw the control of the means of production through the socialist State as a means of creating *socialist man*. Whilst it is a persistent theme in Marx's critique of capitalism that the control of the means of production by the capitalist class prevents the achievement of social, political and economic equality, it is also a persistent theme that the division of labour (through its creation of a class for whom work is instrumental rather than part of their natural activity) dehumanises and alienates men and women and prevents the development of what Marx called the 'whole man'.[105] Additionally, the production of goods for profit means that work becomes the activity which consumes most of man's waking hours and leaves little opportunity for the development of other areas of human existence.[106] The socialist State, according to Marx, would act by the production of goods for need rather than profit and, by the utilisation of technology to shorten working hours, to provide opportunity for the development of man's capacities for the production of enjoyment and his potential for creative intellectual work.[107]

For Marx, then, the primary goal of the socialist State is to socialize the means of production in order to abolish the division of labour which characterises capitalist society. The socialization of the means of production in socialist society would, in Marx's view:

1. Prevent the exploitation of one class by another and therefore aid the achievement of economic and social equality, and of communism.

2. Transform the nature of work from an instrumental alienating activity into one human activity in a potentially many sided human repertoire, thereby aiding the development of the whole productive, creative and intellectual man.

It is quite obvious, however, that any attempt in an emergent socialist society to effect the socialization of the means of production – involving the removal of the dichotomy between ruling and ruled classes and between mental and manual work – would depend, in part, upon certain functions being performed by the educational system. In our opinion these functions would be fourfold. First, the educational system in a socialist society would need to perform the function of generating, in the general population, the intellectual capacity and level of general technological knowledge which would enable the majority to exercise an informed control of the State and its decisions concerning the means by which production might be socialized. Second, the educational system would need to produce, from the majority class, technological and other specialists to plan the socialization of the means of production. Third, the educational system would need to function to facilitate the process of developing socialism into communism by means of the socialisation of individuals into the morality of collectivism so that economic and political decisions which are taken by State workers, specialists and others are in the interests of the collectivity rather than in the interests of individuals or groups in that society. Finally, the educational system would need to function to ensure equal access for all to educational institutions which offer the possibility of acquiring high status knowledge. This function we believe would be crucial not only to preclude the stratification of socialist society into 'thinkers' and 'workers' but also to maximise the possibility of all developing the intellectual capacities which Marx believed concomitant with the all round development of individuals.[108]

If our analysis is correct, it is difficult to escape the conclusion that the educational prescriptions of the new radicalism within the contemporary sociology of education are dysfunctional not only in effecting the transformation from capitalism to socialism but also in the development of socialist society into communist society. Whilst it seems clear that a socialist education system in a socialist society would be characterised by an external structure and internal organisation which precluded the early categorisation of children as possessing high academic potential or low academic potential, it also seems clear that, in order to perform the functions demanded of it, it would retain the commitment to the stratification of knowledge into 'more useful' and 'less useful' knowledge and to the employment of traditional bourgeois rationality.

Conclusion

We have outlined in this paper a classical Marxist socialist resolution to the paradigmatic confusion of current British sociology of education. The paradigm of the 1960s was broadly functionalist in theoretical orientation, in method positivistic and in its prescription basically Fabian in implication. The 'new wave' sociology of education of the 1970s has been informed, by contrast, by the interpretive approach of both the phenomenologists and the ethnomethodologists. In its methodology, this sociology of education is unscientific and lacking in rigour. In its analytic mode, it is either naïvely Idealist or in emphasis excessively Materialist. In its prescriptions, it is in our view profoundly unsocialist, increasingly flirting with the disestablishment of the school system, the tolerance of the eccentricities of bourgeois individualism and the acceptance of a wide variety of 'cultures' as adequate and worthy of study.

It seems clear that the appearance of these new radical perspectives of the last decade seems to have occurred as a reaction to several factors. As a consequence of the failure of attempts to equalise access to school defined 'excellent' culture and 'valid' knowledge that became evident after the apparent failure of the liberal reforms, a reactionary perspective developed which began to question the very rationale of such attempted reforms. The new sociology of education, therefore, became characterised by a fundamental questioning of the concept of stratified knowledge and a growing conviction that much of the knowledge base that the schools wished to transmit may not have been worth transmitting. The growing conviction that many forms of within-school and without-school culture appeared equally valid led, in turn, to a rejection of the need for the existence of a compulsory system of education and, amongst those who still saw the need for an educational system, to the rejection of externally imposed definitions of goals and means for pupils in schools.

It is easy to link these explicit educational prescriptions of the new radicalism, formed by a reaction to the failure of the social policy reforms of the 1960s, to the more implicit political orientation of members of the paradigm. Reacting to the failure of 'Soviet bloc' countries to achieve fully socialist or communist goals and reacting against the restrictions upon personal freedoms and personal liberties that seem entailed by the operation of such State socialist societies, much of the new radical literature seems libertarian, anarchistic or occasionally *syndicaliste* in orientation. Conventional forms of political and social action to take over the existing State apparatus appear to have been rejected by large numbers of socialists. Society, they believe, can be effectively changed only by means of a personal and quasi-spiritual revolution in which individuals – through an awareness of those factors that have formed their lives and their nature – changed the nature of their society by changing their own individual consciousness. Disestablished, culturally diverse and individually-determined forms of education or self-education would, it was believed by members of the new radicalism, facilitate such a greening of capitalism.

In this paper, we have tried to suggest that the new directions that have been travelled in the last decade's journey may have been the wrong directions. We argue, instead, for a scientific method of description, for a balance between crude Materialism and naive Idealism in analysis and for the embracing of classic socialist goals and means as our discipline's prescriptions. We believe basically that the transformation of the society in which we live is unlikely to take place if the prescriptions of the new radicalism are followed. The blocking of access of pupils to the rationality and content of an allegedly bourgeois curriculum impedes rather than advances revolutionary change and fails to understand that the socially shrewd bourgeois regard some forms of knowledge and thought as superior and therefore worth learning simply because they *are* cognitively and intellectually superior.

By contrast, an educational prescription – which ensures open access to a determined, structured and compulsory system of schools, retaining the rationality and content, though not the values, of contemporary bourgeois culture – is argued in this paper to be facilitating for the transformation from capitalism to socialism. Whilst proponents of the new radicalism promote a fascistic society characterised by the dictatorship of the anti-intellectual and of the uneducated, the prescriptions implicit in our socialist sociology of education promote the contrasting idea of a society controlled and developed by the democracy of the universally, compulsorily and excellently educated.

Notes and References

1 FLOUD, J. (1961) 'Sociology and Education', in *Sociological Review Monograph*, University of Keele, p. 6.
2 Adherents to this paradigm included within the sociology of education Jean Floud (see *Ibid.*), Halsey, [see FLOUD, J. and HALSEY, A.H. (1958) 'The Sociology of Education', in *Current Sociology*,] Vol. 7, No. 3 [and VAIZEY] see VAIZEY, J. (1966), *Education for Tomorrow*, Harmondsworth, Penguin.
3 FLOUD, J. (1961) 'Social Class Factors in Educational Achievement', in *Ability and Educational Opportunity*, Paris Organisation for Economic Co-operation and Development, pp. 108 and 91.
4 WILBY, P. (1977) in 'Education and Equality', *New Statesman*, 16th October comments aptly that '... no other induced social change has attracted quite the same degree of liberal enthusiasm and faith and vision ... educational equality was an attempt to achieve social change by proxy. More and better education was more politically palatable and less socially disruptive than direct measures of tackling inequality. So was economic growth ... Education was a cornucopia, so prolific of good things that nobody would need any longer to ask awkward questions about who got what'.
5 See FLOUD, J. and HALSEY, A.H. (1956) *Social Class and Educational Opportunity*, London, Heinemann; and DEPARTMENT OF EDUCATION AND SCIENCE, (1959) *Report of the Central Advisory Council for Education*, London, HMSO.
6 See, for example, PEDLEY, R. (1963) *The Comprehensive School*, Harmondsworth, Penguin; ARMSTRONG, M. and YOUNG, M. (1964) *New Look at Comprehensives*, London, Fabian Society; JACKSON, B. and MARSDEN, D. (1962) *Education and the Working Class*, London, Routledge and Kegan Paul; and TAYLOR, W. (1963) *The Secondary Modern School*, London, Faber and Faber.
7 DEPARTMENT OF EDUCATION AND SCIENCE (1963) *Report of the Central Advisory Council for Education (Newsom Report): Half Our Future*, London, HMSO, p. 6.
8 See the evidence quoted in KOGAN, M. (1974) *The Politics of Education*, Harmondsworth, Penguin.
9 These typologies of State Welfare provision are those developed by Richard Titmuss (1974). See his *Social Policy*, London, George Allen and Unwin, Chapter 2.
10 For evidence see FINN, D. GRANT, N. and JOHNSON, R. (1977) 'Social Democracy, Education and the Crisis', in Centre for Contemporary Cultural Studies, *Working Papers in Cultural Studies No. 10 – On Ideology*, Birmingham, CCCS pp. 160–162.
11 CROSLAND, A. (1974) *Socialism Now and Other Essays*, London, Jonathan Cape p. 165.
12 For further details of the Circular and of the immediate factors leading up to it see BENN, C. and SIMON, B. (1970) *Half Way There*, Harmondsworth, Penguin.
13 CENTRAL ADVISORY COUNCIL FOR EDUCATION, (1967) *Children and Their Primary Schools (Plowden Report)*, London, HMSO.
14 For an excellent treatment of the challenges to the old sociology of education (which this section draws on) see BERNBAUM, G. (1977) *Knowledge and Ideology in the Sociology of Education*, London, Macmillan.
15 BERNBAUM, G. *Ibid.*, p. 44.
16 See WESTERGAARD, J. and RESLER, H. (1976) *Class in a Capitalist Society*, Harmondsworth, Penguin, Part Four.
17 WESTERGAARD, J. and RESLER, H. *Ibid.*, p. 230.
18 See the review of the impressionistic evidence in WRIGHT, N. (1977) *Progress in Education*, London, Croom Helm, Chapter 4; and the detailed London study of FORD, J. (1969) *Social Class and the Comprehensive School*, London, Routledge and Kegan Paul.
19 For a review of the American compensatory programmes that concludes they were generally ineffective see BRONFENNBRENNER, U. (1974) *Is Early Intervention Effective? A Report on the Longitudinal Evaluation of Pre School Programmes*, Washington, US Dept. of Health, Education and Welfare, Chapter 2 and the Conclusion.
20 See the review of evidence in COONS, J.E. and SUGARMAN, S.D. (1978) *Education by Choice*, Berkeley, University of California Press.
21 See WHITESIDE, T. (1978) *The Sociology of Educational Innovation*, London, Methuen.
22 For evidence as to the independence of individual labour market position and academic qualifications see BERG, I. (1973) *Education and Jobs: The Great Training Robbery*, Harmondsworth, Penguin. For information about one particular malfunctioning institution – William Tyndale school – see the evidence in AULD, R. (1976) *William Tyndale Junior and Infants School Public Enquiry: A Report to the Inner London Education Authority*, London, Inner London Education Authority.
23 See, for example, GOULDNER, A.W. (1971) *The Coming Crisis of Western Sociology*, London, Heinemann.

24 YOUNG, M.F.D. (Ed.) (1971) *Knowledge and Control: New Directions for the Sociology of Education*, London, Macmillan.

25 *Ibid.*, p. 2.

26 BERNBAUM, G. *op. cit.*, p. 60.

27 BARTON, L. and WALKER, S. (1978) 'Sociology of Education at the Crossroads', *Educational Review*, Vol. 30. No. 3.

28 SHARP, R. and GREEN, A. (1975) *Education and Social Control*, London, Routledge and Kegan Paul.

29 WILLIS, P. (1977) *Learning to Labour*, Farnborough, Saxon House.

30 KARABEL, J. and HALSEY, A.H. (Eds.) (1977) *Power and Ideology in Education*, New York, Oxford University Press, p. 54 and p. 55.

31 See for example, the generation and testing of ideas in SHARP and GREEN *op. cit.* These authors began their data collection from an interactionist position, later changed their perspective to a more structuralist/Marxist perspective and then found this new perspective supported and validated by the data that had caused them to adopt their new structuralist perspective in the first place! Further treatment of this theme is to be found in REYNOLDS, D. and SULLIVAN, M. (1979) 'The Limitations of the British Ethnographic Approach' and EVANS, J. (1979) 'Criteria of Validity in Social Research: Exploring the Ground Between Ethnographic and Quantitative Approaches', both papers delivered to the SSRC sponsored 'Ethnography of the School' Conference at Oxford in September 1979 and to be published in the resulting collection of Conference papers to be edited by HAMMERSLEY, M.

32 See YOUNG, M. *op. cit.*, YOUNG, M.F.D. (1973) 'Taking Sides Against the Probable Problems of Relativism and Commitment in Teaching and the Sociology of Knowledge', *Educational Review*, Vol. 25, No. 3; and GORBUTT, D.A. (1972) 'The New Sociology of Education', *Education for Teaching*, November.

33 See LAWTON, D. (1977) *Education and Social Justice*, London, Sage Publishing Chapter 5 for a discussion of this theme which has strongly influenced our discussion here.

34 PRING, R. (1977) 'Knowledge Out of Control' quoted in Lawton *Ibid.*, pp. 104–105.

35 NYBERG, D. (1978) 'Ambiguity and Constraint in the "Freedom" of Free Schools', in STRIKE, K.A. and EGAN, K. (Eds.), *Ethics and Educational Policy*, London, Routledge and Kegan Paul, p. 138.

36 MARX, K. (1845) *The German Ideology*, 1845–6, Vol. 1, pp. 35–36. Moscow, Progress Publishers.

37 See the discussions, and the evidence cited, in WOODS, P. and HAMMERSLEY, M. (Eds.) (1976) *The Process of Schooling*, London, Routledge and Kegan Paul, Introduction; and WOODS, P. and HAMMERSLEY, M. (Eds.) (1977) *School Experience*, London, Croom Helm, Introduction: 'School Experience, Explorations in the Sociology of Education'.

38 WHITTY, G. and YOUNG, M.F.D. (Eds.) (1976) *Explorations in the Politics of Educational Knowledge*, Driffield, Nafferton Press, p. 2.

39 SHARP, R. and GREEN, A. *op. cit.*, p. 27.

40 YOUNG, M.F.D. and WHITTY, G. (Eds.) (1977) *Society, State and Schooling*, Ringmer, Falmer Press, p. 7.

41 ALTHUSSER, L. (1971) 'Ideology and Ideological State Apparatuses', in *Lenin, and Philosophy and Other Essays*, London, New Left Books.

42 *Ibid.*, p. 131

43 BOWLES, S. and GINTIS, H. (1976) *Schooling in Capitalist America*, London, Routledge and Kegan Paul.

44 *Ibid.*, p. 131.

45 See the evidence in JOLL, J. (1977) *Gramsci*, London, Fontana, Chapters 8 and 9 especially.

46 MARX, K. quoted in Joll, J. *Ibid.*, p. 84.

47 ENGELS, F. quoted in Joll, J. *Ibid.*, p. 84.

48 GRAMSCI, A. quoted in Joll, J. *Ibid.*, p. 85.

49 BERNSTEIN, B. (1977) 'Aspects of the Relations Between Education and Production', in *Class, Codes and Control*, Vol. 3, London, Routledge and Kegan Paul.

50 BOURDIEU, P. and PASSERON, J.P. (1977) *Reproduction in Education, Society and Culture*, London, Sage.

51 WILLIS, P. *op. cit.*

52 Details of work in South Wales can be found in REYNOLDS, D. and SULLIVAN, M. (1979) 'Bringing Schools Back In', in BARTON, L. and MEIGHAN, R. (Eds.), *Schools, Pupils and Deviance*, Driffield, Nafferton, and in the references for that article. Further details of the work are forthcoming.

53 Many of the neo-Marxist writers popular within the recent sociology of education, such as Althusser or Bowles and Gintis, seem to misunderstand the fact that Marx himself wished for a *balance* between Idealism and Materialism in the explanation of social phenomena. His (and Engels) conception of history was that '. . . all forms and products of consciousness cannot be dissolved by mental criticism, but only by the practical overthrow of the actual social relations which give rise to this idealistic trickery . . . (and) shows that circumstances make man *just as much as* (our emphasis) men make circumstances', Marx, quoted in WHITTY, G. (1977) 'Sociology and the Problem of Radical Educational

Change', in YOUNG, M. and WHITTY, G. *op. cit.*, p. 45.

54 ILLICH, I. (1973) *De-schooling Society*, Harmondsworth, Penguin Books.

55 See for discussion of the old progressive tradition BARROW, R. (1978) *Radical Education*, London, Martin Robertson; and for a discussion of the reformed tradition see HARGREAVES, D. (1974) 'Deschoolers and New Romantics', in FLUDE, M. and AHIER, J. (Eds.) *Educability, Schools and Ideology*, London, Croom Helm.

56 See HARRIS, K. (1980) *Education and Knowledge*, London, Routledge and Kegan Paul, as an example.

57 ILLICH, I. *op. cit.*, p. 52.

58 ILLICH, I. (1973) *Celebration of Awareness*, Harmondsworth, Penguin Books.

59 ILLICH, I. *Ibid.*

60 ILLICH, I. *De-schooling Society*, Chapter 1.

61 ILLICH, I. *Ibid.*

62 REIMER, E. (1971) *School is Dead*, Harmondsworth, Penguin.

63 FREIRE, P. (1970) *Pedagogy of the Oppressed*, New York, Herder and Herder.

64 YOUNG, M.F.D. and WHITTY, G. (1980) quoted in DEMAINE, J. 'Politics and the Left in Britain', *British Journal of Sociology of Education*, Vol. 1, No. 1., p. 28.

65 See, in addition to Harris, Illich, Reimer, Freire, Young and Whitty *op. cit.*, HOLLY, D. (1971) *Society, Schools and Humanity*, London, MacGibbon and Kee, for a general discussion of the process of the secondary education system as 'alienation from oneself' (*sic*.); and see HUSEN, T. (1979) *The School in Question*, Oxford, Oxford University Press especially Chapter 2, pp. 25–34.

66 HARGREAVES, D. *op. cit.*

67 HOLT, J. (1964) *How Children Fail*, Harmondsworth, Penguin.

68 GOODMAN, P. (1962) *Compulsory Miseducation*, Harmondsworth, Penguin.

69 KOZOL, J. (1972) *Free Schools*, Boston, Houghton Mifflin.

70 See the review in HARGREAVES, D. *op. cit.*

71 FROMM, E. (1965) *Escape From Freedom*, New York, Avon.

72 ROGERS, C.R. (1961) *On Becoming A Person*, London, Constable.

73 JACKSON, B. and MARSDEN, D. (1962) *Education and the Working Class*, Harmondsworth, Penguin.

74 JACKSON, B. (1968) *Working Class Community*, London, Routledge and Kegan Paul.

75 HOLLY, D. *op. cit.*, p. 146.

76 MIDWINTER, E. (1972) *Social Environment and the Urban School*, London, Ward Lock.

77 KEDDIE, N. (1973) *Tinker, Tailor ... The Myth of Cultural Deprivation*, Harmondsworth, Penguin.

78 *Ibid.* pp. 8–9.

79 *Ibid.*, Introduction.

80 YOUNG, M.F.D. and WHITTY, G. *op. cit.*, Introduction: 'Perspectives on Education and Society'.

81 HARRIS, K. *op. cit.*

82 *Ibid.*, pp. 63–4 and back cover.

83 *Ibid.*, p. 188.

84 *Ibid.*, p. 88.

85 A rehearsal of some of the arguments against deschooling are to be found in SIMON, B. (1978) *Intelligence, Psychology and Education: A Marxist Critique*, London, Lawrence and Wishart, pp. 272–281.

86 See BANKS, O. (1971) *Sociology of Education*, London, Batsford, pp. 61–83 for a review of the evidence of the effects of differential social and class environments on educational attainment.

87 British Marxists, in particular British communists, played an active and sometimes leading role in promoting the idea of comprehensive secondary education in the period 1945–65. See for instance FENWICK, I.G.K. (1976) *The Comprehensive School 1944–1970*, London, Methuen, pp. 68–89. See also, for an illustration of the British Communist Party's commitment to a universalised high status secondary education system, Communist Party of Great Britain E.C. Education Sub-Committee, (1978) *The Comprehensive School*, London, Communist Party of Great Britain.

88 See MARX, K. and ENGELS, F. (1976) *The German Ideology* in *Marx and Engels, Collected Works Vol. 5*, Moscow, Progress Publishers p. 439 for a discussion of this point.

89 DURKHEIM, E. (1952) *Suicide*, London, Routledge and Kegan Paul, p. 209.

90 MARX, K. and Engels, F. (1952) *Manifesto of the Communist Party*, Moscow, Progress Publishers, pp. 48–49.

91 For elaboration of this point see MARX, K. (1977) *Critique of the Gotha Program*, in *Marx and Engels Selected Works*, London, Lawrence and Wishart, pp. 311–337.

92 See MARX, K. *Ibid.*

93 For Marx's discussion of the development of a socialist consciousness which transforms the working class into a revolutionary class, see MARX, K. *The Poverty of Philosophy*, Moscow, Progress Publisher, n.d., pp. 140 and 195.

94 LENIN, V.I. (1952) *What is to be done?* Moscow, Progress Publishers, p. 30.
95 LENIN, V.I. (1943) *Proletarian Culture* in *Lenin, Selected Works Vol. 9*, New York, International Publishers, p. 485.
96 LENIN, V.I. (1943) *The Tasks of the Youth Leagues* in *Lenin, Selected Works Vol. 9*, New York, International Publishers, pp. 467–468.
97 GRAMSCI, A. (1977), *Prison Notebooks*, London, Lawrence and Wishart, pp. 33–34.
98 *Ibid.*, pp. 396–397.
99 GRAMSCI, A. (1976) *La Formazione dell' Uomo: Scriti di Pedagogia*, Rome, Editore Riuniti, p. 95.
100 That the socialist society envisaged by Marx, unlike that envisaged by the de-schoolers, would utilise and expand technology is demonstrated in his own writings. See for example MARX, K. (1959) *Capital, Vol. 3*, Moscow, Foreign Languages Publishing House, pp. 177–178.
101 For the distinction between Socialism and Communism see MARX, K. (1977) *Critique of the Gotha Programme* in *Marx and Engels Selected Works*, London, Lawrence and Wishart, p. 319.
102 MARX, K. *Ibid.*, p. 327.
103 MARX, K. and ENGELS, F. (1952) *Manifesto of the Communist Party*, Moscow, Progress Publishers, pp. 59, 74.
104 MARX, K. and ENGELS, F. (1976) *The German Ideology* in *Marx and Engels Collected Works Vol. 5*, Moscow, Progress Publishers, p. 441.
105 See MARX, K. *Critique of the Gotha Programme, op. cit.*, p. 315–316.
106 See MARX, K. (1963) *Economic and Philosophical Manuscripts* reproduced in BOTTOMORE, T. *Karl Marx: Early Writings*, London, C.A. Watts, p. 126.
107 For a useful short review of Marx's work on the concepts of alienation, the division of labour and the whole man, see FISCHER, E. (1975) *Marx in his Own Words*, Harmondsworth, Penguin, pp. 15–51.
108 It is, of course, reasonable to question the extent to which the education systems of contemporary 'communist' states conform to the Marxist blueprint outlined. Commentators have noted that, whilst the education systems of the European Communist Community retain the definitions of valid knowledge and the curriculum content of 'bourgeois' culture, there are doubts about the extent to which this high status education is universally available. See for example, CASTLES, S. and WUSTENBERG, W. (1979) *The Education of the Future*, London, Pluto Press, pp. 43–100. Others have suggested the existence of a new elite within these countries comprising those individuals who have gained access to such high status education. Such criticisms are well made and indicate, perhaps, that these societies are still in the transitional stage of *Socialism* (where inequalities persist) rather than in the ultimate stage of *Communist* organisation, where such inequalities would be eliminated. Another question which readers may ask concerns the extent to which Non-European socialist societies (for example China), whose industrial and cultural development is historically different from the development of European nations, have adopted classical Marxist prescriptions in their education systems. Whilst it is possible, through a feat of intellectual agility, to characterise the Chinese Cultural Revolution as carrying with it undertones of cultural relativism, it is impossible to escape the conclusion that the overall goals of Chinese education and its knowledge base are similar to those in the Non-Maoist communist world. The access to high status education, once limited to the Mandarin class, has been broadened. Education is utilised as a socialist instrument of socialization and the traditional 'bourgeois' curriculum is much in evidence: 'Every child learns the basic cultural techniques of reading, writing and mathematics. He also receives instruction in history, geography, basic natural sciences and politics. Every child learns the culture of his country ... A child learns to accept social control and criticism ... to subordinate his own needs to those of the collective. Discipline and self-discipline are important educational aims'. CASTLES, S. and WUSTENBERG, W. (1979) *The Education of the Future*, London, Pluto Press, pp. 133–134.

Contributors

Michael Apple	Professor of Curriculum and Instruction at the University of Wisconsin – Madison, USA.
Len Barton	Senior Lecturer in Sociology of Education at Westhill College, Birmingham.
Samuel Bowles	Professor of Economics at the University of Massachusetts, USA.
Christine Brown	Lecturer in Educational Studies, Faculty of Education, The Polytechic, Wolverhampton.
Rosemary Chessum	Research Fellow, Educational Studies Unit, Brunel University, Middlesex.
Gary Easthope	Lecturer, School of Economic and Social Studies, University of East Anglia, Norwich.
Tony Edwards	Professor of Education at the University of Newcastle-upon-Tyne.
Geoff Esland	Lecturer, Faculty of Educational Studies, Open University, Milton Keynes.
Herbert Gintis	Professor of Economics at the University of Massachusetts, USA.
Madaleine MacDonald	Lecturer, Faculty of Educational Studies, Open University, Milton Keynes.
Roland Meighan	Lecturer in Sociology of Education, Faculty of Education, University of Birminghan.
Peter Musgrave	Professor of Education, Faculty of Education, Monash University, Australia.
David Reynolds	Lecturer in Social Administration in the Department of Social Administration, University College Cardiff.
Janet Strivens	Lecturer, School of Education, University of Liverpool.
Mike Sullivan	Tutorial Fellow, Department of Social Administration, University College, Cardiff.
Stephen Walker	Senior Lecturer in Sociology of Education at Newman College, Birmingham.

Author Index

Subject Index